A Book of Lists

(500 Lists of 50 Things!)

Paul Marks

For reference

Not to be taken from the room.

This book is dedicated to:
**Tazmyn & Lola,
and all the 'list-makers' out there...**

Authors
On Line

Visit us online at www.authorsonline.co.uk

ISBN 0 7552 0251 1

Authors OnLine Ltd
19 The Cinques
Gamlingay, Sandy
Bedfordshire SG19 3NU
England

This book is also available in e-book format, details of which are available at
www.authorsonline.co.uk

About the Author:

Paul Marks was born and educated in Upminster, Essex. In the mid 1970's he began a career in advertising, working in several London art studios. He moved to London in the 1980's and during this time wrote a trilogy of novels that remained unpublished and were subsequently destroyed. Marks trained as a teacher in the late 1980's and worked in education for ten years. He bore two daughters with his first partner and married his second partner in the early 1990's. Finally, a novel; Flowerwolf was published in 1999 followed by a book of short stories; The Sky Was Full of Screaming Birds in 2003. Marks lives and works as a musician and writer in Camden, London: reading, listening to music, watching Star Trek, and collecting Penguin Modern Classics, LP's on vinyl, black-leather bookmarks and polka-dot shirts.

Acknowledgements:

Thanks go to many, many friends and family members who helped come up with 'list categories' for this momentous task.

Thanks again to those who actually supplied lists all on their own or prodded and poked by me into action; particularly; Veronica Dajani and Neil Cross.

Special thanks go especially to **Michael Marks** who so painstakingly helped proof-read and correct the whole book!

Contents:

50 Musical Instruments..........page 9
50 Breeds of Dog.........9
50 Bones in the Human Body..........10
50 Bands, Groups and Musicians beginning with
    -'S'..........10
50 Different Meals.........11
50 Things Guy Fawkes might have done while
    -waiting to blow up Parliament.........11
50 T. Rex Songs.........12
50 Board and Table Games.........12
50 Varieties of Trees.........13
50 Kings and Queens of England.........13
50 States of America..........14
50 Modes of Land Transport..........14
50 Types of Seacraft.........15
50 DIY Tools..........15
50 Fruits..........16
50 Arterial Roads........16
50 Church Features.........17
50 Kitchen Items..........17
50 Illnesses and Diseases in the Middle
    -Ages.........18
50 Star Trek Characters..........18
50 TV Programmes from the 1960's..........19
50 Number One Song Titles..........19
50 Colours..........20
50 Criminal Offences..........20
50 Things you'd find on a Farm..........21
50 American Baseball Teams..........21
50 Things the World could do Without..........22
50 Ranks within the Armed Forces..........22
50 Film Monsters..........23
50 Things to think about when fielding 'Deep
    -Fine Leg'..........23
50 Words to describe 'Cold'..........24
50 Well-known Cricketers from 1938..........24
50 Gangster Movies from the 1960's and
    -'70's..........25
50 White Wines..........25
50 Grand National Winners..........26
50 Gangster Movies from the 1930's and
    -'40's..........26
50 Breakfasts..........27
50 Ways to say 'I Love You'..........27
50 Capital Cities of the World..........28
50 Items of Clothing..........28
50 Things Red Riding Hood might have taken to
    -Grandma's..........29
50 Triple-Barrel Words and Phrases..........29
50 Vegetables..........30
50 Things to 'Hold'..........30
50 Species of Birds..........31
50 Ways to Die..........31
50 Painters and Artists..........32

50 'Off' and 'Out' Phrases..........32
50 Breeds of Cats..........33
50 Old London Street Cries..........33
50 Central London Street Names..........34
50 British Prime Ministers..........34
50 Breeds of Horses and Ponies..........35
50 Things Sleeping Beauty might have said
    -when woken by the Prince..........35
50 Film Actors..........36
50 Well-known Buildings..........36
50 English Authors..........37
50 Contemporary Illnesses and
    -Diseases..........37
50 Alternative ways to Earn a Living..........38
50 Ways to Murder Someone..........38
50 Materials and Fabrics..........39
50 Countries..........39
50 Embarrassing things to Buy..........40
50 Mammals..........40
50 British Fish..........41
50 Flowers..........41
50 Paintings by Botticelli..........42
50 Savoury Meat Dishes..........42
50 Things to say if you ever met the
    -Queen..........43
50 Serial Killers..........43
50 Mountains and Volcanoes..........44
50 Rivers..........44
50 Moons..........45
50 Film Actresses..........45
50 Discoveries and Inventions..........46
50 Car Manufacturers..........46
50 Tiny Islands around the World..........47
50 Things to put on your Face..........47
50 Types of Weights and Measures..........48
50 Things to put on your Head..........48
50 Dinosaurs..........49
50 Insects..........49
50 Coronation Street Characters..........50
50 Weapons..........50
50 Feelings..........51
50 Shakespeare Characters..........51
50 Things you should never, ever, ever
    -Do..........52
50 Muscles of the Body..........52
50 Chemical Elements..........53
50 Fashion Designers..........53
50 Miss World Winners..........54
50 Gooseberry Varieties..........54
50 Olympic Gold Medallists..........55
50 Most useless Items..........55
50 Well-known Ships and Boats..........56
50 Rocks and Minerals..........56
50 Outdoor Sports and Games..........57
50 Common Ailments..........57
50 Indoor Games..........58

50 Film Genres..........58
50 Painting Movements..........59
50 Football Teams..........59
50 Mr. Men..........60
50 Waters around the UK..........60
50 Mildly Blasphemous Expressions..........61
50 Airlines..........61
50 Rugby Teams..........62
50 Roman Emperors..........62
50 Traditional Trades and Professions..........63
50 Well-known Novels..........63
50 Forms of Evening Entertainment..........64
50 Motorways..........64
50 Geographical Features..........65
50 Items of Street Furniture..........65
50 Cities and large Towns in the UK..........66
50 TV Comedy Programmes..........66
50 British Seaside Towns..........67
50 Things 'not to say' when entering a Church
-..........67
50 Boring things to do at Home on a Dark Night
-..........68
50 Mushrooms and Fungi..........68
50 Types of Dwelling..........69
50 Classical Composers..........69
50 Things to do on a hot Summer's Day..........70
50 Sweets..........70
50 Philosophers/Political Thinkers..........71
50 Words for Man..........71
50 Chocolate Bars..........72
50 Soft Drinks..........72
50 Alcoholic Drinks..........73
50 Styles of Music..........73
50 Languages..........74
50 Races..........74
50 Battles..........75
50 Sins..........75
50 Virtues..........76
50 More Discoveries and Inventions..........76
50 Freshwater Aquarium Fish..........77
50 Film Directors..........77
50 Football League Managers..........78
50 Things the World couldn't do Without..........78
50 Things that make our lives just that little bit
-Easier..........79
50 Characters from Classical Mythology..........79
50 Ways to get Arrested..........80
50 Ways to Communicate..........80
50 Ways to avoid People..........81
50 Foreign Footballers..........81
50 Popes..........82
50 Things to do as an Eskimo..........82
50 Dances..........83
50 Pubs with Silly Names..........83
50 London Theatres..........84
50 Things you could buy from a Victorian Chemist
-..........84
50 Nuts..........85

50 Patterns..........85
50 Operas..........86
50 Cockney Rhyming Slang Phrases..........86
50 Things you can buy at the Bakers..........87
50 Forms of Therapy..........87
50·Types of Aircraft..........88
50 Newspapers..........88
50 Magazines..........89
50 Parts of a Bicycle..........89
50 Supermodels..........90
50 Armed Forces..........90
50 Things we use in the Bathroom..........91
50 Sports Items..........91
50 Traditional Children's Toys..........92
50 Cartoon Characters..........92
50 Comic Characters..........93
50 Items of Furniture..........93
50 Types of Footwear..........94
50 Types of Hats..........94
50 Kinds of Coats and Jackets..........95
50 Electrical Appliances..........95
50 Roman Towns..........96
50 Well-known Films..........96
50 Types of Skirts and Dresses..........97
50 Michael Jackson Songs..........97
50 Beatles Songs..........98
50 Rolling Stones Songs..........98
50 Madonna Songs..........99
50 Playwrights..........99
50 London Postal Areas..........100
50 Circus Acts..........100
50 Popular Zoo Animals..........101
50 Comedians..........101
50 Places worth a Visit..........102
50 TV Programmes from the 1980's..........102
50 Double-Acts..........103
50 Radio Shows from the 1930's –
-1960's..........103
50 Characters from the Bible..........104
50 Explorers..........104
50 Traditional Children's Story
-Characters..........105
50 Novel Characters..........105
50 Fictional Detectives..........106
50 Dicken's Characters..........106
50 'Ologies..........107
50 Poets..........107
50 Olympic Events..........108
50 Things to do on a boring Sunday Afternoon
-..........108
50 Things to Collect..........109
50 Pets..........109
50 Footballers who have played for England
-..........110
50 Bottled Waters..........110
50 Cricketers who have played for England
-..........111
50 Forms of Small-Talk..........111

50 Shakespeare Insults..........112
50 Outdoor Leisure Pursuits..........112
50 Things to use in the Gym..........113
50 Counties in Britain and Ireland..........113
50 Things to do at the Seaside..........114
50 Castles..........114
50 Prime Numbers..........115
50 Musical Terms..........115
50 Sails..........116
50 Parts of the Ear..........116
50 Famous Deaths..........117
50 Banks and Building Society Names..........117
50 Knots..........118
50 Easy DIY Jobs..........118
50 Cheeses..........119
50 Bacteria and Viruses..........119
50 Types of Weather..........120
50 Well-known 'Sayings' from the
    - Cinema..........120
50 Breeds of Pig..........121
50 Breeds of Cattle..........121
50 Pieces of Armour..........122
50 Chain-Stores..........122
50 Words to describe 'Hot'..........123
50 Words to use instead of 'Nice'..........123
50 Names of Stars..........124
50 Books of the Bible..........124
50 Dr. Who Monsters..........125
50 Vampire Films..........125
50 Cowboy Films..........126
50 Things to do at 'Camp'..........126
50 Phobias..........127
50 Common Medicines..........127
50 Words beginning with 'X'..........128
50 Films starring John Wayne..........128
50 TV Catchphrases..........129
50 Record Labels..........129
50 Book Publishers..........130
50 Football Grounds..........130
50 Designer Labels..........131
50 Perfumes..........131
50 Electrical Brand Names..........132
50 Words for 'Dirt'..........132
50 Words for 'Dark'..........133
50 Words for 'White'..........133
50 2nd. World War Films..........134
50 'Space' Films..........134
50 Songs with the word 'Love' in the
    -Title..........135
50 Songs with the word 'Boy' or 'Girl' in the Title
    -..........135
50 Boys Names..........136
50 Girls Names..........136
50 Well-known Surnames..........137
50 Pet Names..........137
50 Beers and Lagers..........138
50 Whiskeys..........138
50 Green things to Eat..........139

50 Types of Bags and Cases..........139
50 Different Ages..........140
50 Things to do on Summer Holiday..........140
50 Things to do in the Town..........141
50 Obscure words beginning with 'Q'..........141
50 Words beginning with 'Zoo...'..........142
50 Estate Agents..........142
50 Things not to say in an Interview..........143
50 Good People..........143
50 Tastes..........144
50 Swords..........144
50 Sounds..........145
50 Smells..........145
50 Touchy/Feely Words..........146
50 Things you'd find on the Dinner
    -Table..........146
50 Things the Seven Dwarfs might have done if
    -Snow White hadn't woken Up..........147
50 Infamous People..........147
50 Things Cinderella might have done if the
    -Glass Slipper hadn't Fit..........148
50 Comedy Films..........148
50 Disaster Movies..........149
50 Films starring Bette Davies..........149
50 Anglers..........150
50 Films starring Jack Nicholson..........150
50 Films starring Katherine Hepburn..........151
50 Baby Items..........151
50 Cleaning Implements..........152
50 Wedding Gifts..........152
50 Reality TV Shows..........153
50 Names not to call your Funeral
    -Service..........153
50 Funeral Items..........154
50 Things to 'Catch'..........154
50 Archers..........155
50 Things to 'Throw'..........155
50 Chores..........156
50 Parts of the Body..........156
50 Parts of the outside of a House..........157
50 Things we do with our Bodies..........157
50 Days out with the Kids..........158
50 Popular Sayings and Phrases..........158
50 Skip Hire Firms..........159
50 Ways to shout 'Run'..........159
50 World Record Holders..........160
50 Things not to do on a 'First Date'..........160
50 Medals and Awards..........161
50 Cubs and Scouts Badges..........161
50 Hobbies..........162
50 Kid's Programmes..........162
50 Things you might find in a Castle..........163
50 Types of Tea..........163
50 Things you might say when arriving at the
    -Gates of Hell..........164
50 Yellow Things to Eat..........164
50 Things not to say on your Wedding
    -Night..........165

50 Things a man shouldn't say when present at -the Birth of his Child..........165
50 Darts Players..........166
50 Things not to say when you first meet your -Girlfriend's Parents..........166
50 Words beginning with 'Sun...'..........167
50 Things the Queen might say when -Waking..........167
50 Religious Festivals around the World..........168
50 Fashion Accessories..........168
50 Different 'Balls'..........169
50 Mathematical Terms..........169
50 Scientific Terms..........170
50 Geographical Terms..........170
50 Historical Terms..........171
50 London Underground Stations..........171
50 Satellite TV Channels..........172
50 Playstation Games..........172
50 Moon Crater Names..........173
50 Jobs, Trades and Professions A-L..........173
50 Jobs, Trades and Professions M-Z..........174
50 Bands and Singers from the 1950's..........174
50 Bands and Groups from the 1970's..........175
50 Scottish Football Teams..........175
50 Bands and Groups from the 1990's..........176
50 TV Presenters and Personalities..........176
50 Sports Personalities..........177
50 Silent Movie Stars..........177
50 Film Stars from the 1960's..........178
50 Contemporary Film Stars..........178
50 Things not to say when stopped by the -Police..........179
50 Types of Biscuit..........179
50 Tinned Items..........180
50 Fonts..........180
50 Signs and Symbols..........181
50 Shapes..........181
50 Haircuts and Hairstyles..........182
50 Racing Greyhounds..........182
50 Supermarkets..........183
50 London Churches in the Middle Ages..........183
50 London Parks..........184
50 Ballets..........184
50 Golfers..........185
50 Musicals..........185
50 Salvador Dali Paintings..........186
50 Picasso Paintings..........186
50 Forms of Lighting..........187
50 Forms of Heating..........187
50 Computer Commands..........188
50 Science Fiction B-Movies..........188
50 Best selling Novels..........189
50 Frank Sinatra Songs..........189
50 Star Wars Characters..........190
50 Simpson's Characters..........190
50 Beans and Pulses..........191
50 London Bus Routes..........191
50 Vegetarian Dishes..........192

50 Butterflies and Moths..........192
50 Molluscs..........193
50 Memorable Dates and Days..........193
50 Slang words for Money..........194
50 Words for Woman..........194
50 Bridges..........195
50 Words for 'Bottom'..........195
50 Electrical Goods Shops..........196
50 Office Jobs..........196
50 Words for 'Big'..........197
50 Racing Car Drivers..........197
50 Words for 'Small'..........198
50 Barbara Cartland Novels..........198
50 Things the Wolf might have said to gain -entrance to the Three Little Pigs -House..........199
50 Things you might say if you met -Jesus..........199
50 Parts of the Eye..........200
50 Things taught at School..........200
50 Danielle Steele Novels..........201
50 Nautical Terms..........201
50 David Bowie Songs..........202
50 Famous Numbers..........202
50 Possible Wives for Henry VIII..........203
50 Aerial Terms..........203
50 Mints and Chewing Gums..........204
50 Lollies and Ice-Creams..........204
50 Police-Drama/Detective -Programmes..........205
50 Boxers..........205
50 British Towns and Villages with Silly Names -A-G..........206
50 British Towns and Villages with Silly Names -G-N..........206
50 British Towns and Villages with Silly Names -N-Z..........207
50 Oceans and Seas..........207
50 Lakes..........208
50 Drawing, Painting and Writing -Implements..........208
50 Gems and Precious Stones..........209
50 Items of Jewellery..........209
50 Disasters..........210
50 Cakes and Puddings..........210
50 Meats..........211
50 Thoughts from a Burglars -Perspective..........211
50 Places to find a Crowd..........212
50 Places you'd find Deserted..........212
50 Accidents and Mishaps..........213
50 Well-known Soldiers..........213
50 Gasses..........214
50 Witchcraft Artefacts..........214
50 Proverbs..........215
50 Little-known Animals..........215
50 HMS Ships..........216
50 'Anger' Words..........216

50 'Love' Words..........217
50 Theatrical Terms..........217
50 Heavens and Hells..........218
50 Angels and Fairies..........218
50 Devils, Demons and Monsters..........219
50 Forms of Torture..........219
50 Words and Phrases to express
    -Drunkenness..........220
50 Words and Phrases to express
    -Craziness..........220
50 Relations..........221
50 Receptacles..........221
50 Scottish Clans..........222
50 Things to do in a 1950's Sitting-Room..........222
50 Sounds we can make with our
    -Voices..........223
50 World Leaders..........223
50 Political Parties..........224
50 Places to have Fun..........224
50 Houses of Detention..........225
50 Traditional Cocktails..........225
50 Gods and Goddesses..........226
50 Holy Days..........226
50 Vitamins, Minerals and Nutrients..........227
50 Food Colourings and Additives..........227
50 Herbs and Spices..........228
50 Theatre Styles..........228
50 Things you might find at the Bus Stop..........229
50 Sweeteners..........229
50 Packets of Crisps..........230
50 Types of Fuel..........230
50 People that come to our Door..........231
50 Farm Crops..........231
50 Clergy Terms..........232
50 Clock and Timepieces..........232
50 Nursery Rhymes..........233
50 Snakes..........233
50 Things to put on a Shelf..........234
50 Tacky Christmas Presents..........234
50 Weird and wonderful Band Names..........235
50 Bands, Groups and Musicians beginning with
    -'U'..........235
50 Sayings..........236
50 Things to be found in a Victorian
    -Kitchen..........236
50 Primary Schools in London..........237
50 Paris Street Names..........237
50 Biggest things on Earth..........238
50 Dead Pop Stars..........238
50 Smallest things on Earth..........239
50 Forms of Greeting..........239
50 Roman Numerals..........240
50 Things to think about when playing Centre
    -Forward..........240
50 'In' and 'On' Phrases..........241
50 Liqueurs..........241
50 Women Wimbledon Players..........242
50 Bicycles..........242

50 Female Characters from History..........243
50 Facial Expressions..........243
50 Tropical Marine Fish..........244
50 Collective Nouns and Group
    -Names..........244
50 Greyhound Racing Trainers..........245
50 Some Historical Events..........245
50 Aesop Fables..........246
50 Animal Homes..........246
50 Rooms..........247
50 Things in a Forest..........247
50 Things to Drop..........248
50 Things Charles I might have thought on the
    -morning of his Beheading..........248
50 Guitar Manufacturers..........249
50 Things to sit On..........249
50 Metals and Metal Compounds..........250
50 Things in a Ladies Handbag..........250
50 Things in a Man's Pocket..........251
50 Made-up Words..........251
50 Bushes..........252
50 Floor Coverings..........252
50 Council Departments..........253
50 Areas in the Houses of Parliament..........253
50 Times of the Day..........254
50 Sharks..........254
50 Card Games..........255
50 Things to look Through..........255
50 Sums..........256
50 Well-known Plays..........256
50 Countries in Africa..........257
50 Bizarre Beliefs..........257
50 Fast-Food Outlets..........258
50 Useless Lists..........258

50 Musical Instruments

Piano
Guitar
Trumpet
Harp
Tuba
Saxophone
Glockenspiel
Tambourine
Drums
Double Bass
Piccolo
Oboe
Ukulele
French Horn
Bagpipes
Banjo
Flute
Cello
Accordion
Mouth-Organ
Triangle
Violin
Tubular Bells
Sackbut
Cor Anglais
Xylophone
Mandolin
Clarinet
Bass Guitar
Alpenhorn
Tom-Tom
Balalaika
Dulcimer
Concertina
Castanets
Bassoon
Viola
Trombone
Cornet
Clavichord
Spinet
Lute
Flageolet
Vibraphone
Lyre
Recorder
Keyboard
Zither
Organ
Penny whistle

50 Breeds of Dog

Alsatian
Corgi
Dingo
Terrier
Chow
Greyhound
Asian Pariah
Spaniel
Bloodhound
Golden Retriever
Pekinese
Bulldog
Pug
Newfoundland
Shepherd
Mastiff
Borzoi
St. Bernard
Afghan Hound
Great Dane
Poodle
Saluki
Doberman Pinscher
Dalmatian
Whippet
Beagle
Dachshund
Labrador
Irish Setter
Chihuahua
Husky
Boxer
Basset
Old English Sheepdog
Pinscher
Wolfhound
Pointer
Gorden Setter
Sealyham
Bull Terrier
Pomeranian
Coyote
Cocker Spaniel
Fox Terrier
Collie
Labrador Retriever
Courser
Staghound
King Charles Spaniel
Welsh Corgi

50 Bones in the Human Body	50 Bands, Groups and Musicians beginning with 'S'
Skull	Slade
Sternum	The Shadows
Humerus	Smashing Pumpkins
Rib	Patti Smith
Radius	Stereophonics
Ulna	Soul Asylum
Carpus	David Soul
Metacarpal	The Seekers
Distal phalanx	The Saints
Proximal phalanx	Soul Wax
Coccyx	Steelers Wheel
Sacrum	Sad Café
Pelvis	Sassafrass
Patella	Seal
Tibia	Alvin Stardust
Fibula	Smash Mouth
Middle phalanx	Slowdive
Tarsus	Frank Sinatra
Metatarsal	Soundgarden
Clavicle	Scissor Sisters
Thoracic vertebra	Slipknot
Intervertebral disc	The Searchers
Ilium	Sonic Youth
Ischium	Britney Spears
Mandible	The Strokes
Hamate	Suede
Pisiform	Barbara Streisand
Capitate	Supergrass
Triquetral	Sex Pistols
Lunate	Sham 69
Scaphoid	Shalamar
Trapezoid	Siouxsie and The Banshees
Femur	Sick Of It All
Trapezium	Slayer
Calcaneus	Steppenwolf
Talus	Smokie
Cuboid	Section 25
Navicular	Sugercubes
Cuneiform	Swell Maps
Hammer	Cat Stevens
Anvil	Sister Sledge
Stirrup	Swervedriver
Lumbar vertebra	Subway Sect
Scapula	Sum 41
Atlas	The Sundays
Axis	Soft Machine
Pubis	The Supremes
Cervical vertebra	Sparks
Distal phalanx of hallux	The Stranglers
Proximal phalanx of hallux	Simple Minds

50 Different Meals

Fish and chips
Beans on toast
Toad in the hole
Egg and bacon
Beef lasagne
Shepherd's pie
Steak and kidney pie
Lamb casserole
Bubble and squeak
Bangers and mash
Hotpot
Caesar salad
Waldorf salad
Ploughman's lunch
Irish stew
Cornish pasty
Omelette
Welsh rarebit
Boiled egg and soldiers
Chicken broth
Baked potato
Fish fingers
Egg and chips
Roast beef and Yorkshire pudding
Boiled beef and carrots
Haggis
Hamburger
Pork pie and pickle
Bath chap
Fry-up
Pot-roast
Spaghetti bolognaise
Pizza
Macaroni cheese
Donor kebab
Egg soufflé
Jellied eels and liquor
Cottage pie
Ham and eggs
Chicken chow mien
Chop suey
Goulash
Vegetable curry
Bombay duck
Lobster
Roast turkey and Brussels sprouts
Steak and chips
Sausage and onions
Meat and two veg.
Cannelloni

50 Things Guy Fawkes might have done while waiting to blow up Parliament

Picked his nose
Sneezed
Coughed
Bit his nails
Counted the rats
Checked his matches
Drummed with his fingers
Sat and dozed
Paced up and down
Realised he was scared of spiders
Thought of his sweetheart
Cursed Robert Catesby
Combed his hair
Counted his money
Ate some bread and cheese
Slept
Wondered if he'd ever get famous
Considered how much he hated James 1
Muttered a Catholic prayer
Worried if he'd fed the cat
Tutted at the price of a good pair of gaiters
Drew idly in the dust
Farted
Got spooked in the dark
Turned out his pockets
Wondered if he'd thrown out his slops
Whistled a popular ditty
Rubbed his head in his hands
Got cramp
Stretched
Dropped and did twenty press-ups
Ground his teeth
Sighed
Smoked
Became intolerably bored
Sighed again
Fiddled with his lace cuffs
Clinked his tunic buttons
Slapped his thighs
Pondered how he'd got mixed up in all of this
Thought about becoming a Christian
Cleaned out his ears
Tapped his foot
Re-counted the gunpowder kegs
Leant on a wall
Squatted
Knelt
Tried to touch the ceiling
Thought about what people would be doing on
-Nov. 5th in years to come
Wondered what 1606 would bring

50 T. Rex Songs

Children of the Revolution
Chariot Choogle
Metal Guru
Jitterbug Boogie
Baby Strange
One Inch Rock
Jeepster
Zip Gun Boogie
Soul of My Suit
Dreamy Lady
Lady
Christmas Bop
I Love to Boogie
Hot Love
The Groover
Venus Loon
Sound Pit
Planet Queen
Woodland Rock
20th. Century Boy
New York City
King of the Rumbling Spires
By the Light of the Magical Moon
Girl
Shock Rock
Get it On
Life's a Gas
Raw Ramp/Electric Boogie
Painless Persuasion
Cosmic Dancer
Telegram Sam
Solid Gold Easy Action
London Boys
Calling All Destroyers
Jupiter Liar
Dandy in the Underworld
Rabbit Fighter
Debora
Sunken Rags
Ride a White Swan
Sailors of the Highway
Born to Boogie
Thunderwing
Spaceball Ricochet
Electric Slim and the Factory Hen
Rapids
Carsmile Smith and the Old One
Mambo Sun
Baby Boomerang
Buick Mackane and the Babe Shadow

50 Board and Table Games

Monopoly
Totopoly
Antique Collector
Connect Four
Chartbuster
Buccaneer
Snail's Race
Mine-a-Million
Mary-Kate & Ashley Friendship Connection
-Game
Operation
Formula One
Campaign
Scrabble
Mr. and Mrs.
Chess
Draughts
Mr. Potato Head
Battleships
Shove-Ha'penny
Tidily-Winks
Buckaroo
Yahtzee
Pro Jax
Backgammon
Ludo
Coppitt
Snakes and Ladders
In Your Face
Go
Fox and Hounds
Crown and Anchor
Treasures and Trapdoors
Cludo
Trivial Pursuit
Mastermind
Stratego
Guess Who
Hungry Hippos
Mousetrap
Ker-Plunk
Jack Straws
The New Avengers Board Game
4 in a Row
Halls of Hogwarts
Bingo
Bagatelle
Magnetic Fish
Crossfire
Beat the Warden – Motoring Dice Game
Rawhide –Cattle Drive Game

50 Varieties of Trees	50 Kings and Queens of England
Common oak	Elizabeth 1
Holly	Edward 11
Ash	Henry 1V
Thula	Ethelred 1
Evergreen Oak	John
Lombardy Poplar	Charles 111
Willow Service Tree	Henry V11
Strawberry	Mary 1
Lawson Cyprus	Edmund Ironside
White Willow	Edwy
Pear	Harold 11
Plane	Victoria
Beech	Elizabeth 11
Sweet Chestnut	William 11
Black Poplar	Stephen
Lime	Richard 111
Norway Spruce	Anne
Larch	Ethelwulf
Box	Ethelbald
Weeping Willow	Alfred the Great
Horse Chestnut	Harold Harefoot
Field Elm	George 1
Sycamore	Henry V
Birch	Edward 1
Cherry	George 1V
Crab-Apple	Edward V111
Yew	Edward the Confessor
Douglas fir	Edward the Elder
Ginkgo	Edred
Goat Willow	Charles 11
Field Maple	George 111
Walnut	William 111
Acacia	Edmund 1
Alder	William 1V
Lebanon Cedar	Henry V1
Swamp Cyprus	Richard 11
Scots Pine	Henry 111
Silver Fir	Egbert
Aspen Poplar	Athelstan
Hornbeam	Edgar the Peaceful
Mountain Ash	Edward the Martyr
Whitebeam	James 11
Wych Elm	George V1
Corsican Pine	Henry V111
Wellingtonia	Canute
Copper Beech	Richard 1
Linden	Henry 1
Pussy Willow	Edward V11
Sallow	William 1
Rowan	Ethelred the Unready

50 States of America	50 Modes of Land Transport
Washington	Pony and trap
Montana	Horse bus
North Dakota	Tractor
Minnesota	Donkey
Wisconsin	Articulated vehicle
Michigan	Tram
Oregon	Penny-farthing
Idaho	Buggy
Wyoming	Hay cart
South Dakota	Car
Nebraska	Fire engine
New York	Litter
Iowa	Elephant
Maine	Steam carriage
New Hampshire	Horse
Vermont	Break-down lorry
California	Trolley bus
Alaska	Bus
Nevada	Coach
Utah	Furniture van
Colorado	Camel
Kansas	Huskies and sleigh
Missouri	Stage coach
Illinois	Handsome cab
Indiana	Hackney carriage
Ohio	Police van
Kentucky	Ambulance
Arizona	Road tanker
New Mexico	Van
Texas	Minibus
Oklahoma	Bicycle
Arkansas	Milk float
Louisiana	Unicycle
Tennessee	Horse and cart
North Carolina	Taxi
Alabama	Omnibus
Georgia	Steam traction engine
Florida	Mule
South Carolina	Pony
West Virginia	Lorry
Mississippi	Motorbike
Connecticut	Charabanc
District of Columbia	Sedan chair
Delaware	Chariot
Maryland	Tricycle
Massachusetts	Scooter
New Jersey	Wagon
Virginia	4-wheel drive
Rhode Island	Yak
Pennsylvania	Go-cart

50 Types of Seacraft

Clipper
Egyptian Dahabiah
Catamarran
Ocean liner
Dredger
Landing craft
Aircraft-carrier
Dug-out canoe
Schooner
Arab Felucca
Philippine raft
Racing yacht
Hovercraft
Tramp steamer
Ice-breaker
Frigate
Submarine
Whale catcher
Ferry
Viking Longboat
Spanish Galleon
Paddle ship
Rowing boat
Barge
Rubber dinghy
Nile Gaiassa
Tigris Gufa
Gondola
Troopship
Grain ship
Pilot boat
Cable-laying ship
Lifeboat
Destroyer
Battleship
Whale factory ship
Roman galley ship
Cruiser
Chinese Junk
Eastern Sampan
Rubber ring
Speedboat
Kayak
Welsh Coracle
Fishing boat
Mississippi Stern-Wheeler
Monitor
Light-ship
Research ship
Tug

50 DIY Tools

Hand axe
Bowsaw
Ratchet
Cold chisel
Electric drill
Wrench
Sander
Mallet
Wire brush
Adjustable spanner
Vice
Bench grinder
Hacksaw
Shears
Long nosed pliers
Scriber
Claw hammer
Spirit level
Craft knife
Bearing separator
Wrecking bar
Screwdriver
Long-reach scraper
Spring callipers
Socket set
3-Legged glaze breaker
Spanner
Piston ring pliers
Suction dent puller
Clip-grip tool
Wheel brace
HD riveter
Diagonal side cutters
Tin snips
Cupped nail punch
Bolt cutters
Knife
Ball pein hammer
Tape measure
Levelling plate
Trowel
Crowbar
Shovel
Sledge hammer
Paint brush
Spade
Bradawl
Bow shackle
Wire stripper
Soldering iron

50 Fruits	**50 Arterial Roads**
Apple	A19
Gooseberry	A68
Currant	A606
Apricot	A2
Strawberry	A53
Peach	A5
Raspberry	A12
Redcurrant	A14
Nectarine	A127
Plum	A1
Loganberry	A256
Greengage	A272
Damson	A3024
Blackberry	A3088
Blackcurrant	A40
Stone fruit	A39
Cherry	A30
Pippin	A87
Russet	A9
Pear	A99
Bilberry	A882
Mulberry	A977
Cantaloupe	A697
Mango	A1068
Orange	A69
Grapefruit	A96
Avocado	A171
Lemon	A4
Melon	A16
Banana	A1173
Tangerine	A180
Fig	A58
Citron	A65
Star fruit	A683
Lime	A590
Clementine	A10
Mandarin	A15
Paw-paw	A52
Papaya	A60
Pineapple	A61
Grape	A515
Rhubarb	A523
Date	A4600
Raisin	A25
Prune	A6
Pomegranate	A55
Sultana	A470
Passion fruit	A4010
Guava	A28
Lychee	A102

50 Church Features

Finial
Flying buttress
Altar
Turret
Buttress
Cornice
Porch
Gable
Octafoil
Processional path
Side chapel
Sacristy
Transept
Octahedral turret
Weathering
Spire
Aureole
Trefoil in a spandrel
Parapet
Arch
Crocket
Pinnacle
Pulpit
Organ
Arcade pier
Main vessel
Reredos
Crossing pier
Stained glass
Confessional
Mullion
Gargoyle
Niche
Nave
Attached colonette
Romanesque capital
Vaulting shaft
Embrasure
Vestibule
Oculus
Bay
Domed rib-vault
Hammer-beam roof
Tower
Steeple
Lesene
Weather-vane
Blind gabled arch
Archivolt
Cloister

50 Kitchen Items

Microwave
Potato peeler
Tureen
Garlic crusher
Saucepan
Refrigerator
Kettle
Knife
Fork
Ladle
Eggcup
Oven
Toaster
Teaspoon
Plate
Dish
Larder
Set of scales
Steamer
Pudding basin
Extractor fan
Dessert spoon
Colander
Egg timer
Washing-up brush
Wok
Jug
Spice rack
Tablespoon
Tin opener
Cup and saucer
Mug
Roasting tray
Glasses
Soupspoon
Eggspoon
Bread knife
Chopping board
Mixing bowl
Gravy boat
Bin
Sink and drainer
Washing-up bowl
Egg whisk
Baking tray
Wine rack
Copper
Frying pan
Casserole dish
Teapot

50 Illnesses and Diseases in the Middle Ages

Ague
Dropsy
Colic
Typhus
Apoplexy
Worms
Cancer
Quincy
Scurvy
Chicken pox
Kwashiorkor
Smallpox
Leprosy
Canker
St. Anthony's fire
Measles
Gripe
Consumption
Gonorrhoea
Rickets
Palsy
Syphilis
Whooping cough
Diabetes
Pleurisy
Tuberculosis
Pneumonia
Bubonic plague
Gout
Scarlet fever
Thrush
Purple fever
Spotted fever
Imposthume
Asthma
Malignant fever
Fistulas
Infantile diarrhoea
Diphtheria
Mumps
Bronchitis
Lunacy
Jaundice
Gangrene
Cholera
Typhoid
Twisting of the guts
Convulsion
Tympany
Grief

50 Star Trek Characters

Fek'lhr
Beverley Crusher
The Caretaker
Kes
Benjamin Sisko
Captain Kirk
Tom Paris
Mr. Spock
Kozak
Jean-Luc Picard
Q
Dr. Julian Bashir
Guinan
Vorik
Lieutenant Uhura
Worf
Dr. Leonard McCoy (Bones)
Admiral Mendak
Data
M-113 Creature
Seven of Nine
Gem
Odo
Locutus of Borg
Neelix
B'Elanna Torres
Christopher Pike
Pralor Automated Personnel Unit 3947
Yeoman Martha Landor
Khan
Harry Kim
Quark
Yeoman Janice Rand
Cyrus Redblock
Commander Toreth
Captain Kathryn Janeway
Hugh
Mr Sulu
The Emergency Medical Hologram (EMH)
Gul Dukat
Jadzia Dax
Geordi La Forge
Zefram Cochrane
Pavel Chekov
Chakotay
Borg Queen
William T. Riker
Montgomery Scott (Scotty)
Homm
Kahless the Unforgettable

50 TV Programmes from the 1960's

Z – Cars
Supercar
Fireball XL5
Danger Man
The Man from U.N.C.L.E.
Coronation Street
Pogles Wood
That Was The Week That Was
Monty Python's Flying Circus
Stingray
Dr. Who
The Saint
Thunderbirds
The Monkees
Dr. Kildare
Trumpton
The Morecambe and Wise Show
The Likely Lads
Softly Softly
The Girl from U.N.C.L.E.
Not Only … But Also
The Flintstones
Captain Scarlet and the Mysterons
Huckleberry Hound
The Avengers
The Addams Family
Till Death Us Do Part
Steptoe and Son
Joe 90
The Magic Roundabout
The Prisoner
Sooty and Sweep
Daktari
The Forsyte Saga
Dad's Army
Dr. Finlay's Casebook
Camberwick Green
The Jetsons
Basil Brush
What's My Line?
Saturday Night at the London Palladium
The I Love Lucy Show
The Tonight Programme
Watch with Mother
Star Trek
Crossroads
Play School
The Harry Worth Show
The Munsters
The Golden Shot

50 Number One Song Titles

You Belong to Me
Barbados
How Much is that Doggie in the Window
Mamma Mia
Unchained Melody
Mull of Kintyre
Rock Around the Clock
Rivers of Babylon
Whatever Will Be Will Be
Y.M.C.A.
Yes Tonight, Josephine
Ashes to Ashes
Great Balls of Fire
Shaddap Your Face
Beetlebum
Come on Eileen
My Old Man's a Dustman
Karma Chameleon
Poetry in Motion
99 Red Balloons
Return to Sender
19
I Want to Hold Your Hand
The Lady in Red
Always on My Mind
I'd Like to Teach the World to Sing
Baby Love
Pump Up the Volume
Mr. Tambourine Man
I Should Be So Lucky
These Boots are Made for Walking
Do They Know it's Christmas?
Release Me
Ice Ice Baby
Jumpin' Jack Flash
Oh Carolina
Lily the Pink
Gangsta's Paradise
Spirit in the Sky
Firestarter
Grandad
Barbie Girl
Long Haired Lover from Liverpool
If You Tolerate this Your Children Will be Next
Cum on Feel the Noize
Perfect Moment
Kung Fu Fighting
Should I Stay or Should I Go
Three Coins In the Fountain
I Will Always Love You

50 Colours	*50 Criminal Offences*
Black	Murder
Crimson	Indecent assault
Grey	Illegal use of firearms
Ochre	Attempted murder
Cyan	Rape
Purple	Wounding/GBH with intent
Amber	Arson
Blue	Criminal damage endangering life
Olive	Sexual assault
Scarlet	Violent assault
White	Resisting arrest
Red	Robbery
Silver	Burglary
Turquoise	Robbery with violence
Navy	Causing an affray
Yellow	Aggravated burglary
Lime	Drug dealing
Gold	Drug supplying
Ginger	Taking a vehicle without consent
Cerise	Stealing
Burnt Sienna	Perjury
Beige	Criminal damage to property
Violet	Theft
Ultramarine	Anti-social behaviour
Khaki	Disturbance of the peace
Cream	Rioting
Green	Racial harassment
Orange	Domestic violence
Magnolia	Actual bodily harm
Copper	Treason
Brown	Found in possession of a deadly weapon
Azure	Manslaughter
Pink	Driving without due care or attention
Fawn	Failure to stop following a motor accident
Tangerine	Impersonating a police officer
Burgundy	Smuggling
Emerald	Harbouring a known criminal
Maroon	Terrorism
Lilac	Trespassing
Pearl	Soliciting
Sable	Poaching
Sepia	Failing to report a crime
Tan	Tax evasion
Carmine	Fraud
Cerulean	Drunk and disorderly
Magenta	Attempted suicide
Bronze	Cannibalism
Heliotrope	Drunk in charge of a minor
Vermilion	Embezzlement
Auburn	Crime of passion

50 Things you'd find on a Farm	*50 American Baseball Teams*
Pigs	Anaheim Angels
Tractor	Pittsburgh Pirates
Sheep	Boston Red Sox
Dutch barn	Minnesota Twins
Hay	Brooklyn Trolley Dodgers
Harrow	Buffalo Buffeds
Wheat	Houston Astros
Silo tower	Tampa Bay Devil Rays
Cattle	California Angels
Milking shed	Chicago Cubs
Bales of straw	Atlanta Braves
Fallow land	Boston Bees
Duck pond	Chicago Indians
Farm house	San Francisco Giants
Orchard	Los Angeles Angels of Anaheim
Combine harvester	Cincinnati Reds
Corn rick	Kansas City Packers
Seed drill	Colorado Rockies
Horses	Detroit Tigers
Pigsty	Arizona Diamondbacks
Cow shed	Philadelphia Phillies
Poultry	St. Louis Cardinals
Plough	Washington Nationals
Grain	Baltimore Orioles
Farmers	Florida Marlins
Lambs	Houston Colt .45's
Stable	Toronto Blue Jays
Old donkey	Indianapolis Hoosiers
Hay cart	Chicago Whales
Pasture land	Kansas City Royals
Chickens	Brooklyn Tip-Tops
Barley	Los Angeles Dodgers
Foals	Milwaukee Brewers
Kale	New York Mets
Disk harrow	Chicago Orphans
Roller	Boston Beaneaters
Geese	Newark Peppers
Corn	Cleveland Indians
Hay rick	Oakland Athletics
Straw rick	Pittsburgh Rebels
Farm hands and labourers	San Diego Padres
Threshing machine	Baltimore Terrapins
Milk churns	New York Yankees
Calves	Seattle Mariners
Bucket	St. Louis Perfectors
Chick incubator	Montreal Expos
Water trough	Brooklyn Robins
Binder	St. Louis Terriers
Out buildings	Chicago White Sox
Ducks	Texas Rangers

50 Things the World could do Without

Mobile phones
Tony Blair
Thugs
Cracked pavements
OK magazine
Terry Wogan
The Simpsons
Pigeons
Youths on street corners
Dust
Toilet paper that rips instead of tears
Horses that walk away when you go up to pat them
People that talk too loud on buses
Rip-off merchants
Automated phone systems that lead you nowhere
Dog shit
Teletubbies
Another new music format
Gangs of loud-mouthed school girls
Builders
Posh and Becks
Traffic wardens
Trainers
People that walk in front of you when you're about
-to take a photo
Motorway tolls
Crime
Pollution
Monday mornings
People asking for 20p spare change
Harry Potter
Tourists
The tax-man
Leaky roofs
Smoking
Sudden rain
Rats
Dandruff
Albums re-released on CD with just one bonus track
Films re-released on DVD with 1 min. 20 secs. of
-never seen before footage
You just miss a train and the next two are cancelled
Computer pop-up windows
Spam
The Spice Girls
Brut aftershave
Despots, Tyrants and Dictators
Bird Flu
The government extending the retirement age to 67
Gas and electric bills
Coughs and colds
Mother's Day

50 Ranks within the Armed Forces

Brigadier
Major-General
Squadron Leader
Lieutenant-Commander
Sea Lord
Centurion
Group Captain
Admiral of the Fleet
Seraskier
Generalissimo
Rear-Admiral
Sergeant
Corporal
Aide-De-Camp
Commodore
Flag-Lieutenant
Brevet Officer
Marshall
Colonel
Sergeant Major
Subahdar
Decurion
Petty Officer
Commander-In-Chief
Chiliarch
Marshal of the Royal Air Force
Wing Commander
Hipparch
Leading Seaman
Captain
Subaltern
Ensign
Quatermaster
Colour Sergeant
Non-Commissioned Officer
Flight Lieutenant
Warrant Officer
Field Marshal
Vice-Admiral
Lieutenant-General
Company Sergeant Major
Orderly Officer
Imperator
Private
Lance Corporal
Sub-Lieutenant
Cornet
Lieutenant-Colonel
Trierarch
Navarch

50 Film Monsters

The Werewolf
Dracula
Freddie Kruger
Frankenstein's Monster
The Phantom of the Opera
The Abominable Snowman
The Cannibal Man
The Elephant Man
Gremlins
The Devil Bat
Blood Dolls
The Creature from the Black Lagoon
The Daleks
King Kong
Dr. Caligari
The Thing
Beetlejuice
The Mummy
The Abominable Dr. Phibes
The Alien
The Golem
The 50-Foot Woman
The Beast with Five Fingers
The Blob
The Candyman
Jaws
Doctor X
Dr. Giggles
Mr. Hyde
The Driller Killer
Edward Scissorhands
The Gorgon
The Zombie
Elvira, Mistress of Darkness
The Fiend without a Face
The Wolf Man
Frankenweenie
The Wendigo
Godzilla
Michael Myers
Orlac
Hannibal Lector
The Haunted Strangler
The Hollow Man
The Hunchback of Notre Dame
Dr Moreau
Jack The Ripper
Mr. Sardonicus
Nosferatu
The Winged Serpent

50 Things to think about when fielding 'Deep Fine Leg'

I'm bowling next
The sun's in my eyes
There's grass stains on my knees
Hope my bum looks good in these trousers
Wish that kid would stop screaming
Another jumper round his waist and he'll fall over
I count six seagulls
That roof needs repairing
Not another advert for athlete's foot powder
Did I leave the gas on?
What if I miss an easy catch?
Wow, it's getting hot
Why me
Did I pay my credit card bill?
Must put a new button on this shirt
Should have brought some sunglasses
I always draw the short straw
Haven't these people got anything better to do?
This is a good way to get paid for doing nothing
Should I buy the new Ford Fiesta?
Wonder what me wife Karen's up to?
I count five crows
Am I gonna be standing here every Sunday?
What if it suddenly rains?
Must concentrate
Interesting clouds
Karen said she'd be back at six
Hope I don't get clamped
At least I'll be the first one back inside if it rains
Getting peckish now
One magpie…is that unlucky
Is that Sheila in the red top?
Karen was out very late last night
Should I have brought an umbrella?
Oh Lord! Here it comes…
Cheers, good catch, even if I say so myself
What's he staring at
Must get around to clearing out the garage
How does the umpire know where Karen was last
-night?
There goes ol' baggy pants
Those onions are repeating on me
Two magpie's, that's better
Did I shut down the computer?
Uh-oh, ere comes a '6!'
Shit…-well you try better!
Now it is raining
Hope I've not got a parking ticket
Come to think of it wasn't the umpire's jumper in
-the back of Karen's car last week?!
…I don't feel like bowling next

50 Words to describe 'Cold'	50 Well-known Cricketers from 1938
Chilly	Leslie Ames
Nippy	R.W.V. Robins
Chapping	Charlie Barnett
Draughty	Jim Sims
Blitz	Les Berry
Freezing	C.I.J. Smith
Not warm	Denis Compton
Windy	Denis Smith
It's a bit 'tatters	Peter Smith
Brass monkeys	Don Bradman
Wintry	Bill Copson
Blue	E. Davies
Icy	John Timms
Frigid	Bill Edrich
Gelid	Kenneth Farnes
Frosty	Hedley Verity
Like Siberia	Harold Gimblett
Zero	Bill Voce
Like the grave	Tom Goddard
Bitter	Cyril Washbrook
Biting	Alf Gover
Like the North Pole	Arthur Wellard
Raw	Wally Hammond
Keen	Tom Worthington
Like the arctic	Joe Herdstaff
Cool	R.E.S. Wyatt
Parky	Len Hutton
Fresh	Norman Yardley
Inclement	James Langridge
Brumal	C.L. Badcock
Perishing	M.G. Waite
Chilled to the bone	Maurice Leyland
Shivery	H. E. Dollery
Teeth chattering	Sydney Barnes
Sub-zero	Neil McCorkell
Like an ice-box	B.A. Barnett
Zone-out	Jim Parks
Polar	E.L. McCormick
Like stone	Eddie Paynter
Goosebumped-up	Stan McCabe
Jack Frost's about	Reg Perks
Icicles	Lindsay Hassett
Like January	George Pope
Bleak	Leary Constantine
Numbing	L. Fleetwood-Smith
Chilled to the marrow	E.S. White
Algid	Frank Ward
Bleak	C.W. Walker
Glacial	Bill O'Reilly
	Jack Fingleton

50 Gangster Movies from the 1960's and '70's

Dirty Harry
The French Connection
The Valachi Papers
Magnum Force
Precinct 45
The Getaway
McQ
The Salzburg Connection
Madigan
Tony Rome
La Samourai
Bonnie and Clyde
The St. Valentine's Day Massacre
Shamus
Harper
Murder Incorporated
Alphaville
Bloody Mama
Klute
The Grisson Gang
Ma Baker's Killer Brood
The Long Goodbye
Superfly
Bullet
Robbery
The Heist
The Burglars
The Mechanic
The Criminal
Get Carter
99 and 44/100% Dead
Shaft
Portrait of a Mobster
Le Doulos
Spin of a Coin
New Face from Hell
Blue Gardinia
Ocean's 11
The Stone Killer
Prime Cut
The Godfather
Pulp
Johnny Cool
The Italian Job
French Connection II
The Last Run
Puppet on a Chain
The Cincinnati Kid
Lady in Cement
Borsalino

50 White Wines

Chablis
Sancerre
Pouilly Fuisse
Chardonnay
Alsace Riesling
Franken Wines
Trebbiano
Dao
Alsace Silvaner
Rulander
Verdicchio
Minho
Chenin Blanc
Anjou
Vernaccia
Rioja
Riesling
Muscadet
Valdepenas
Sauvignon
Pouilly Blanc Furne
Steen
Labouré-Roi
Saumur
Bergerac
Leibfraumilch
Castelli Romani
Entre Deux Mers
Frascati
Barsac
Passito
Tokay
Muscat
Hermitage
Graves
Corvo Bianco
Malvasia
Piesporter
Cerons
Gewurztraminer
Macon Blanc
Vouvray
Spatlese Wines
Monbazillac
Malaga
Asti Spumante
Eiswein
Bonnezeaux
Trockenbeerenaus Lese Wines
Abboccato Wines

50 Grand National Winners

Ally Sloder
Ambush
Ascetics Silver
Ballymacad
Battleship
Ben Nevis
Bogskar
Covertcoat
Double Chance
Drogheda
Drumcree
Eremon
Forbra
Freebooter
Glenside
Golden Miller
Grackle
Gregalach
Grudon
Jack Horner
Jenkinstown
Jerry M
Kellsboro' Jack
Kirkland
L'Escargot
Lutteur 111
Manifesto
Master Robert
Moifaa
Music Hall
Nickel Silver
Party Politics
Poethlyn
Red Alligator
Red Rum
Reynoldstown
Royal Mail
Rubic
Sergeant Murphy
Shannon Lass
Shaun Goilin
Shaun Spadah
Sheila's Cottage
Sprig
Sunloch
The Soarer
Tipperary Tim
Troytown
Vermouth
Workman

50 Gangster Movies from the 1930's and '40's

Little Caesar
Scarface
Public Enemy
On Wing of Song
Angels with Dirty Faces
Doorway to Hell
The Roaring Twenties
The Petrified Forest
The Maltese Falcon
Sleep, My Love
Walk a Crooked Mile
The Killers
Five Star Find
Kiss of Death
Public Hero No. 1
The Thin Man
Hot Spot
Nick Carter, Master Detective
Farewell My Lovely
The High Window
Lady in the Lake
The Big Sleep
Night After Night
White Heat
No Orchids for Miss Blandish
Algiers
The Last Gangster
The Gangster
False Faces
Brighton Rock
The Big Steal
The Blue Dahlia
A Walk in the Sun
Cry of the City
Noose
The Spanish Cape Mystery
The Mandarin Mystery
Eyes in the Night
The Hidden Eye
The Falcon Takes Over
New Face in Hell
Johnny Stool Pigeon
Double Indemnity
False Witness
The Detective
Lady in the Trunk
Murder on a Train
Sleeping Car to Trieste
Pepe Le Moko
Uneasy Terms

50 Breakfasts

Egg and bacon
Cup of tea
Cornflakes
Sausage and egg
Black pudding
Egg on toast
Rice Crispies
Wild mushrooms on toast
Cup of coffee and a biscuit
Yoghurt
Boiled egg
Coco Pops
Pop Tarts
Two boiled eggs
Sultana Bran
Poached egg on toast
All-Bran
Vegetable juice
Piece of fruit
Sausage and beans
Toast and marmalade
Toast and jam
Tinned tomatoes on toast
Bacon sarni
Sausage, egg and bacon
Rivita
Selection of cold meats and cheeses
Champagne
Sugar Puffs
Half a grapefruit
Crunchy Nut Cornflakes
Kippers
Apple juice
Porridge
Wheatabix
Shredded Wheat
Shreddies
Glass of freshly squeezed orange juice
Beans on toast
Egg, bacon and beans
Muffin
Cereal bar
Yoghurt bar
Last nights leftover curry
Stewed fruit
Glass of milk
Ready Brek
"Darling I never rise before noon"
Two sausages, egg, bacon, beans and mushrooms,
Tomato juice

50 Ways to say 'I Love You'

Je t'aime
Ich liebe dich
Ti amo
.. / .-.. --- ...- . / -.-- --- ..-
My darling
T'estimo
Noi makokonda; Ndimakukonda
Here's looking at you kid
Will you marry me
Ya tebya lyublyu
Mi amas vin
Minä rakastan sinua
Let's get hitched
Tha gradh agam ort
Se erotao
Maney tamari satey pyar che
Honey
Aloha i'a au oe; Aloha au la o'e
Sweetheart
Ik hou van je
Aishite imasu
I adore you
Iway ovelay ouyay
Kocham cie
I love ya
Eu te amo
Keyagorata
My dearest
Ani ohev otach
Mai tumaha pyar karta hu
I wouldn't trade you for the world
'Rwy'n dy garu di
Khoshim awee
As tave myliu
Mahn dousett daram; Ushegheh-tam
Te iubesc
My sweet angel
Jag älskar dig
Ek her jou lief
Sugar-pie, honey-pie
Ohhe-buk
Nin ko nga chitde; Chit pa de
Ngor oi ley
Volim te; Ljubim te
Ndinoluda
I Chaa di Garn
Iniibig kita; Mahal kita
Phom Rak Khun
You're bad buff
Seni seviyorum

50 Capital Cities of the World	**50 Items of Clothing**
Phnom Penh	Vest
Panama City	Trousers
Bridgetown	Corset
Lisbon	Smock
Paris	Dungarees
Roseau	Mini skirt
Kigali	Sarong
London	Pants
Tegucigalpa	Pinafore dress
Riga	Zoot suit
Copenhagen	Coat
Brasilia	Sari
Mexico City	Jeans
Bergen	Tights
T'bilisi	Crinoline
Helsinki	Sweatshirt
Lusaka	Catsuit
Dhaka	Tracksuit
Moscow	Socks
Cairo	Waistcoat
Washington D. C.	Kimono
Tokyo	Jacket
Ouagadougou	Pullover
Dublin	Camisole
Vienna	Shirt
Athens	Skirt
Saint George's	Tank top
Guatemala City	Oxford bags
Vaduz	Blouse
Ulaanbaatar	Caftan
San Salvador	Toga
Prague	T-shirt
Windhoek	Blazer
San Marino	Shorts
Santiago	Leotard
Ottawa	Knickers
Oslo	Cassock
Stockholm	Anorak
Madrid	Overalls
Ljubljana	Galligaskins
Rome	Knickerbockers
Zagreb	Cocktail dress
Berlin	Tie
Warsaw	Cravat
Sofia	Slacks
Bratislava	Slippers
Budapest	Dressing gown
Ashkhabad	Frock
Sarajevo	Woolly
Skopje	Cardigan

50 Things Red Riding Hood might have taken to Grandma's

Home-baked bread
Some nice Swiss cheese
Firelighters
Mrs. Riding Hood's home-made jam
Bottle of lemonade
Matches
Milk
To The Lighthouse novel by Virginia Woolf
Local paper
Sponge cake
Some soft butter
Crossword puzzle book
Grapes
Company of Wolves film on DVD
Scones
Hot water bottle
Newly knitted shawl
Crumpets
New computer game software
Council tax bill
Torch for coming home with later
Map of the forest
Woodcutters number on her mobile
Magazine
Spare hood
Umbrella
Freshly washed and ironed nightie for grandma
Paracetamol
Coal
Something for an upset stomach
Blanket
B/w werewolf video
Dancing with Wolves starring: Kevin Costner
Slippers
Soup
Reading glasses
Batteries for grandma's iPod
Change of clothes and lipstick
Bed socks
Bed pan
Sweets
Mr. Riding Hood's home-brewed beetroot wine
Harmonica
Thermometer
Apple pie
Kindling
Bobble hat
Travel alarm clock
Compass
Rendezvous point for meeting the woodcutter

50 Triple-Barrel Words and Phrases

Cul-de-sac
Had-I-wist
Jack-a-dandy
Fleur-de-lys
Put-and-take
Jig-a-jig
Smash-and-grab
Horse-god-mother
Cul-de-four
Bric-a-brac
Make-or-break
Slug-foot-second
Cock-a-doodle
Jack-o'-lantern
Tac-au-tac
Cat-and-mouse
King-of-arms
Egg-and-tongue
Vis-à-vis
Cul-de-lampe
Flower-de-luce
All-play-all
Jack-a-Lent
Wink-a-peep
Knife-and-fork
Face-to-face
Out-and-out
Pied-a-terre
Tête-à-tête
Cock-a-hoop
Ups-a-daisy
Heart-to-heart
In-and-out
Dog-eat-dog
Jack-in-office
Egg-and-spoon
Cat-and-dog
Kiss-me-quick
Slug-a-bed
Cock-and-bull
Dog's-tail-grass
Hen-and-chickens
Horse-and-buggy
Off-the-peg
Pitch-and-putt
Cock-a-bondy
Rat-a-tat
Hard-a-lee
One-to-one
Up-to-date

50 Vegetables	50 Things to 'Hold'
Pea	Pen
Beetroot	Bat
Cabbage	Club
Potato	Racquet
Carrot	Hands
Leek	Sword
Sorrel	A dinner and dance
Lettuce	Fork
Onion	Money
Spring onion	Rifle
Aubergine	Stick
Eggplant	The front page
Swede	Golf club
Turnip	Reins
Okra	Scissors
Spinach	Gun
Chilli	Brush
Brussels sprout	Pencil
Broccoli	Steering wheel
Jerusalem artichoke	Programme
Parsnip	Rattle
Beansprouts	Cigarette
Runner bean	A demonstration
Squash	Newspaper
Pumpkin	Dog lead
Yam	Dagger
Courgette	Lighter
Edible seaweed	Ball
Cauliflower	A world record
Sweetcorn	Phone
Broadbean	Oar
Garlic	Spoon
Chicory	An election
Red cabbage	Toothbrush
Mustard and cress	Walking stick
Sweet potato	Comb
Calabrese	Scrubbing brush
Mangetout	Knife
Asparagus	Remote control
Shallots	A meeting
Chinese cabbage	Magazine
Marrow	Bag
Celery	Saw
Cucumber	Magnifying glass
Endive	Calculator
Radish	Match
Love-apple	Cigar
Watercress	Camera
Sauerkraut	A raffle
Curly kale	The bus up

50 Species of Birds	50 Ways to Die
50 Species of Birds	*50 Ways to Die*

<table>
<tr><td>Cormorant</td><td>Hung</td></tr>
<tr><td>Mallard</td><td>Garrotted</td></tr>
<tr><td>Red-necked Grebe</td><td>Beheaded</td></tr>
<tr><td>Black Grouse</td><td>Ducking</td></tr>
<tr><td>Cuckoo</td><td>Burnt at the stake</td></tr>
<tr><td>Kingfisher</td><td>Buried alive</td></tr>
<tr><td>Swift</td><td>Made to walk the plank</td></tr>
<tr><td>Ostrich</td><td>Pushed under a train</td></tr>
<tr><td>Lesser Spotted Woodpecker</td><td>Hung, drawn and quartered</td></tr>
<tr><td>Avocet</td><td>In front of a firing squad</td></tr>
<tr><td>Rock Pipet</td><td>Flayed alive</td></tr>
<tr><td>Robin</td><td>Boiled alive</td></tr>
<tr><td>Chaffinch</td><td>Bitten by a snake</td></tr>
<tr><td>Corn Bunting</td><td>Thrown over a cliff</td></tr>
<tr><td>Raven</td><td>Guillotined</td></tr>
<tr><td>Sandwich Tern</td><td>AIDS</td></tr>
<tr><td>Puffin</td><td>A fall from a horse</td></tr>
<tr><td>Heron</td><td>Shot</td></tr>
<tr><td>Egyptian Goose</td><td>Strangled</td></tr>
<tr><td>Smew</td><td>Lost at sea</td></tr>
<tr><td>Parrot</td><td>By electric chair</td></tr>
<tr><td>Honey Buzzard</td><td>Eaten alive by piranhas</td></tr>
<tr><td>Kite</td><td>Stoned</td></tr>
<tr><td>Turtle Dove</td><td>Crucified</td></tr>
<tr><td>Golden Eagle</td><td>Death on the wheel</td></tr>
<tr><td>Swan</td><td>Dismembered</td></tr>
<tr><td>Lady Amherst's Pheasant</td><td>Impaled</td></tr>
<tr><td>Barn Owl</td><td>Gas chamber</td></tr>
<tr><td>Toucan</td><td>Eaten by a shark</td></tr>
<tr><td>Jack Snipe</td><td>Genocide</td></tr>
<tr><td>Blackbird</td><td>Left to rot in prison</td></tr>
<tr><td>Starling</td><td>Gored by a bull</td></tr>
<tr><td>Dartford Warbler</td><td>Run over by a car</td></tr>
<tr><td>Wren</td><td>By lethal injection</td></tr>
<tr><td>Skylark</td><td>Poisoned</td></tr>
<tr><td>House Martin</td><td>Death by a thousand cuts</td></tr>
<tr><td>Jay</td><td>To die a traitors death</td></tr>
<tr><td>Magpie</td><td>Bird flu</td></tr>
<tr><td>Kiwi</td><td>Bow-strung</td></tr>
<tr><td>Great Northern Diver</td><td>Overdose</td></tr>
<tr><td>Scaup</td><td>Auto de fe</td></tr>
<tr><td>Kestrel</td><td>Asphyxiation</td></tr>
<tr><td>Marsh Harrier</td><td>Drowned</td></tr>
<tr><td>Quail</td><td>Heart attack</td></tr>
<tr><td>Ruff</td><td>Run over by a bus</td></tr>
<tr><td>Great Tit</td><td>Bludgeoned</td></tr>
<tr><td>Carrion Crow</td><td>Run through with a sword</td></tr>
<tr><td>Macaw</td><td>In the lion's den</td></tr>
<tr><td>Oystercatcher</td><td>A nagging wife</td></tr>
<tr><td>Bar-Tailed Godwit</td><td>Trampled underfoot</td></tr>
</table>

50 Painters and Artists	**50 'Off' and 'Out' Phrases**
Claude Monet	Out of order
Edouard Manet	Off the cuff
Max Ernst	Out-of-date
Marcel Du Champs	Off the beam
Renoir	Out-of-doors
Matisse	Off his head
Joseph Beuys	Out-of-body
Caravaggio	Off his face
Joseph Turner	Out and out
John Constable	Off the wall
Frida Kahlo	Out by nine
Salvador Dali	Off-ground-touch
Andy Warhol	Out you go
Picasso	Off-and-on
Stanley Spencer	Out-of-work
David Hockney	Off beam below
Mondrain	Out-board motor
August Strindberg	Off the road
Frans Hals	Out run her
Robert Crumb	Off-putting
Damien Hurst	Out of season
Rembrant	Off shore leave
Michelangelo	Out of breath
Jan van Eyck	Off-the-peg
Rachel Whiteread	Out of time
Leonardo da Vinci	Off-street parking
Gainsborough	Out-side in
Raphael	Off you go
Titian	Outside edge
Valasquez	Off one's oats
Rubens	Outside left
Hogarth	Offset printing
David Cox	Out of use
Augustus John	Off the wrist
Vincent Van Gogh	Out of service
Wu Chen	Off his food
Pieter Bruegel	Out of bounds
James McNeill Whistler	Off to market
Tracey Emin	Out of stock
Roy Lichtenstein	Off at night
Bridget Riley	Out by miles
Jackson Pollock	Off to bed
Masaccio	Off his trolley
Botticelli	Out of favour
Sarah Lucas	Off shore purchase
Hieronymus Bosch	Out tonight?
Albrecht Durer	Off she walked
Rene Magritte	Out on patrol
Toulouse-Lautrec	Off to the shops
Hokusai	Out of milk

50 Breeds of Cats	50 Old London Street Cries
Ocelot	'Flowers, penny a bunch'
Turkish Van	'Buy a fine singing bird'
Oriental Shorthair	'3 rows a penny pins. Short, whites an' middlings'
Wildcat	Fine writeing ink'
Persian Longhair	'Old shoes for some broomes'
California Spangled	'Past one o'clock, an' a fine morning'
Lion	'Buy a fork or a fire shovel'
Birman	'Twelve pence a peck, oysters'
Clico cat	'2 pence to London Bridge, 3 pence to the Strand'
Korat	'Crab, crab, any crab'
Bobcat	'Buy a very fyne mousetrap, or a rat-trap or a
Somali Sorrel	-tormentor for your fleas'
Ragdoll	'Any old iron take money for'
Tiger	'New River water'
Maine Coon	'My bell I keep ringing, and walk about merrily
Colour Pointed Longhair	-singing – my muffins'
Japanese Bobtail	'Ye maidens and men, come for what ye lack, and
American Wirehair	-buy the fair ballads I have in my pack'
Cheshire Cat	'Milk below, maids'
Leopard	'What d'ye lack, what d'ye lack my masters'
Burmese	'Letters for post'
Turkish Angora	'Taters all 'ot'
Tortoiseshell cat	'Dumplings ho'
British shorthair	'Who'l have a dip and a wallop for a bawbee'
Cheetah	'Barcelona philberts'
Balinese	'Chimney Swepes'
Javanese	'Sixpence a pound, fair cherryes'
Egyptian Mau	'Lantorne Candellyht'
Panther	'New-born eggs, 8 a grout, crack 'em an' try 'em'
Somali Silver	'Bonnets for to fit English heads'
Scottish Fold	'Buy my wash balls Gemmen and Ladies'
Lynx	'Good sausages'
Siamese	'The bear bayting'
Puma	'Hote mutton poys'
Marmalade cat	'Jaw-work, a whole pot for a ha'penny, hazelnuts'
Exotic	'Quick periwinckels'
Manx	'Rype chesnuts'
American Shorthair	'Songs, penny a sheet'
Felix the Cat	'Buy any pompcons'
Jaguar	'Buy a longe brush'
Colour Pointed British Shorthair	'Hote eele pyes'
Cornish Rex	'Holloway cheese cakes'
Chartreux	'Cat's meat, dawg's meat'
Cougar	'A penny stick to beat your wives'
Tonkinese	'Hearts, liver or lights'
Havana Brown	'Come buy my nettle-tops'
Abyssinian	'Old chairs to mend'
Crown Classic Tabby	Strawberrys, scarlet strawberrys'
Chocolate Point Siamese	'Round & sound, 5 pence a pound, Duke cherries'
Russian Shorthair	'Clean yer boots, shine 'em, Sir'
	'Fresh cabbidge'
	'Hokey Pokey'
	'O' clo'

50 Central London Street Names

Bond Street
Gray's Inn Road
Aldwych
Soho Square
The Mall
Queen's Gate Terrace
Regent Street
Stew Lane
Gutter Lane
Oxford Street
Clerkenwell Road
Victoria Embankment
The Cut
Duke of Wellington Place
Shaftesbury Avenue
Old Kent Road
Northumberland Avenue
Old Fish Street
Haunch of Venison Yard
Wardour Street
Ironmonger Lane
The Strand
Chancery Lane
High Holborn
Lansborough Place
Tottenham Court Road
Hanover Square
Falconberg Court
Park Lane
Edgware Road
Whitechapel High Street
Poultry
Piccadilly
Turpentine Lane
Angel Passage
Crutched Friars
Old Street
Great Titchfield Street
Duck Lane
Cumberland Terrace Mews
New Cavendish Street
Gunpowder Square
Garlick Hill
Charing Cross Road
All Souls Place
Bull Inn Court
Knightsbridge
Catherine Wheel Yard
Liverpool Street
Porchester Terrace

50 British Prime Ministers

Henry Pelham
John Major
Viscount Palmerston
Earl of Rosebery
Margaret Thatcher
Edward Stanley
T. Pelham-Holles
Tony Blair
James Callaghan
G. Hamilton-Gordon
Harold Wilson
John Russell
Edward Heath
Sir Robert Peel
William Lamb
Alec Douglas-Home
Harold Macmillan
Sir Anthony Eden
Arthur Wellesley
Winston Churchill
Charles Grey
Clement Attlee
Neville Chamberlain
Frederick Robinson
Stanley Baldwin
George Canning
Ramsay MacDonald
Robert Jenkinson
Spencer Perceval
William Bentinck
Andrew Bonar Law
Henry Addington
William Grenville
David Lloyd George
Herbert Asquith
William Pitt (the Younger)
H. Campbell-Bannerman
William FitzMaurice
Arthur Balfour
C. Watson-Wentworth
Marquess of Salisbury
Fredrick North
Augustus Fitzroy
William Gladstone
Benjamin Disraeli
William Pitt (the Elder)
George Grenville
John Stuart
William Cavendish
Sir Robert Walpole

50 Breeds of Horses and Ponies

Irish Draught
Dartmoor
Saddlebred
Clydesdale
Connemara
Australian Stock horse
Exmoor
Kabarda
Pinto
Vlaamperd
American Shetland
Shire
Camargue
Australian pony
Welsh Cob
Kiger Mustang
Welsh Mountain pony
Hackney horse
Percheron
Cart-horse
Riwoche Wild horse
Shetland
Lipizzaner
Brumbie
Barbary horse
Highland
Morgan
Minature pony
Icelandic horse
Andalucian
Ardennais
New Forest pony
Tennessee Walking horse
Fjord
Carriage-horse
Hanoverian
Falabella
Appaloosa
Suffolk Punch
Quarter horse
Arab
Orlov Trotter
Thoroughbred
Barb
Onegar
Belgium Draught
Przewalski's Wild horse
Hunter
Cleveland Bay
Pit pony

50 Things Sleeping Beauty Might have Said when Woken by the Prince

Cor, what a liberty!
Well you took your time!
Did you shave this morning?
Arr, my back's killing me
I was right in the middle of a good dream then
You ugly git!
There's just no privacy in these old castles!
Slobber, slobber!
Hello darling!
Is it Tuesday?
Next time, don't dribble all over me
ID?
I'm starving!
(Fart…)
Is that what they're wearing these days?
Nice arse!
Next time, come a bit sooner
Have you been eating pickled onions?
What time is it?
Ahh! I've got cramp!
That tree's grown
Just wait till I get my hands on that damn witch!
Cheers, the wind's been blowing up my skirt all
-month
Didn't you pass by last week?
Hi
Typical, I might have known it was you
I could murder a burger
Nice kiss. Don't stop!
At least you're not a dwarf!
Come on in!
Haven't I seen you up at the palace?
I hope you're not one of those pretend princes?
What nice eyes… coloured contacts?
How long have I been sleeping?
Did you knock?
(Burp…)
Your nasal hair needs a good clipping
Got a mint
Gee, I really need the loo!
Please! No tongues
Oh well, beggars can't be choosers
Hey, hey! Don't get too carried away
Nice tunic
Is that a nightingale or a skylark over in that tree?
You could have at least asked
Typical! Send a boy to do a man's job!
What a nightmare!
Well you certainly know how to keep a girl
-waiting!
Hello, fat boy!
And that's your horse…

50 Film Actors	50 Well-known Buildings
Dustin Hoffman	Notre Dame
John Hurt	St. Paul's Cathedral
John Gielgud	Palacio de las Cadenas
Tom Cruise	The Eiffel Tower
Brad Pitt	Capilla del Salvador
Robert Redford	St. Basil's Cathedral
Anthony Hopkins	The Temple of Artemis
William Hurt	Milan Cathedral
Clark Gable	The Tower of London
Ewan McGregor	Bauhaus Building
Michael Douglas	Guggenheim Museum
Dennis Hopper	Mausoleum at Halicarnassus
Paul Newman	Gran Via
Bruce Willis	Statue of Liberty
Benn Afflick	Century Tower
Jack Nicholson	Palace of the Statues
Peter Sellers	The Great Pyramid
Johnny Depp	Chrysler Building
Charles Bronson	The Leaning Tower of Pisa
Mel Gibson	Great Arch
Patrick Stewart	Seagram Building
Michael Caine	Sydney Opera House
Robert DeNiro	Empire State Building
Peter Ustinov	The Pantheon
Richard Burton	Taj Mahal
Laurence Olivier	Houses of Parliament
Robert Carlyle	The Colosseum
Christopher Lee	The Hanging Gardens of Babylon
Ray Winston	Church of the Spilled Blood
Bela Lugosi	Buckingham Palace
Sean Connery	The Vatican
James Fox	Canary Wharf
Marlon Brando	Dome of the Rock
Gene Hackman	Sacré Coeur
Ralph Richardson	Florence Cathedral
Charles Laughton	The Parthenon
Harvey Kietel	Santiago de Compostela
Anthony Perkins	Pharos of Alexandria
Gary Oldman	The Globe Theatre
Sylvester Stallone	Solomon's Temple
Dirk Bogarde	The Acropolis
Humphrey Bogart	Alexander Nevsky Cathedral
Sean Penn	The Pentagon
Victor Mature	The Dancing Building
John Mills	Yamoussoukro Basilica
Richard Attenborough	Temple of Luxor
Oliver Reed	Château Frontenac
Jim Carrey	Brighton Pavilion
Danny De Vito	Rijksmuseum
Willem Dafoe	La Sagrada Familia

50 English Authors

Virginia Woolf
Henry Fielding
Emily Bronte
Iian Sinclair
Christopher Isherwood
R. D. Blackmore
Anna Sewell
Geoffrey Chaucer
Ian Rankin
Daniel Defoe
Poppy Z. Brite
Joseph O'Connor
Charles Dickens
Frances Hodgson Burnett
Dan Brown
Alan Sillitoe
George Orwell
Oscar Wilde
JK Rowling
G. K. Chesterton
Aldous Huxley
William Shakespeare
Ian McEwan
Kenneth Grahame
Irving Welsh
George Eliot
Ben Jonson
Rudyard Kipling
Lionel Shriver
Anthony Trollop
Louisa May Alcott
D. H. Lawrence
Thomas Hardy
Sir Arthur Conan Doyle
Jane Austen
Richard Adams
Mark Twain
Anthony Burgess
William Golding
Mary Shelly
Charles Kingsley
Martina Cole
Graham Greene
J. M. Barrie
Lewis Carroll
Robert Louis Stevenson
Sir H. Rider Haggard
Jerome K. Jerome
Andrea Levy
Evelyn Waugh

50 Contemporary Illnesses and Diseases

Glandular fever
Chicken pox
German measles
Bird flu
Mumps
Muscular-skeletal disease
Rubella
Scabies
Human immunodeficiency virus (HIV)
Shingles
Attention deficit hyperactivity disorder (AD/HD)
Asperges syndrome
Cardio-vascular disease
Tourettes syndrome
Chlamydia
Anorexia nervosa
Autism
Cancer
Respiratory disease
Bulimia nervosa
Hepatitis A, B or C
Acquired immune deficiency syndrome (AIDS)
Diabetes
Gastro-intestinal disease
Meningitis
Fibrosis
Diphtheria
Whooping-cough
Small pox
Scarlet fever
Typhus
Polio
Tetanus
Rabies
Drug addiction
Asian flu
Obesity
Repetitive compulsive disorder (RCD)
Pneumonia
Rickets
Purple fever
Hypochondria
Pre-menstrual tension (PMT)
Alcoholism
Cystitis
Bronchitis
Prostatitis
Migraine
Epilepsy
Encephalitis

50 Alternative ways to Earn a Living	**_50 Ways to Murder Someone_**
Artist	Shoot
Thief	Throttle
Confidence trickster	Bludgeon
Royalty	Push over a cliff
Burglar	Suffocate
Housewife	Strangle
Pole dancer	Stab
Musician	Poison
Hangman	Shove under a train
Acrobat	Starve
Prostitute	Garrotte
Spy	Stone
Saboteur	Hang
Monk	Behead
Busking	Tamper with the brakes of a car
Stripper	Drown
eBay powerseller	Crucify
Extra	Burn at the stake
Life class model	Guillotine
Belly dancing	Gas
Begging	Axe
Research guinea pig	Bayonet
Leaflet distributor	Bomb
Baked potato peddler	Electrocute
Look-alike	Bury alive
Lap dancer	Flay alive
Nun	Cut their throat
Juggler	Run through with the sword
Street actor	Hang, draw and quarter
Drug dealer	Knife
Envelope stuffer	Walk the plank
Paper boy	Play Des O'Conner records continuously
Strawberry picker	Frighten to death
Smuggler	Beat to a pulp
Fire-eater	Acid bath
Astronaut	Push out of a 10-storey window
Shoe shiner	Blow up
Whaler	Impale
Slave	Hit and run
Ice-cream seller	Overdose
Mole catcher	Lock in the cellar
Chimney sweep	Boiled alive
Clown	Death by weights
Coffin maker	Keel-haul
Rat catcher	Throw to the lions
Queen's guardsman	A duel
Taxidermist	Death on the wheel
Fumigator	Slingshot
Goat herdsman	Set fire to
Grave digger	Trampled

50 Materials and Fabrics	50 Countries
Cotton	Andorra
Rayon	Canada
Velvet	Albania
Hessian	United Sates of America
Towelling	Austria
Calico	Mexico
Muslin	St. Vincent and the Grenadines
Damask	Azerbaijan
Wool	Greenland
Denim	Bangladesh
Tweed	United Kingdom
Brocade	Belgium
Khaki	Norway
Gingham	Benin
Seersucker	Mongolia
Lace	Herzegovina
Chintz	Brazil
Serge	Antigua and Barbuda
Crepe de chine	Burundi
Grosgrain	France
Chenille	Central African Republic
Mohair	Spain
Corduroy	Croatia
Suede	Kazakhstan
Cashmere	Chad
Leather	Sudan
Satin	Paraguay
Cheesecloth	Cyprus
Alpaca	Czech Republic
Bombazine	Ivory Coast
Oilskin	Denmark
Gabardine	Dominican Republic
Vicuna	Australia
Silk	Equatorial Guinea
Terylene	Trinidad and Tobago
Angora	Germany
Worsted	Ghana
Baize	Hungary
Doeskin	Lebanon
Flannel	Lithuania
Swansdown	Luxembourg
Buckskin	Macedonia
Winceyette	Netherlands
Jute	Russia
Homespun	Rwanda
Duffel	Slovakia
Paisley	Switzerland
Flannelette	Togo
Velour	United Arab Emirates
Drill	Yugoslavia

50 Embarrassing things to Buy

Flip-flops
KY Jelly
Best of Donny Osmond CD
Anusol cream
My Little Pony box set
Condoms –size small
Economy size toilet rolls x12
Top shelf magazine
Hush Puppies
Brut aftershave
Knitting Weekly
Roland Rat boxer shorts
Huge bag of cat litter
Pooper scooper
Mr. Blobby wallpaper
Box set of Harry Potter books
Loo brush
Old Bruce Forsyth record
Woman's Weekly
Giant cuddly toy won at the fair
Teenage Mutant Hero Turtle yoghurt
Leg-warmers
Lard
A support truss
Miss Piggy duvet cover
Can of ginger beer
On The Buses DVD
Lavatory air freshener
Anti-flatulence tablets
Big box of Teletubbies nappies
Bright yellow trainers
Kiss-me-quick hat
Sing-A-Long The Sound of Music tickets
Carry On Camping DVD
Woolworth's electric guitar
Pop socks
Scooby Doo spaghetti
Shandy
Incontinence pants
A divorce
Viagra
Cassette tape recorder
The Simpson's tie
The 'morning after' pill
A Daffy Duck T-shirt
Spot cream
Colonic irrigation session
A pouffe
Dentures
Cilla Black biography

50 Mammals

Ibex
Giraffe
Horse
Gorilla
Fox
Tiger
Mongoose
Red Squirrel
Lion
Deer
Hyena
Zebra
Tapir
Armadillo
Rat
Wolf
Monkey
Duck-Billed Platypus
Leopard
Rhino
Polar Bear
Walrus
Jackal
Otter
Skunk
Elk
Hippopotamus
Bison
Shrew
Wild boar
Ring-Tailed Lemur
Chimpanzee
Buffalo
Giant Panda
Kangaroo
Stoat
Mouse
Gazelle
Hedgehog
Weasel
Sloth
Great Ant-Eater
Koala Bear
Badger
Porcupine
Rabbit
Gibbon
Greenland Whale
Arabian Camel
Gnu

50 British Fish	50 Flowers
Eel	Comfrey
Grayling	Lily-of-the-Valley
Pike	Star of Bethlehem
Roach	Daffodil
Bib	Broom
Tompot Blenny	Bluebell
Plaice	Ivy-Leaved Toadflax
Five-Bearded Rockling	Poppy
Salmon	Foxglove
Dace	Squinancywort
Bronze Bream	Deadly Nightshade
Rainbow Trout	Dog's Mercury
Cod	Hairy Rock-Cress
Butterfish	Rose
Cuckoo Wrasse	Traveller's Joy
Grey Mullet	Daisy
Perch	Sneezewort
Twaid Shad	Gorse
Gudgeon	Archangel
Stickleback	Creeping Jenny
Conger	Dandelion
Flounder	Buddleia
Dab	Pansy
Smelt	Forget-Me-Not
Basking Shark	Fuchsia
Trout	Honesty
Chub	Thyme
Tench	Night-Flowering Catchfly
Zander	Stinging Nettle
Carp	Snowdrop
Rock Goby	Pellitory-of-the-Wall
Worm pipefish	Mother-of-Thousands
Sturgeon	Stinking Hellebore
Weever	Good King Henry
Minnow	Fat Hen
Rudd	Blackberry
Wels	Dusty Miller
Dory	Raspberry
Tub Gurnard	White Clover
Blue Shark	Wallflower
Saithe	Primrose
Dragonet	Tulip
Whitefish Vendace	Marsh Marigold
Barbel	Meadow Buttercup
Stone Loach	Tansy
Bulthead	Crocus
Silver Bream	Venus's-Looking-Glass
Painted Goby	Cornflower
Roker	Thistle
Lumpsucker	Crowberry

50 Paintings by Botticelli

Adoration of the Magi
The Virgin and Child with an Angel
The Cestello Annunciation
The Return of Judith to Bethulia
The Discovery of the Dead Holofernes
Temperantia
Fortitudo
Virgin of the Eucharist
Sebastian
The Virgin and Child with Six Saints
Portrait of a Man
Portrait of a Lady (Smeralda Brandini?)
Portrait of Giuliano de' Medici
Madonna del Magnificat
The Virgin Teaching the Child to Read
Madonna del Libro
St Augustine
St. Jerome
The Annunciation
The Rebellion Against the Laws of Moses
Jewish Sacrifice and the Temptation of Christ
Scenes from the Life of Moses
Portrait of Simonetta Vespucci
Primavera
Pallas and the Centaur
Venus and Mars
The Story of Nastagio degli Pnesti
The Birth of Venus
The Birth of Christ
Springtime
Allegory of Abundance
The Virgin and Child with Six Angels
Virgin and Child Attended by 4 Angels and 6 Saints
Madonna of the Pomegranate
Virgin & Child with the Young St. John the Baptist
The Virgin and Child with Two Angels
The Virgin Adoring the Child
Lamentation Over the Dead Christ
Lamentation Over the Dead Christ with St.
-Jerome, St. Paul and St. Peter
The Calumny of Apelles
St. Augustine Writes in His Cell
Portrait of a Young Man
Inferno, Canto XVIII
The Mystical Nativity
Three Miracles of St. Zenobius
The Agony in the Garden
The Last Communion of St. Jerome
The Execution of Savonarola on the Piazza
-della Signoria
Girolama Savonarola (1452-1498)
Judith Leaving the Tent of Holofernes

50 Savoury Meat Dishes

Corned beef hash
Bubble and squeak
Steak and kidney pie
Toad-in-the-hole
Beef stew
Jugged hare
Braised shoulder of lamb
Boiled mutton
Lamb hotpot
Irish stew
Mock goose
Stewed knuckle of veal
Ragoût of mutton
Lamb cutlets
Roast beef and Yorkshire pudding
Casserole of liver
Devilled kidneys
Liver and onions
Tripe and bacon
Roast chicken
Stewed rabbit
Beef patties
Pork chops
Cornish pasty
Mutton pudding
Pork pie
Rabbit pie
Sausage roll
Veal and ham pie
Hasty pie
Rissoles
Shepherd's pie
Beef bourguignon
Braised pheasant
Carrots in a blanket
Porcupine meatballs
Salmi of grouse
Spiced pot roast
Boiled beef and dumplings
Pork and bean dinner
Lancashire hot pot
Melton Mowbray pie
Fidget pie
Haggis
Sheep's head mould
Ox tongue
Grouse soufflé
Hunter's pie
Stuffed heart
Pig's face

50 Things to say if you ever met the Queen

Hi! How's tricks?
Didn't I see you in Tesco's the other week?
What's the best way to get to Dalston?
Fancy a pint sometime?
There's never any toilet paper in those loos
Have you seen the price of petrol these days?
Could you give me a hand with these boxes?
Alright, how's the kids?
What's happening up at the palace these days?
Got a light?
There's a great 2 for 1 offer down at Boots
Is that really you on all those coins?
Alright luv?
Can you spare us 20p?
Look what the cat dragged in
Sorry, I can't stop. Got to get to the Post
-Office before it shuts
What time do you make it?
Ooh, where d'you get your nails done?
I used to have a Corgi once
Don't forget to wave
I've just had to buy a new washing machine,
-don't know if the old one's any good to you?
My daughter's name's Diana
How much is a Queen's pension these days?
Have you come on your own?
You're much shorter than I thought
Can I text you later?
What d'you think of the new High St. buses?
Did you watch Emmerdale last night?
What, no kiss?
You look better in lemon
Can you split a 'fiver' by any chance?
Love the wig
Here, have some gum
D'you like the new Ford hatchbacks?
Someone got mugged here last week
Who's the tall guy with you, with the walkie-talkie?
I noticed Philip has put on a bit of weight
You were great in that thong advert
These dinner/dances make me feel so bloated
You staying at the Travel Inn as well?
What ever you do, don't use the end toilet
You'll have to speak up old girl
...Er, sorry, I've been eating onions
Can I use your napkin?
No hubby tonight?
Is that a Newcastle accent?
So how long have you been top bitch now?
Just call me 'Pazza'
D'you want my cucumber?
Guess what; I've just seen the real Queen!

50 Serial Killers

Jack the Ripper
Fred and Rosemary West
Henry Lee Lucas
The Green River Killer
Ramirez, The Night Stalker
Erskine, The Stockwell Strangler
The Yorkshire Ripper
Bela Kiss, The Hungarian Bluebeard
Neil Cream
The Camden Ripper
Earle Nelson, The Dark Strangler
The Cleveland Torso Killer
Fernandez and Beck, The Lonely Hearts Killers
Ian Brady & Myra Hindley, The Moors Murderers
Bruno Lüdke
Dennis Nilsen
Charles Manson
Staniak, The Red Spider
John Duffy, The Railway Rapist
Ed Gein, The Necrophile
Joseph Vacher
Anna Zwanziger
Peter Kurten, The Dusseldorf Sadist
Albert DeSalvo
Albert Fish
Beverley Allitt
Jeffrey Dahmer
Gordon Fredrick
Charles Starkweather
Ted Bundy
The Ratcliffe Highway Murderer
Lacenaire
Georg Grossmann
Werner Boost, The Double Killer
John Gacy
Jeanne Weber, The Ogress of the Goutte D'Or
Fritz Haarmann of Hanover
Thierry Paulin, The Paris Phantom
Melvin Rees
John Collins, The Ypsilanti Killer
David Canter
Leonard Lake
The Axeman of New Orleans
Kenneth Bianchi & Angelo Buono, The Hillside
-Stranglers
The Boston Strangler
Reginald Christie
Ludwig Tessnow
Aileen Wurnoss
H. H. Holmes

50 Mountains and Volcanoes

Everest
K2
Kanchenjunga
Lhotse
Vesuvius
Eiger
Yalung Kang
Makalu
Gasherbrum II
St. Helens
Matterhorn
Annapurna
Dhaulagiri
Manaslu
Snowdon
Glittertind
Quiescent
Cotopaxi
Cho Oyu
Aneto Peak
Olympus
Etna
Nanga Parbat
Llullaillaco
Pobeda
Aconcagua
McKinley
Kilimanjaro
Wu-lu-k'o-mu-shih
Elbrus
Vinson Massif
Broad Peak
Kosciusko
Whitney
Fujiyama
Antisana
Ben Nevis
Robson
Neblina Peak
Hvannadalshnúkur
Svartisen
Puy de Dôme
Puy de Sancy
Fan Si Pan
Shishapangma
Camaroon
Thabana-Ntlenyana
Yu Shan
Iwaki
Chimborazo

50 Rivers

Mackenzie
Glåma
South Saskatchewan
Danube
Bug
Doubs
Niger
Angerman
Mississippi
Naktong
Darling
Snake
Rjórsa
Thames
Hari Rud
Gambia
Rio Grande de Santiago
Amazon
Xingu
Shannon
Limpopo
Colorado
Seine
Great Ouse
Clutha
Guadalquivir
Aliakmon
Seven
Po
Ob
Xi
Rhine
Vistula
Syr Darya
Orange
Ganges
Chang
Kizil Irmak
Nile
Senegal
You
Chao Phraya
Kitakami
Murrumbidgee
Volga
Peace
Orinoco
Mekong
Back
Trent

50 Moons	50 Film Actresses
Deimos	Bette Davis
Phobos	Sigourney Weaver
Ganymede	Sharon Stone
Europa	Renée Zellweger
Io	Jane Fonda
Sinope	Joan Crawford
Pasiphae	Katherine Hepburn
Carme	Theda Bara
Earth's moon	Winona Ryder
Ananke	Lillian Gish
Elara	Audrey Hepburn
Pandora	Gwyneth Paltrow
Lysithea	Jodie Foster
Himalia	Janet Leigh
Leda	Julia Roberts
Phoebe	Sadie Frost
Desdemona	Kim Bassinger
Iapetus	Susan George
Hyperion	Olivia Newton-John
Callisto	Kathy Burke
Titan	Jennifer Aniston
Dione	Tatum O'Neal
Helene	Hali Berri
Tethys	Meg Ryan
Telestro	Rosanna Arquette
Calypso	Sissy Spacek
Juliet	Julie Andrews
Enceladus	Elizabeth Taylor
Mimas	Julie Christie
Epimetheus	Catherine Deneuve
Janus	Sandra Bullock
Prometheus	Lesley-Anne Down
Atlas	Raquel Welch
Oberon	Nastassja Kinski
Titania	Anna Friel
Ariel	Greta Garbo
Miranda	Marilyn Monroe
Larissa	Jane Russell
Puck	Britt Ekland
Belinda	Barbra Streisand
Rosalind	Deborah Kerr
Portia	Betty Grable
Cressida	Glenn Close
Bianca	Sarah Jessica Parker
Orphelia	Catherine Zeta-Jones
Cordelia	Cate Blanchett
Charon	Ann-Margret
Triton	Michelle Pfeiffer
Proteus	Meryl Streep
Despoina	Julianne Moore

50 Discoveries and Inventions

Watt's steam engine (1765)
Caxton's printing press (1476)
Edison's incandescent lamp (1879)
T. Adam's and W. Wrigley invent gum (1870)
Culpeper's microscope (1735)
Shole's typewriter (1867)
Eastman's invents celluloid roll-film (1889)
Anderson invents the windscreen wiper (1903)
Trevethick's first steam locomotive (1801)
Marconi's wireless telegraphy (1896)
Röntgen's discovery of x-rays (1895)
Dickson invents the common plaster (1920)
Archimedes Archimedean Screw (200 BC)
The Curie's discovery of Radium (1898)
Savery's water pump (1698)
Silver and Woodland invent the bar code (1948)
Carothers invents nylon (1934)
Parson's steam turbine (1897)
RCA invent the compact disc (CD) (1972)
William Harvey discovers that blood circulates
-around the body (1628)
Singer's sewing machine (1851)
Ronald's electrostatic telegraph (1816)
Hero's water clock (1st. Century AD)
Elisha G. Otis invents the lift (1852)
Laennec's stethoscope (1816)
Poulsen's tape-recording of sound (1898)
Dunlop's pneumatic tyre (1888)
Drake's discovery of petroleum (1859)
Clarence Birdseye first froze food (1924)
Paper was invented in China (100 AD)
Diesel's first small engines (1909)
Hertz discovery of radio waves (1888)
Chadwick discovers the neutron (1932)
Eastman's first camera (1888)
Montgolfier brothers' hot-air balloon (1783)
Wright brothers' first powered air flight (1903)
Salk produces Polio vaccine (1952)
Cosmetics were first used in Egypt (4000 BC)
Cockerell's hovercraft (1959)
Oppenheimer's atomic bomb (1945)
Simpson's discovery of chloroform as an
-anaesthetic (1847)
Pascal's calculating machine (1642)
Galen discovers that muscles are controlled by
-the brain (130 AD)
Galileo's thermometer (1590)
The plow was invented (2,500-3,000 BC)
Gordon shows the effects of 'germs' (1795)
Linus Yale invented the cylinder lock (1851)
Louis S. Lenormand parachute (1783)
Cristofori invented the Hammerklavier piano (1709)
E. Budding and J. Ferrabee invent the lawn mower
-(1830)

50 Car Manufacturers

Ford
BMW
Alfa Romeo
Rolls Royce
Triumph
Audi
Citroën
Hyundai
Austin
Volkswagon
Nissan
Bentley
Skoda
Lotus
Daewoo
Peugeot
Chevrolet
Renault
Caterham
Suzoki
Jensen
Ferrari
Mercedes-Benz
Chrysler
Lancia
Yugo
Rover
Vauxhall
Morris
Fiat
Honda
Jaguar
Mazda
SAAB
Mitsubishi
Bristol
Izuzu
Porsche
Toyota
Kia
Lamborghini
Nash
Seat
Volvo
Daimler
Lada
Datsun
Aston Martin
MGA
Wolseley

50 Tiny Islands around the World

Pag
Great Barrier Island
Cephalonia
Formentera
Roti
Johnston Atoll
Stewart Island
Isles of Scilly
Cheju
Simeulue
Tok
Hoy
Little Andaman
Annobon
Nunivak Island
Isla de la Juventud
Ceram
Tokelau
Bonin Island
Enggano
French Polynesia
Unst
October Revolution
Rügen
Pitcairn
Volcano Island
Timor
New Ireland
Wake Island
Martinique
Cocos
Juan Fernandez Island
St. Peter and St. Paul Rocks
Guam
Ullung
King Island
Biak
Admirality Islands
Bougainville
Norfolk Island
Wetar
Sylt
Kangaroo Island
Yell
Vesteralen
Bolshevik
Masirah
Banks Island
Falklands
Brac

50 Things to put on your Face

Lipstick
Nose-ring
Beard
Eyeliner
Sideburns
Blusher
Sneer
Contact lens
Tattoo
Beauty spot
Glasses
Eyeshadow
Frown
Mascara
Goatee
Lipbalm
Moisturiser
Quiff
Veil
Lipgloss
Snarl
Monocle
War paint
Concealer
Visor
Moustache
Rouge
Puzzled look
Mask
Clown nose
Nose stud
Eyebrow pencil
Sunglasses
Foundation
Whiskers
Sun cream
Face mask
Flannel
Shaving cream
Goggles
Fringe
Spot cream
Soap
Grimace
Stubble
Eye-patch
Smile
Powder
Look of horror
Lines

50 Types of Weights and Measures

Feet
Fathom
Inch
Millimetre
Anker
Firkin
Pondo
Furlong
Chain
Centimetre
Yard
Hogshead
Dram
Decimetre
Gill
Metre
Pony
Kilometre
Butt
Thimbleful
Square mile
Peck
Hectolitre
Acre
Mile
Teaspoon
Nip
Hectare
Chaldron
Pint
Quart
Gallon
Litre
Ounce
Puncheon
Shot
Pound
Fluid ounce
Stone
Hundredweight
Kilderkin
Ton
Gram
Kilogram
Barrel
Tonne
Bushel
Tablespoon
Flagon
Cubic metre

50 Things to Put on Your Head

Head scarf
Wig
Crown
Balaclava
Cupule
Tarboosh
Bandanna
Toupee
Hankie
Headphones
Yashmak
Hairspray
Ribbons
Your hands
Headband
Halo
Kiss-me-quick hat
Viking helmet
Hood
Head-dress
Hairnet
Party hat
Tiara
Hair gel
Shako
Dunce's cap
False ears
Shampoo
Water carrier
Bundle
Sunglasses
Goggles
Balanced books
Pet bird
Devil's horns
Cowl
Heated rollers
Extensions
Hair cream
Snood
Clown hat
Pirate hat
The weight of the world
A carried child
Bows
Fencing mask
Conditioner
Feathers
Hairpiece
Ear muffs

50 Dinosaurs	50 Insects
Baryonyx	Ground beetle
Eustreptospondylus	Glow-Worm
Panoplosaurus	Ladybird
Triceratops	Snail beetle
Edmontonia	Caddis fly
Titanosaurid	Earwig
Dromiceiomimus	Soldier beetle
Massospondylus	Devil's Coach Horse
Stegosaurus	Nut weevil
Iguanodon	Dragonfly
Ouranosaurus	Cockroach
Psittacosaurus	Churchyard beetle
Garudimimus	Hornet
Yanghuanosaurus	Cockchafer
Tyrannosaurus	Aphid
Muttaburrasaurus	Moth
Allosaurus	Ked
Brachiosaurus	Firebrat
Brontasaurus	Cardinal beetle
Leptoceratops	Silverfish
Tuojiangosaurus	Gnat
Chirostenotes	Large Marsh grasshopper
Lufengosaurus	Bumble bee
Huayangosaurus	Louse
Kentrosaurus	Death-Watch beetle
Riojasaurus	Common wasp
Camptosaurus	House cricket
Albertosaurus	Powder Post beetle
Melanorosaurus	Mayfly
Wuerhosaurus	Water stick-insect
Anchisaurus	Bluebottle
Pinacosaurus	Wood-Boring beetle
Minmi	Lacewing
Polacanthus	Thrip
Struthiomimus	Stag beetle
Avimimus	Ant
Procompsognathus	Bloody-Nosed beetle
Coelurus	Great Green bush-cricket
Camarasaurus	Flea
Cetiosaurus	Water Boatman
Shunosaurus	Australian Fungus beetle
Ankylosaurus	Springtail
Diplodocus	Scorpion fly
Gallimimus	Apple Blossom weevil
Archaeopteryx	Colorado beetle
Herrerasaurus	Snake fly
Probactrosaurus	Scavenger beetle
Plateosaurus	Honey bee
Saltasaurus	Hawthorn Shield bug
Euoplocephalus	Great Diving beetle

50 Coronation Street Characters	**50 Weapons**
Albert Tatlock	Revolver
Jack Duckworth	Bow and arrow
Reg Holdsworth	Dagger
Harry Flagg	Blow-pipe
Archie Shuttleworth	Battering ram
Rita Littlewood	Hand-grenade
Bet Lynch	Tomahawk
Cilla Brown	Staff
Danny Baldwin	Duelling pistol
Billy Walker	Sword
Elsie Tanner	Harpoon
Des Barnes	Atom bomb
Detective Sergeant Cross	Club
Eddie Yates	Lasso
Annie Walker	Boomerang
Eileen Grimshaw	Halbert
Doctor Graham	Crossbow
Ena Sharples	Truncheon
Frank Roper	Catapult
Mike Baldwin	Sawn-off shotgun
Rosie Webster	Nuclear bomb
Amy Barlow	Knuckle-duster
Gail Porter	Nerve gas
Hilda Ogden	Cutlass
Ian Davenport	Bazooka
Betty Turpin	Cosh
Ivy Nelson	M 60 Machine gun
Tommy Harris	Greek fire
Jack Walker	Cruise missile
Deirdre Hunt	Intercontinental ballistic missile
Judy Mallett	Mace
Ken Barlow	Battle-axe
Steve McDonald	Lance
Len Fairclough	Knife
Les Battersby	Landmine
Maria Sutherland	Blunderbuss
Natalie Horrocks	Rifle
Ted Sullivan	Flame-thrower
Mavis Riley	Booby trap
Maxine Heavey	Molotov cocktail
Mrs. Snape	Mustard gas
Norman 'Curley' Watts	Bolas
PC Wilcox	Rocket
Percy Sugden	Surface-to-air missile
Ron Jenkins	War-hammer
Spider (Geoffrey) Nugent	Blackjack
Jed Stone	Tommy gun
Stan Ogden	Doodlebug
Tanya Pooley	Colt 45
Vicky Arden	Sabre

50 Feelings	50 Shakespeare Characters
Happy	Prospero
Exuberant	Speed
Bored	Proteus
Tired	Macbeth
Lonely	Sir John Falstaff
Angry	Mistress Quickly
Jealous	Pistol
Passionate	Froth
Shocked	Titus Andronicus
Joyful	Mistress Overdone
Sensuous	Elbow
Terrified	Hamlet
Sympathetic	Friar Francis
Horrified	Borachio
Affectionate	Don Adriano De Armado
Vivacious	Moth
Lively	Bottom
Sensitive	Philostrate
Vibrant	Romeo
Sentimental	Prince of Arragon
Envious	Old Gobbo
Romantic	Touchstone
Impetuous	Sir Oliver Mar-text
Thrilled	Bianca
Aroused	Marcus Brutus
Excited	Petruchio
Awed	Countess of Rousillon
Shy	Sir Toby Belch
Sly	Hermione
Inspired	Polixenes
Depressed	Robert Faulconbridge
Eager	Duke of Austria
Earnest	Richard II
Zealous	Green
Livid	Sir Stephen Scroop
Enthusiastic	Lady Percy
Indifferent	Prince Humphrey of Gloster
Impatient	Silence
Hysterical	Fang
Abashed	Cassio
Delirious	Henry V
Awkward	Richard Plantagenet
Estatic	Joan La Pucelle
Proud	Duke of Norfolk
Amused	Patience
Hurt	Cardinel Wolsey
Perplexed	Troilus
Confused	Caius Marcius Coriolanus
Bemused	Ophelia
Sad	Posthumus

50 Things you should never, ever, ever Do

Walk under a ladder
Give your pin number to someone
Wave a red handkerchief at a bull
Cross the road without looking
Lend someone money
Talk to strangers in a dark alley
Eat a big meal just after eating a big meal
Shout out, 'I smell bacon!' in a police station
Wear tights over your trousers
Look down the nozzle of a hosepipe
Stop the bus by sticking your foot out
Shake hands with a leper
Pick a fight with a WWF wrestler
Play with matches in a petrol station
Howl at the moon
Put your head in a lion's mouth
Shout out, 'fire!' in a fire station
Walk barefoot on hot coals
Ask where FM is on a plane's cockpit radio
Ask for a pork pie at a Jewish wedding
Fart in a shared bath
Tie your shoelaces while driving
Give a comb as a Xmas present to a bald man
Lock yourself out
Knock yourself out
Wear the same hat to a wedding as the bride's mother
Attend a funeral with a coffin-shaped shoulder bag
Light the gas before getting the matches out
Kiss a frog
Boil and egg without water
Put a metal spoon in the microwave
Eat garlic, chillies and onions before a date
Jump in the deep-end if you can't swim
Offer a pair of tap shoes to a one-legged man
Drive a car wearing a blindfold
Read a book upside-down
Stroke a tarantula
Play air-violin at a classical concert
Walk under a horse
Ride in a car without wearing a seat belt
Jump out of a 10-storey block window
Paint floorboards from doorway to corner
Re-freeze meat
Park on a hill without using the handbrake
Answer the door naked
Talk to yourself in the street
Run down the stairs backwards
Argue with a policeman
Wear an '80's shell-suit
Try to pin a tail on a real donkey

50 Muscles of the Body

Adductor longus
Biseps brachii
Brachialis
Brachioradialis
Buccinator
Corrugator supercilii
Cricothyroid
Deltoid
Depressor anguli oris
Depressor labii inferioris
Extensors of hand
External oblique
Flexors of forearm
Flexors of hand
Frontalis
Gluteus maximus
Gracilis
Ileum
Illiopsoas
Infraspinatus
Iris
Latissimus dorsi
Levator anguli oris
Linea alba
Masseter
Mentalis
Nasalis
Occipitofrontalis
Orbicularis oculi
Pectoralis major
Peronius brevis
Platysma
Procerus
Rectus abdominis
Rectus femoris
Rhomboideus major
Risorius
Scalenus medius
Semitendinosus
Sternocleidomastoid
Temporalis
Tensor fasciae latae
Teres major
Teres minor
Tibialis anterior
Tongue
Trapezius
Triceps brachii
Vastus medialis
Zygomaticus major

50 Chemical Elements	50 Fashion Designers
Hydrogen	Giorgio Armani
Lithium	Cristobal Balenciaga
Carbon	Issey Miyake
Nitrogen	Dirk Bikkembergs
Oxygen	Tommy Nutter
Fluorine	Paco Rabanne
Neon	Barbara Bui
Sodium	Coco Chanel
Magnesium	Christian Lacroix
Aluminium	Emma Cook
Silicon	Stella McCartney
Phosphorous	Vivienne Westwood
Sulphur	Hubert Givenchy
Chlorine	John Galliano
Argon	Christian Dior
Potassium	Domenico Dolce & Venetian Cabbana
Scandium	Erotokritos
Titanium	Nicole Farhi
Vanadium	Bill Gibbs
Chromium	Guccio Gucci
Manganese	Juimmy Choo
Iron	Anand Jon
Cobalt	Calvin Klein
Nickel	Karl Lagerfeld
Copper	Jill Sander
Zinc	Alexander McQueen
Gallium	Mary Quant
Arsenic	Claude Montana
Krypton	Bruce Oldfield
Zirconium	Christina Perrin
Niobium	Ralph Lauren
Molybdenum	Zandra Rhodes
Rhodium	Yves Saint-Laurent
Palladium	David Shilling
Silver	Anna Sul
Tin	Valentino Garavani
Antimony	Gianni Versace
Xenon	Mathew Williamson
Iridium	Xuly Bët
Platinum	Yohji Yamamoto
Lead	Amy Zoller
Mercury	Agatha Ruiz Deha Prada
Uranium	Emillo Pucci
Radon	Sir Paul Smith
Astatine	Bill Blass
Unnilquadium	Ebru Ercon
Tantalum	Caroline Herrera
Berkelium	Julien MacDonald
Iodine	Jessica Ogden
Barium	Zac Posen

50 Miss World Winners

Kiki Haakonson, Sweden, 1951
Mary Stavin, Sweden, 1977
Denise Perrier, France, 1953
Gina Swainson, Bermuda, 1979
Carmen Zubillaga, Venezuela, 1955
Pilin Leon, Venezuela, 1981
Marita Linahl, Finland, 1957
Sarah Jane Hutt, United Kingdom, 1983
Corine Rottschafer, Holland, 1959
Hofi Karlsdottir, Iceland, 1985
Rosemarie Frankland, United Kingdom, 1961
Ulla Weigerstorfer, Austria, 1987
Carole Crawford, Jamaica, 1963
Andeta Kreglicka, Poland, 1989
Reita Faria, India, 1966
Julia Kourotchkina, Russia, 1992
Penelope Plummer, Australia, 1968
Aishwariya Rai, India, 1994
Jennifer Hosten, Grenada, 1970
Irene Skliva, Greece, 1996
Belinda Green, Australia, 1972
Linor Abargil, Israel, 1998
Anneline Kriel, South Africa, 1974
Priyanka Chopra, India, 2000
Winelia Merced, Puerto Rico, 1975
Azra Akin, Turkey, 2002
May Louise Flodin, Sweden, 1952
Silvana Suarez, Argentina, 1978
Antigone Costanda, Egypt, 1954
Kimberly Santos, Guam, 1980
Petra Schurmann, Germany, 1956
Mariasela Lebron, Dominican Republic, 1982
Penelope Coelen, South Africa, 1958
Astrid Herrera, Venezuela, 1984
Norma Cappagli, Argentina, 1960
Giselle Laronde, Trinidad, 1986
Catherine Lodders, Holland, 1962
Linda Petursdottir, Iceland, 1988
Ann Sidney, United Kingdom, 1964
Gina Marie Tolleson, USA, 1990
Lesley Langley, United Kingdom, 1965
Ninebeth Jiminez, Venezuela, 1991
Madeiline Hartog Bel, Peru, 1967
Lisa Hanna, Jamaica, 1993
Eva Reuber Staier, Austria, 1969
Jacqueline Aquilera, Venezuela, 1995
Lucia Petterie, Brazil, 1971
Diana Hayden, India, 1997
Marjorie Wallace, USA, 1973
Yukta Mookhey, India, 1999

50 Gooseberry Varieties

Bellona
Careless
Australia
Cousin's Seedling
Admiral Beattie
Woodpecker
Dan's Mistake
Early Sulphur
Firbob
Aston Red
Broom Girl
Green Gem
Guido
Heart of Oak
Marigold
Criterion
Howard's Lancer
Ironmonger
Jubilee
Keepsake
Blucher
Talford
King of Trumps
Lancashire Lad
White Lion
Clayton
London
Alma
Hero of the Nile
Lord Kitchener
Macherauch's Seedling
Gunner
Sultan Juror
Matchless
Speedwell
White Eagle
Crown Bob
May Duke
Plunder
Green Ocean
Queen of Hearts
Sir George Brown
Suter Johnny
Trumpeter
Whinham's Industry
Freedom
Leveller
Lord Derby
Whitesmith
Yellow Champagne

50 Olympic Gold Medallists	50 Most useless Items
Jesse Owens	One chopstick
Jim Hines	Chocolate teapot
Harold Whitlock	Rubber screwdriver
Irena Szewinska	TV Times from 1968
Steve Redgrave	Sandpit in the desert
Fanny Blankers-Koen	Fridge in the arctic
Lasse Viren	Bouncer for Mothercare
Tamara Press	10/- note
Sergei Bubka	8 track tape recorder
Kid Keino	Cricket bat on a tennis court
Bob Beamon	Bank robbers' see-through balaclava
Mary Peters	Guitar without strings
Jack Lovelock	Duffel coat in the jungle
Cassius Clay	One shoe
Wilma Rudolph	Comb for a bald man
Carl Lewis	Divorce lawyers phone number at a wedding
Dawn Fraser	Book of Green Shield Stamps
Paavo Nurmi	Doll's house chair when confronted by a lion
Marion Jones	Holiday brochure in prison
Harold Abrahams	Paperweight made of paper
Jean-Claude Killy	Pogo stick in a swamp
Ed Moses	Clown's outfit on a battlefield
Linford Christie	The 'Pill' for a pregnant woman
Olga Korbut	Pen without ink
Mark Spitz	Football on a rugby field
Petra Felke	Can of 2 stroke petrol
Tessa Sanderson	Snake detector with Dolby
Daley Thompson	Garlic to ward off a vampire
Peter Snell	Sunglasses in a cinema
Florence Griffith-Joyner	Lawnmower in a high-rise flat
Emil Zatopek	Central heating in Singapore
Mary Rand	Lead balloon
Sebastian Coe	Pencil skirt for a running race
Lynn Davies	Gas cooker in a home supplied with electricity
Marita Koch	Ashtray on a motorbike
Babe Didrikson	Bus map in a train station
Herb Elliott	French dictionary in Norway
Harrison Dillard	New music released on a 78 rpm record
Haile Gebrselassie	Bucket with a hole in it
Arthur Wint	One-bladed scissors
Kelly Holmes	Paper hammer
Al Oerter	One sock
Otis Davis	Grapes for a 'nil by mouth' patient
Iolanda Balas	Comedian at a funeral
Mohamed Gammoudi	Boomerang in a lift
Jayne Torvill	Beachball in a coalmine
Matt Biondi	Table-tennis bat on a cricket pitch
Sally Gunnell	Handle without a basket
Michael Johnson	Pram in a youth club
Gail Devers	Unleaded pencil

50 Well-known Ships and Boats

The Mayflower
The Discovery
HMS Victory
The Cutty Sark
Gypsy Moth
The Santa Maria
HMS Belfast
Noah's Ark
The Marie Celeste
The QE2
The Bismark
The Graf Spey
The Ark Royal
The Hood
Argo
Contiki
The Bounty
The Torey Canyon
The Pinta
HMS Wellington
The African Queen
The Belgrano
The Marie Rose
Lusitania
Mauritania
The Queen Mary
The Sea Wolf
The Nina
HMS Dreadnought
The Golden Hind
The Beagle
The U.S.S Enterprise
The Victoria
HMS President
The Ariel
The Oriano
The Peter
The Terra Nova
HMS Nevasa
Ma Robert
The Resolution
The Trinidad
HMS Endeavour
The Adventure
The Star of India
The Sea Hawk
The Royal George
HMS Warrior
The Minas Geraes
The Titanic

50 Rocks and Minerals

Flourite
Slate
Pegmatite
Chalcopyrite
Jasper
Marble
Porphyry
Iron
Granite
Schist
Pyrite nodules
Lead
Olivine
Silica
Barite
Sphalerite
Luxullianite
Quartzite
Jet
Calcite
Basalt
Serpentine
Cairngorm
Gneiss
Haematite
Flint
Pyroxene
Hornblende
Quartz
Carboniferous limestone
Red sandstone
Agate
Gypsum
Tremolite
Galena
Amethyst
Breccia
Connemara marble
Smoky quartz
Garnet
Amber
Blue John
Selenite
Chalcedony
Zinc
Bastite
Chromeite
Feldspar
Mica
Tourmaline

50 Outdoor Sports and Games

Football
Trampoline
Jump rope
Volleyball
Frisbee
Tennis
Baseball
Egg-and-spoon race
Badminton
Rugby
Dodgeball
Rounders
Skipping
Piggy-in-the-middle
Cricket
Hopscotch
Basketball
Roller-skating
Relay race
5-a-side football
Hop, skip and a jump
Hockey
Greyhound racing
Javelin
Farmer in the dell
Sticky-mitt
Lacrosse
Long jump
Netball
Hide and seek
Croquet
Horse racing
Motor racing
High jump
Boating
Discus
Marbles
Crazy golf
Three-legged race
Shooting
Softball
Bowls
Speedway racing
Sack race
Pole-vaulting
Tug-of-war
Red light/Green light
Stuck in the mud
Stickball
Catch

50 Common Ailments

Sore throat
Viral infection
Anxiety
Anaemia
Insomnia
Chest infection
Headache
Depression
Bronchitis
Indigestion
Nausea
Mouth ulcers
Backache
Kidney infection
Verruca
Stye
Dandruff
Piles
Tonsillitis
Pulled muscle
Angina
Asthma
Laryngitis
Toothache
Stomach ache
Constipation
Abscess
Hernia
Bruise
Fever
Cut
Migraine
Sinusitis
Muscle strain
Earache
Arthritis
Cramp
Influenza
Panic attack
Acne
Rash
Cold sore
Eczema
Warts
Conjunctivitis
Common cold
Stress
Wind
Fungal infection
Ingrowing toenail

50 Indoor Games

I Spy
Hide the Thimble
Murder in the Dark
20 Questions
Pass the Parcel
Sleeping Lions
Hide-and-Seek
Bear and the Honeypot
Tag
Musical Bumps
Postman's Knock
Kiss in the Ring
Oranges and Lemons
Sardines
Nuts in May
Rabbits
Forfeits
Guessing Game
Quiz
Charades
Consequences
Rocking Horse
Ring-a-Ring-o'-Roses
Simon Says
Blind Man's Buff
Off-Ground-Touch
Who am I?
Musical Statues
Bricks
Dolls
He
I went to the shops and I bought…
Model Making
Parson's Cat
Riddles
Doll's House
Teddies
Spinning Top
Yo-Yo
Skittles
Jacks
Musical Chairs
Hoopla
It
Toy Soldiers
Hunt the Slipper
Crambo
Follow-the-Leader
Hares and Hounds
Marbles

50 Film Genres

Horror
Western
Chiller
Comedy
Melodrama
Gangster
Romance
Animation
Spaghetti western
Thriller
Love story
Documentary
Slapstick comedy
Weepy
Computer animation
Road movie
Children's
B-Movie
Cartoon
War
Kung-fu
Science fiction
Supernatural thriller
Musical
Rockumentary
Action
Adventure
Swashbuckling
Silent
Comedy drama
Travelogue
Art film
Biblical epic
Creepie
Spinechiller
Suspense
Futuristic
Blue movie
Cult horror
Biopic
Space opera
Cops and robbers
Experimental
Historical drama
Black comedy
Spy film
Film noir
Fairy tale
Disaster movie
Murder mystery

50 Painting Movements	50 Football Teams
Abstract Art	West Ham United
Suprematism	Aston Villa
Mannerism	Preston North End
Abstract Expressionism	Arsenal
Post-impressionism	Manchester United
Action Painting	Leeds United
Neo-impressionism	Chelsea
Pre-Raphaelite Brotherhood	Tottenham Hotspur
Primitive	Liverpool
Art Nouveau	Nottingham Forest
Baroque	Accrington Stanley
Minimalism	Middlesbrough
Bauhaus	Sheffield United
Cavaggisti	Swansea
Neo-plasticism	Leicester City
Classicism	Reading
Avant-garde	Everton
Constructivism	Wigan Athletic
Realism	Sunderland
Cubism	AFC Bournemouth
Dada	Newcastle United
Vorticism	Blackburn Rovers
Expressionism	West Bromwich Albion
Surrealism	Huddersfield Town
Futurism	Sheffield Wednesday
German Expressionism	Manchester City
Renaissance	Cardiff City
High Victorian Art	Portsmouth
Impressionism	Wolverhampton Wanderers
Gothic	Swindon Town
Neo-classicism	Burnley
Metaphysical School	Ipswich Town
Pop Art	Norwich City
Rococo	Brighton & Hove Albion
Neue Sachlichkeit	Exeter City
Op Art	Derby County
Socialist Realism	Bolton Wanderers
Pointillism	Fulham
Romanticism	Hull City
De Stijl	Luton Town
Symbolism	Oldham Athletic
Watercolour	Scunthorpe United
Young British Artists	Tranmere Rovers
Barbizon School	Barnet
Colorfield Painting	Halifax Town
Happening	Rushden & Diamonds
International Gothic	Yeovil Town
Ready-made	Stockport County
Tenebrism	MK Dons
Art Brut	Charlton Athletic

50 Mr. Men	50 Waters around the UK
Mr. Wrong	North Sea
Mr. Tickle	English Channel
Mr. Silly	Bideford Bay
Mr. Rush	Strait of Dover
Mr. Quiet	The Wash
Mr. Bump	Sound of Rum
Mr. Perfect	Mouth of the Humber
Mr. Grumpy	Thames Estuary
Mr. Worry	Firth of Forth
Mr. Slow	Scapa Flow
Mr. Cool	Firth of Tay
Mr. Cheerful	Moray Firth
Mr. Nosey	Cramerty Firth
Mr. Sneeze	The Solent
Mr. Muddle	Poole Bay
Mr. Brave	Larne Lough
Mr. Good	Irish Sea
Mr. Uppity	Lyme Bay
Mr. Grumble	Bristol Channel
Mr. Mischief	Cardigan Bay
Mr. Strong	St. George's Channel
Mr. Noisy	Caernarfon Bay
Mr. Cheeky	Blackwater
Mr. Clumsy	Morecombe Bay
Mr. Lazy	Solway Firth
Mr. Small	North Channel
Mr. Bounce	Loch Ryan
Mr. Jelly	Firth of Clyde
Mr. Forgetful	Sound of Jura
Mr. Tall	Celtic Sea
Mr. Fussy	Ramsey Bay
Mr. Daydream	Kilbrannan Sound
Mr. Rude	Firth of Lorn
Mr. Impossible	Burrows Hole
Mr. Happy	Little Minch
Mr. Clever	Sea of the Hebrides
Mr. Nervous	Pentland Firth
Mr. Messy	Red Wharf Bay
Mr. Skinny	Sound of Bute
Mr. Busy	Fishguard Bay
Mr. Greedy	Belfast Lough
Mr. Topsy-Turvey	Portland Harbour
Mr. Funny	Southampton Water
Mr. Dizzy	Loch of Strathbay
Mr. Christmas	Atlantic Ocean
Mr. Mean	Loch Sunart
Mr. Chatterbox	Sound of Mull
Mr. Nonsense	The Sound
Mr. Snow	Dury Voe
Little Miss Bossy	Loch Boghasdail

50 Mildly Blasphemous Expressions

Good God!
Bouncing bishops
Holy Moses!
Clucking clergymen
Bloody hell!
Dancing deacons
B'Jesus!
Frolicking friars
Harry H. Christ!
Prancing priests
Heavens above!
Pompous Pilate
Hell's teeth!
Jesus wept!
Jumping Jesuits
Stone me!
Jiving Jehovahs
Lord above!
Pogoing popes
Saints alive!
Good Lord!
Vacillating vicars
Holy Joseph!
Moaning monks
Gawd blimey!
Chortling cherubs
Heaven help us!
Suffering seraphs
Gawd help us!
Farting cardinals
Bless my soul
Pouting apostles
Blessed hell!
Bristling Christians
God forbid
Pirouetting Protestants
Holy Mother of Christ!
Effervescent evangelists
May the saints preserve us?
Burping Buddhists
Sweet Jesus!
Jostling Jews
Can you Adam and Eve it?
Marching Muslims
Hopping nuns
Christ almighty!
Lordy Lordy!
Simpering sinners
Coughing congregations
Amen to that!

50 Airlines

SAS
British Airways
RyanAir
Easyjet
Pan-Am
Virgin Atlantic
FedEx
Monarch
Laker Skytrain
B.O.A.C
Egyptair
Iran Air
Buzz
Germanwings
Free Bird International
Air France
Thai Airways
Varig
BEA
Turkish Airlines
SpanAir
Britannia
Flybe
Air Malta
Norwegian Air Space
El Al Isreal Airlines
FlyMe
Nextjet
Malaysia Airlines
European Executive Express
Air Finland
Falcon Air
Lithuanian Airlines
Icelandair
Bmi baby
Czech Airlines
Air Zimbabwe
Korean Air
Qatar Airways
DNL
Estorian Air
Viking Airlines
Pegasus
US Airways
UPS
Estonian Air
Finnair
South African Airways
Lite
Avianca Airlines

50 Rugby Teams	50 Roman Emperors
Batley Bulldogs	Probus
Oldham	Augustus
Swinton	Carus
Halifax RLFC	Nero
Carlisle	Numerian
Broughton Rovers	Tiberius
Warrington Wolves	Carinus
Leeds Rhinos	Caligula
Hull FC	Postumus
Huddersfield Giants	Claudius
Leigh Centurions	Tetricus
Dewsbury	Galba
Rochdale Hornets	Otho
Wigan Warriors	Maximian
Hunslet	Vitellius
Castleford Tigers	Vespasian
St. Marys-Penrith Cougars	Constantius I
London Broncos	Victorinus
Widnes Vikings	Titus
Salford City Reds	Nerva
Bradford Northern	Trajan
Workington T	Maximinus II
Barrow	Julian the Apostate
St. Helens	Maximus
Canterbury Bulls	Victor
Featherstone Rovers	Romulus Augustas
Hull KR	Arcadius
Sheffield E	Septimus Severus
York	Gordian I
Keighley	Declus
Barrow Raiders	Florian
Tweed Heads	Hadrian
London B	Domitian
Bradford Bulls	Marcus Aurelius
Wakefield Trinity Wildcats	Pertinax
Windsor Wolves	Didius Julianus
Les Catalans Dragons	Geta
Newcastle Knights	Balbinus
Harlequins	Philip I the Arabian
Doncaster Dragons	Trebonianus Gallus
Thornhill Trojans	Laelian
Celtic Crusaders	Licinius
Whitehaven	Constans
Toulouse	Quintillus
London Skolars	Aemilian
St. Albans Centurions	Volusian
Hemel Hempstead Stags	Hostilian
Ipswich Jets	Herennius Etruscus
Redcliffe Dolphins	Caracalla
Wales Dragons	Macrinus

50 Traditional Trades and Professions	50 Well-known Novels
Joiner	Dr. No – Ian Flemming
Cartographer	The Catcher in the Rye – JD Salinger
Bowyer	Gigi - Colette
Jobber	Heart of Darkness – Joseph Conrad
Vintner	For Whom the Bell Tolls – Ernest Hemingway
Millwright	American Psycho – Brett Easton Ellis
Cartwright	The Metamorphosis – Franz Kafka
Farrier	The Bell Jar – Sylvia Plath
Cooper	Jane Eyre – Charlotte Brontë
Mercer	Our Man in Havana – Graham Greene
Stenographer	Birds without Wings – Louis de Bernières
Haberdasher	David Copperfield – Charles Dickens
Cordwainer	Blott on the Landscape – Tom Sharpe
Purser	The Wasp Factory – Iain Banks
Costermonger	Of Mice and Men – John Steinbeck
Curator	Harry Potter & the Chamber of Secrets – JK
Draper	-Rowling
Shipwright	The Adventures of Sherlock Holmes – Arthur
Fletcher	-Conan Doyle
Hosier	Jaws – Peter Benchley
Ironmonger	Murder on the Orient Express – Agatha Christie
Bursar	Deception Point – Dan Brown
Steeplejack	Little Women – Louisa May Alcott
Tanner	The Canterbury Tales – Geoffrey Chaucer
Charcutier	On the Road – Jack Kerouac
Wainwright	The Satanic Verses – Salman Rushdie
Chandler	Moll Flanders – Daniel Defoe
Milliner	Vanity Fair – WM Thackeray
Pedagogue	1984 – George Orwell
Gatherer	Noddy – Enid Blyton
Couturier	The Secret Diary of Adrian Mole Aged 13¾
Groom	-Sue Townsend
Publican	Papillon – Henri Charrière
Saddler	Ulysses – James Joyce
Seamstress	The Rats – James Herbert
Cobbler	Lady Chatterley's Lover – DH Lawrence
Founder	Room at the Top – John Braine
Currier	The Scarlet Pimpernel – Baroness Orczy
Horner	A Passage to India – EM Forster
Stationer	The Thirty-Nine Steps – John Buchan
Cabinetmaker	To the Lighthouse – Virginia Woolf
Stevedore	Dracula – Bram Stoker
Scrivener	War and Peace – Leo Tolstoy
Dressmaker	Three Men in a Boat – Jerome K Jerome
Stoker	Watership Down – Richard Adams
Glazier	A Clockwork Orange – Anthony Burgess
Upholsterer	Tinker, Tailor, Soldier, Spy – John Le Carré
Bookbinder	Bridget Jones's Diary – Helen Fielding
Lorimer	Lord of the Flies – William Golding
Wheelwright	The Broker – John Grisham
	The Way of All Flesh – Samuel Butler
	Brave New World – Aldous Huxley
	It – Stephen King

50 Forms of Evening Entertainment	50 Motorways
Cinema	M66
Restaurant	M621
Dog racing	M49
Pub	A64 (M)
Club	M1
Walk	M77
TV	A3(M)
Early night	M58
Gym	M61
Snooker	A66(M)
Drive	M9
Theatre	M50
Opera	M2
Bowling	M876
Take-away	M54
Dance classes	M3
Band	A38(M)
Speedway racing	M56
Dinner and dance	M25
Hanging out	M10
Boxing	M45
Pool	M4
Ice-skating	M42
Midnight swim	M65
Astronomy	A48 (M)
Jigsaw	M73
Reading	M90
Wrestling	M180
Hair-washing	A57(M)
Radio	M69
Listening to music	M5
Night fishing	M11
Sewing	M20
A crossword puzzle	M26
A cross word with the wife	M62
Friends round for dinner	M6
Squash	M57
Playing a musical instrument	M8
Youth club	M23
Working late	M74
On the internet	M606
On the phone	A1(M)
Bath	M80
Walking the dog	M27
Cooking	M40
Model-making	A167(M)
Evening worship	M53
Ghost hunting	M60
Disco	M67
Casino	A58(M)

50 Geographical Features

Hill
Mountain
Escarpment
Oxbow lake
Ravine
Island
Desert
Gully
Continent
Peninsula
Highland
Reef
Ocean
Field
River
Strand
Forest
Ditch
Lagoon
Polder land
Steppe
Slope
Swamp
Beach
Water meadow
Glacier
Scar
Plateau
Wood
Moor
Bay
Oasis
Cliff
Cave
Lowland
Stream
Copse
Wilderness
Loch
Country
Shoreline
Grassland
Crag
Sea
Fen
Quicksand
Mainland
Valley
Prairie
Bush

50 Items of Street Furniture

Traffic light
Fire hydrant
Bollard
Lamp post
Tree
Post box
Level crossing
Plaque
Curb
Sign post
Telephone box
Traffic signs
Milestone
Telegraph pole
Electricity-cable cover
Foundation stone
Litter bin
Drain cover
Water stopcock
Bench
Drain
Weather vane
Telephone junction box
Bus lane
Road workings
Barriers
Coal-hole cover
Zebra crossing
Pawnbroker sign
Pavement
Traffic cone
Stop-valve
Barber's pole
Road markings
Public house sign
Belisha beacon
Pelican crossing
Weir drain
Chemist sign
Gas stopcock
Cycle lane
Traffic island
Cats' eyes
Tram lines
Speed camera
Street names
Railings
Town clock
Grass verge
Bus stop

50 Cities and large Towns in the UK

London
Plymouth
Glasgow
Manchester
Ipswich
Chelmsford
Southampton
Huddersfield
Norwich
Birmingham
Leeds
Coventry
Brighton
Peterborough
Liverpool
Hull
Newcastle-upon-Tyne
Bristol
Nottingham
Luton
Stratford-upon-Avon
York
Portsmouth
Durham
Bournemouth
Aberdeen
Sheffield
Leicester
Sunderland
Edinburgh
South Shields
Canterbury
Torquay
Carlisle
Perth
Exeter
Cardiff
Stoke-on-Trent
Cambridge
Bradford
Dover
Swansea
Bath
Derby
Lincoln
Middlesborough
Blackpool
Dundee
Belfast
Oxford

50 TV Comedy Programmes

Absolutely Fabulous
Are You Being Served
Bewitched
Blackadder
Cheers
Dad's Army
Dinnerladies
The Fall and Rise of Reginald Perrin
Fawlty Towers
The Generation Game
The Golden Girls
Happy Days
The Harry Enfield Show
Hi-De-Hi
I Love Lucy
It Aint Half Hot Mum
Porridge
Keeping Up Appearances
The Likely Lads
Little Britain
Man About the House
Men Behaving Badly
No, Honestly
Not Only But Also
The Office
One Foot in the Grave
On the Buses
Phil Silvers Show
Please Sir
Red Dwarf
Rising Damp
Some Mothers Do 'Ave 'Em
Spitting Image
Steptoe and Son
Till Death Us Do Part
The Vicar of Dibley
The Larkins
The Young Ones
'Allo 'Allo
Drop the Dead Donkey
Friends
Love thy Neighbour
Monty Python's Flying Circus
The Goodies
Not the Nine O' Clock News
Only Fools and Horses
Roseanne
The Royle Family
Sykes
To the Manor Born

50 British Seaside Towns

Southend-on-Sea
Cromer
Clacton-on-Sea
Brighton
Tenby
Southport
Walton-on-Naze
Bognor Regis
Newgale
Cleethorpes
Saltburn-by-the-Sea
Blackpool
Skegness
Girvan
Bangor
Bournemouth
Campbeltown
Torquay
Felixstowe
Bridlington
Aberystwyth
Lowestoft
St. Ives
Newquay
Praa Sands
Frinton-on-Sea
West Looe
Colwyn Bay
Bigbury-on-Sea
Paignton
Budleigh Salterton
Lyme Regis
Poole
Ryde
Barton-on-Sea
Hayling Island
Shoreham-by-Sea
Tywyn
Eastbourne
Bude
Ilfracombe
Burnham-on-Sea
Weston-Super-Mare
Deal
Whitley Bay
Margate
Pwllheli
Hunstanton
Prestatyn
Scarborough

50 Things 'not to say' when entering a Church

Do they sell cappuccino here?
This'll convert well into flats
Where's the toilets mate?
Is there a gift shop?
Jesus; is there no heating in here!
Can I have a go on the organ?
So what happens in here then?
I want to talk to the man at the very top
They don't do it like this in a synagogue
Sorry! I thought you were the gravedigger
What the Devil; it's dark in here!
Thinking of selling?
I'm not kneeling!
Where can I connect up my laptop?
You could run a bar along that wall…
Lord; you call that singing!?
What's a place like this worth?
Sorry to interrupt vic., I've come to read the meter
I prefer the Mosque…
There's not much parking space out there geez
You know I can't sing
Can I still keep my headphones on?
The vicar looks a bit gay
I'm not rising!
Sorry I thought the font was a washbasin
The groom looks pissed already
I'm a Muslim you know
…No curtains over the windows?
These hymns are so tuneless
It's so draughty in here; I'll keep my hat on!
Oops, I thought this was a charity shop!
They could at least put a bit of carpet down!
What the hell's he waffling on about up there
God! Is that the bride? No wonder she's
-wearing a veil!
Wine and crisps! Excellent! I am a bit peckish
I thought you were an Atheist?
Should I turn my phone off?
I'll sit at the back and have a quick 40 winks…
This is the church we broke into as kids
Your slate roof's worth a fortune you know. I
-could swop it for tiles in a weekend?
…D'you sell any beer here mate?
No choir girls,… that's a bit bloody sexist!
The last vicar didn't have body odour
I've forgotten the ring! —Will a ring-pull do?
D'you hire this place out for disco's?
Can't stay long; football's on in half an hour?
Should I take my shoes off; like in a temple?
Where's the cloakroom?
Their Mary looks cross-eyed don't you think
Next time I'll bring a cushion

50 Boring things to do at Home on a Dark Night

Put the cat out
Empty the rubbish
Listen to radio 4
Vacuum
Sharpen some pencils
Do the ironing
Check your spare fuses box
Match up all those odd socks
Dust the squirting boards
Take the dog for a walk
Sew on a button
Clean out the car
Tidy the kitchen draw
Fix the living room pelmet
Polish the cutlery
Re-arrange the ornaments
Draw up a Christmas card list
Clear the draining board
Put your paperbacks in alphabetical order
See which Biro's don't work
Look out the back window
Venture up into the loft
Ring an old cousin
Clean out the fish tank
Re-charge the re-chargeable batteries
Neatly fold all the pillow-slips
Check you've enough spare light bulbs
Clean out the litter-tray
Re-make the bed
Throw out any out-of-date medicines
Clean behind the cooker
Re-stack the saucepans
See which Tupperware lids fit which pots
Play a board game with the kids
Tidy up your address book
Glue on bits of torn wallpaper
Return that drill-bit to your neighbour
Check an old e-mail account
Talk to the wife
Read your star sign
Clean the computer mouse
Wash-up
See what's under the bed
Cut your toenails
Throw out all those old bank statements
Start labelling jars
Post a letter
Look at your old memorabilia collection
Start knitting a scarf
Call the cat in

50 Mushrooms and Fungi

Fly Agaric
Witches' Butter
Earth Star
Elf Cup
Stinkhorn
Dead Men's Fingers
St, George's mushroom
Wood Woolly Foot
Saffron Milk-Cap
Common Puff-Ball
Yellow-staining mushroom
Chanterelle
Horn of Plenty
Jew's Ear fungus
Destroying Angel
Magic mushroom
Edible Boletus
Truffle
Tinder
Oyster fungus
Forest Truffle
Fairy Ring Champignon
Sickener
Death Cap
Blusher
Panther Cap
Common mushroom
Honey fungus
Deceiver
Field mushroom
Black Bulgar
Razor Strop
Beefsteak fungus
Ergot
Grisette
Funnel Cap
Bracket fungus
Wood Blewitt
Winter fungus
Morel
Edible winter fungus
Cep
Wood mushroom
Hyphae
Shaggy Ink Cap
Parasol mushroom
Beech Tuft
Devil's Boletus
Red-staining Inocybe
Crumble Cap

50 Types of Dwelling

Penthouse
Cottage
Croft
Oast house
Council flat
Semi-detached house
Igloo
High-rise flat
Mansion
Castle
Wigwam
Detached house
Farm house
Cave
Convent
Shack
Tent
Palace
Low-rise flat
Caravan
Barracks
Tepee
Apartment
Château
Log cabin
Town house
Pied-à-terre
Chalet
Bivouac
Refugee camp
Kraal
Hotel
Boarding school
Remand centre
Monastery
Villa
Prison
Prefab
Ranch
Bungalow
Stately home
Vicarage
Hacienda
Houseboat
Bed-sit
Tower block
Night shelter
Billet
Terraced house
Hut

50 Classical Composers

Antonio Vivaldi
Johann Sebastian Bach
George Frederick Handel
Wolfgang Amadeus Mozart
Leonard Bernstein
Edward Elgar
Henry Purcell
Richard Wagner
Ludwig van Beethoven
Niccolò Paganini
Hector Berlioz
Pyotr Tchaikovsky
Frédéric Chopin
Robert Schumann
Paul Dukas
Franz Liszt
Giuseppe Verdi
Franz Peter Schubert
Jacques Offenbach
Heinrich Schütz
Felix Mendelssohn
Johann Strauss
Georges Bizet
Modest Mussorgsky
George Gershwin
Christopher Willibald Gluck
Antonin Dvořák
Alessandro Scarlatti
Edvard Grieg
Nikolay Rimsky-Korsakov
Giacomo Puccini
Gustav Mahler
Achille-Claude Debussy
Stephen Sondheim
Domenico Cimarosa
Gustav Holst
Maurice Ravel
Igor Stravinsky
Richard Strauss
Benjamin Britten
Karlheinz Stockhausen
Claudio Monteverdi
Johannes Brahms
Johann Jakob Froberger
Franz Joseph Haydn
John Blow
Giacomo Meyerbeer
Gaetano Donizetti
Alexander Borodin
Karl Nielson

50 Things to do on a hot Summer's Day

Go for a swim
Sunbathe
Frisbee in the park
Barbecue
Beer in a beer garden
Read under the shade of a tree
Play with the kids
Hoe the flowerbeds
Wear flip-flops
Go to the zoo
Have a picnic
Go on a ramble
Wear big, baggy shorts
Go sailing
Put on fake tan
A nice, long walk
Hang out the washing
Prune the roses
Jog along by the canal
Buy an ice cream
Wear that awful Hawaiian shirt
Have a shower to cool down
Go for a bike ride
Football in the park
Go to the garden centre
Summer clothes shopping
Wear a hankie on your head
Water the garden
Play loud music with the windows open
Go on the swings
Play tennis
Eat a salad
Water-skiing
Walk to the next village
River boat ride
Mow the lawn
Drink a coke
Try and find your sunglasses
Yachting
Play cricket
Snog in the park
Go to the seaside
Wash the car
Spring-clean
Wear your favourite T-shirt
Drink designer water
Bird-watching
Rock-climbing
Eat a lolly
Sulk indoors

50 Sweets

Spangles
Jelly tots
Wine gums
Liquorice allsorts
Opal fruits
Fruit pastels
Lemon toffee bonbons
Sweet cigarettes
Jelly babies
Smarties
Fruit gums
Black jacks
Dolly mixtures
Cola bottles
Lollipops
Chewits
Gob-stoppers
Sherbet dip
Angel dust
Marzipan teakes
Starburst
Toffos
Acid drops
Sherbet lemons
Fruit salad
Barley sugar
Coltsfoot rock
Liquorice torpedoes
Sherbet pips
Cough candy
Marshmallows
Fizzy strawberries
Pear drops
Humbugs
Fizzy dummies
Nougat
Treacle dabs
Aniseed balls
Lovehearts
Gold coins
Jelly beans
Milk gums
Midget gems
Aniseed balls
Fizzy wizzy
Palma violets
Mojo fruit chews
Pineapple cubes
Merry Maid caramels
White mice

50 Philosophers/Political Thinkers	50 Words for Man
Pythagoras	Mate
St. Augustine of Hippo	Boy
Immanuel Kant	Pal
Albert Camus	Mr.
Socrates	Master
St. Thomas Aquinas	Lad
Niccolò Machiavelli	Man
Fredrich Wilhelm Nietzsche	Geezer
Sir Francis Bacon	Crony
René Descartes	Jim
Baruch Spinoza	Hunk
John Locke	Bloke
David Hume	Stud
Jean-Jacques Rousseau	Male
Denis Diderot	Spouse
Georg Hegal	Husband
John Stuart Mill	Fella
Plato	Buffer
Seren Kierkegaard	Him
Karl Marx	He
Bertrand Russell	Gentleman
Ludwig Wittgenstein	Sir
Martin Heldegger	Monsieur
Aristotle	Herr
Jean-Paul Satre	Senõr
Willard Quine	Don
Michel Foucault	Comrade
Thales	Squire
Anaximander	Guvnor
Heraclitus	Jock
Lucretius	Buddy
Karl Raimund Popper	Chum
John Duns Scotus	Fellow
Nicholas of Cusa	Guv.
Giordano Bruno	Laddie
Gottfried Wilhelm von Leibniz	Guy
Thomas Paine	Chap
Jeremy Bentham	Gent
Friedrich Schelling	Bachelor
Empedocles	Youngster
Auguste Comte	Bro.
Wilhelm Dilthey	Old dog
Edmund Husseri	Widower
Nishida Kitarõ	Codger
Otto Neurath	Gaffer
György Lukács	Cock
Rudolf Carnap	Johnny
Hans-Georg Gadamer	Blade
Sir Alfred Jules Ayer	Son
Epicurus	Trooper

50 Chocolate Bars

Kit-kat
Mars
Snickers
Marathon
Lion
Picnic
Toblerone
Turkish Delight
Fry's peppermint cream
Revels
Maltesers
Caramac
Cadbury's fruit and nut
Bournville, plain chocolate
Curly Wurly
Minstrels
Bounty
Jacob & Co. Cinema chocolate
Smarties
Galaxy milk chocolate
Crunchie
Sky bar
Toffo's
Milky Way
Nestle's milky bar
Munchies
Cadbury's milk chocolate
Penguin
Punch
Duncan's Hazelnut Wartime chocolate
Kendal Mint Cake
Rolo's
Aero
Buzz
Texan
Rowntree's Motoring milk chocolate
Amazin' Raisin bar
Aztec
Terry's chocolate orange
Flake
Twirl
Cadbury's whole nut
Toffee Crisp
Jacob & Co. Charleston
Bubblo
Nestle's Smokers bittersweet milk chocolate
The Barker & Dobson Tipperary toffee
Ration
Mackintosh's Weekend assortment
Dime bar

50 Soft Drinks

Coca-cola
Tango
Lilt
Orange squash
Pepsi cola
Fruit Shoot
Irn Bru
Apple juice
Lucozade original
Sunkist
Virgin cola
Tizer
Spa Reine
7 Up
Ginger beer
Diet coke
J2O
Fruit spring
Lemonade
Lucozade orange
Cherryade
Ribena
Orange juice
Vimto
Powerade
Drench
Red bull
Sprite
Oasis
Um Bungo
Panda Pops
Tovali
Purdy's
Lucozade sport
Kick
Red Rooster
Aqua-Pura
Dr. Pepper
Umbro X
Fanta
Capri-Sun
Spa Citron
Coca-cola vanilla
Pepsi max
Lucozade tropical
Gatorade
Amé
Ocean Spray
Mr. Juicy
Abbey Well fruits

50 Alcoholic Drinks

Whiskey
Rum
Glenfiddich
Vodka
Gin
Lager
Bitter
Champagne
Sonti
Shandy
Brandy
Pimms No. 1
Armagnac
Curacao
Pale ale
Vermouth
Wheat beer
Stout
Beer
Sherry
Red wine
Maraschino
Cachaça
Martini Rosso
Light ale
Cider
Port
Bock
Tequila
White wine
Scotch
Cognac
Absinthe
Bacardi
Fruit beer
Dry Martini
Saki
Mead
Mulled wine
Bourbon
Cinzanno Bianco
Ouzo
Porter
Raki
Madeira
Schnapps
Mezcal
Dubonnet
Barley wine
Rice beer

50 Styles of Music

Jazz
Jive
Rock 'n' roll
Rock
Blues
Bluegrass
Ska
Folk
Drum and bass
Ragtime
Bebop
Renaissance
Techno
Heavy metal
Progressive
Country
Swing
Reggae
Country and western
Jazz-funk
Soul
Pop
Classical
Rockabilly
Jungle
Rhythm and blues
Trance
Indie
Chamber
Goth
Psychobilly
Death metal
Gospel
Funk
Funkadelic
Atmospheric
Hip-hop
Experimental
Choral
Disco
Muzak
Dixieland
Boogie-woogie
New wave
Trad. jazz
Industrial
Skiffle
Glam
New romantic
Pre-Classical

50 Languages	50 Races
French	100 metre
Greek	Hurdles
Latin	Egg-and-spoon race
Swahili	Greyhound racing
German	200 metres
Bulgarian	Sack race
Spanish	Race to the North Pole
Urdu	Rally driving
Creole	Speedway racing
English	Race into space
Quechua	Regatta
Welsh	Front-crawl
Gujerati	Marathon
Sign language	The Hare and the Tortoise
Norwegian	Wacky Races
Czech	Snail race
Chinese	400 metres
Swedish	Bobsleighing
Pidgin English	Hopping race
Dutch	Butterfly
Turkish	Horse racing
Gaelic	Tour de France
Catalan	The Oxford and Cambridge Boat race
Arabic	Relay
Esperanto	Motor racing
Hungarian	Escalado
Mandarin	London to Brighton Vintage Car Rally
Hindi	Steeplechase
Egyptian	Potato-and-spoon
Macedonian	Sprint
Danish	Cross-country
Icelandic	Stockcar racing
Sanskrit	Boat race
Hebrew	Eights
Italian	Backstroke
Japanese	Ski race
Russian	America's Cup competition
Braille	Three-legged race
Polish	Gold rush
Finnish	800 metres
Bengali	Yacht race
Kirundi	Sprint
Portuguese	Obstacle race
Cheyenne	Point-to-point
Dzongkha	Walking race
Maltese	Dirt track racing
Albanian	Motorcross
Romanian	Track race
Dari	Carrier Pigeon racing
Amharic	Flat race

50 Battles

Battle of Trafalgar – 1805
Crecy - 1346
Battle of Hastings - 1066
Agincourt – 1415
Salamis – 480 BC
Custer's Last Stand – 1876
Siege of Ribodane – 1480
Boston Tea Party - 1773
The Alamo – 1836
Battle of Sluys - 1340
Balaclava – 1854
Defeat of the Moors - 1492
Bosworth Field – 1485
Siege of Metz – 1324
Battle of Britain – 1940-41
Cannae – 216 BC
Storming of the Bastille - 1789
Bombing of Pearl Harbour - 1941
D-Day Landing – 1944
Khartoum – 1885
Zama – 202 BC
Sempach – 1386
Battle of Nieuport -1600
Mafeking – 1899
Medway Invasion – 43 AD
Battle of Lepanto –1571
Defeat of the Spanish Armada -1588
Mortimer's Cross – 1461
The Fall of Rome – 476 AD
Battle on the River Plate – 1939
Battle of Gettysburg - 1863
Shanghai – 1937
Six Day War – 1967
Siege of Toulon - 1793
Battle of the Somme – 1918
Stamford Bridge – 1066
Vinegar Hill – 1798
Waterloo - 1815
Boudicca's Revolt – 61 AD
Leipzig – 1813
Hampton Roads – 1862
Cambrai - 1917
Battle of Ypres – 1915
Marathon – 490 BC
Poitiers – 1356
Battle of Blenheim – 1704
Battle of the Bulge – 1944-45
Austerlitz – 1805
Jena – 1806
Hiroshima - 1945

50 Sins

Gluttony
Greed
Sloth
Pride
Vanity
Laziness
Lust
Envy
Wrath
Jealousy
Lying
Malice
Covetousness
Anger
Debauchery
Corruption
Slander
Persecution
Cruelty
Spitefulness
Trespassing
Theft
Murder
Arrogance
Over confidence
Hate
Spite
Drunkenness
Laundering
Squandering
Perjury
Bullying
Rudeness
Unfaithfulness
Polygamy
Gratuity
Licentiousness
Mockery
Ignorance
Recklessness
Treason
Hoarding
Rape
Vice
Depravity
Villainy
Dishonesty
Contempt
Melancholy
Tyranny

50 Virtues

Honesty
Charity
Helpfulness
Kindness
Hope
Faith
Optimism
Forgiveness
Love
Friendliness
Courage
Sincerity
Openness
Hard working
Cleanliness
Chivalry
Encouragement
Sharing
Giving
Perseverance
Faithfulness
Appreciation
Benevolence
Sympathy
Gratefulness
Godliness
Respectfulness
Happiness
Fairness
Moral strength
Integrity
Rectitude
Honour
Temperance
Conscientiousness
Chastity
Prudence
Justice
Fortitude
Magnanimity
Nobleness
Altruism
Unselfishness
Righteousness
Dutiful
Generosity
Sobriety
Humbleness
Self-respect
Patience

50 More Discoveries and Inventions

The diode – John Ambrose Fleming, 1903
The telephone – Alexander Graham Bell, 1875
Compound microscope – Zacharias Janssen, 1590
The battery – Count Alessandro Volta, 1800
Plastic – Leo Baekeland, 1905
The arc lamp – Humphry Davy, 1809
The bra – Mary Phelps Jacob, 1913
The thermometer – Gabriel Fahrenheit, 1724
The tin can – Peter Durand, 1810
Television – John Logie Baird, 1925
Steam locomotive – George Stephenson, 1814
Cylinder phonograph – Thomas Edison, 1877
The globe – Martin Behaim, 1492
Penicillin – Alexander Fleming, 1928
The microphone – Charles Wheatstone, 1827
The ball point pen – Laszlo Jose Biro, 1938
The typewriter – W. A. Burt, 1829
Microwave oven – Percy LeBaron Spencer, 1946
Gunpowder – Rodger Bacon, 1249
The spinning jenny – James Hargreaves, 1764
Sewing machine – B. Thimonnier, 1830
Velcro – George deMestral, 1948
Drinking straws – Marvin Stone, 1888
Electric dynamo – Michael Faraday, 1831
The light bulb – Joseph Swan, 1878
Micro chip – Jack Kilby, 1958
Mechanical calculator – Charles Babbage, 1835
Barbed wire – Joseph E, Glidden, 1873
Gas lighting – William Murdoch, 1792
Computer mouse – Douglas Englebart, 1964
The revolver – Samuel Colt, 1836
Personal stereo – Akio Morita, 1979
The telegraph – Samuel Morse, 1836
World wide web – Tim Bernes-Lee, 1989
Coca-cola – John Pemberton, 1886
Daguerreotype photography – Louis Daguerre,
-1839
The safety razor – King Camp Gillette, 1901
The stapler – Samuel Slocum, 1841
Antisceptics – Ignaz Semmelweis, 1847
Safety pin – Walter Hunt, 1849
The telescope – Hans Lippershey, 1608
Internal combustion engine – Jean Lenoir, 1858
The automobile – Karl Benz, 1885
The Gramophone – Emile Berliner, 1887
Wireless telegraphy/radio – Guglielmo Marconi,
-1895
Pendulum clock – Christian Huygens, 1656
The cinematographe – Lumiere Brothers, 1895
Carpet sweeper – Melville R. Bissell, 1876
Pianoforte – John Broadwood, 1873
The zipper – W. L. Judson, 1893

50 Freshwater Aquarium Fish

Siamese Fighter
Chocolate Gourami
Barbatus Catfish
Dwarf Otocinclus
Jelly Bean Tetra
Marbled Hatchetfish
Three-Striped Pencilfish
Red Piranha
Blind Cave Fish
Chequerboard Cichlid
Peppered Corydoras
Jade-Eyed Cichlid
Angel
Glowlight Tetra
Blown Julie
Daffodil
Glass Catfish
Filament Barb
Greater Scissortail
Silver Shark
Sparkling Panchax
Fantail Guppy
Platy
Red Rainbowfish
Dwarf Gourami
Sailfin Corydoras
Neon Tetra
Gold Courami
Common Hatchetfish
Angelic Pim
Congo Tetra
Golden Pencilfish
Spotted Headstander
Ram
Kribensis
Oscar
Discus
Lemon Cichlid
Lake Malawi Mbuna
Dwarf Barb
Pearl Danio
Chequer Barb
Zebra Danio
Dwarf Rasbora
Coolie Loach
Red-Tailed Black Shark
Mexican Molly
Black-Bellied Limia
Cape Lopez Lyretail
Tiger Barb

50 Film Directors

Woody Allen
Stanley Kubrick
Fritz Lang
Don Siegel
Mel Brooks
Howard Hawks
Tim Burton
John Carpenter
Alfred Hitchcock
Francis Ford Coppola
Cecil B. De Mille
Brian De Palma
Bill Forsyth
Terry Gilliam
Nicolas Roeg
Peter Greenaway
John Landis
D. W. Griffith
Russ Meyer
Wes Craven
Martin Scorsese
Werner Herzog
Alan Parker
Carol Reed
Ingmar Bergman
Irvin Kershner
Tobe Hooper
Alan J. Pakula
John Huston
Quentin Tarantino
Derek Jarman
Krzysztof Kiéslowski
Sergio Leone
George Miller
Steven Spielberg
Andy Warhol
Sam Peckinpah
David Lynch
Blake Edwards
Guy Richie
Sydney Pollack
Chris Columbus
Ridley Scott
David Cronenberg
Michael Winner
Roman Polanski
Ken Russell
Jean-Luc Godard
Oliver Stone
François Truffaut

50 Football League Managers

George Allison
Tommy Docherty
Brian Clough
Glen Hoddle
Bill Nicholson
Steve Coppell
Harry Redknapp
Matt Busby
Graeme Souness
Bobby Robson
Kenny Dalglish
Herbert Chapman
Alex Ferguson
Keith Burkinshaw
Joe Mercer
Alec Stock
Jimmy Hill
Ted Drake
Martin O'Neill
Dave Mackay
Terry Venables
Graham Taylor
Joe Royle
Walter Winterbottom
Billy Wright
Ron Greenwood
Bob Paisley
Alf Ramsey
Lawrie McMenemy
Stan Cullis
George Swindin
Ted Drake
George Graham
Don Revie
Bill Shankley
Sam Allardyce
Ron Atkinson
Charlie Paynter
Malcolm Allison
Dave Sexton
Kevin Keegan
John Lyall
Harry Johnston
Arthur Rowe
Jimmy Seed
Tom Whittaker
Harry Catterick
Lou Macari
Ron Saunders
Howard Kendall

50 Things the World couldn't do Without

Medicine
Law enforcement
Farming
Transport
Government
Monetary systems
Housing
Mathematics
Hope
Education
Clothing
Electricity
Oxygen
Communications systems
Lighting
Healthcare
Philosophy
Language
Fuel
Entertainments
Ethics
Hospitals
Faith
Food
Food manufacturers
Politics
Justice system
Retail outlets
Water
Heating
Weights and measurements systems
Defence system
Computer systems
Gravity
Science
Psychology
Technology
Leadership
Democracy
Fire
Charity
Sports
A workforce
Undertakers
Recreation facilities
Consumer products
Rat catchers
Hydrogen
Combustion engine
Gossip

50 Things that make our lives just that little bit Easier

Tin-openers
Sliced bread
Mobile phones
Zips
Buttons
Paperclips
Computer mice
Door keys
Washing-up brushes
Potato peelers
Remote controllers
Shoe laces
Paper napkins
Spell-check
Toilet-roll holders
Letter boxes
Pencil sharpeners
Screw top lids
Egg-timers
Cash machines
Drawing pins
Screws
Toothpaste in a tube
Disposable razors
Garlic crushers
Book-marks
Correction fluid
Tea bags
Spoons
Batteries
Ball-point pens
Traffic lights
TV guides
Flossing sticks
Nail-clippers
Soap-on-a-rope
Glue-sticks
Scissors
Clothes pegs
Sticky stamps
Travel card
Popper studs
Belts
Nails
Pockets
Alarm clocks
Torches
Forks
Wet-ones
Combs

50 Characters from Classical Mythology

Jason
Adonis
Icarus
Daedalus
Achilles
Ajax
Perseus
Juno
Pluto
Pandora
Bacchus
Hermes
Hercules
Mercury
Pegasus
Venus
Antigone
Circe
Midas
Vulcan
Aphrodite
Selene
Orpheus
Minerva
Hector
Paris
Janus
Cupid
Agamemnon
Persephone
Cyclopes
Diana
Mars
Hydra
Medusa
Jupiter
Triton
Andromeda
Cassandra
Tantalus
Atlas
Helen
Zeus
Oedipus
Apollo
Priam
Romulus
Remus
Narcissus
Jocasta

50 Ways to get Arrested

Loitering
Theft
Drunk and disorderly
Carrying or possession of an offensive weapon
Murder
Endangering safety at aerodromes
Money laundering
Handling stolen property
Manslaughter
Burglary
Serious harm to the security of the state or to public
-order
Serious interference with the administration of
-justice or the investigation of offences
Physical assault
Abduction
Violent disorder
Affray
Causing fear of violence
Robbery
Disorderly conduct with intent
Criminal damage
Obstructing the police
Rioting
Conspiracy
Production, supply and possession of a controlled
-drug
Damage to property
Refusing to give or giving a false name or address
Unlawful obstruction of the highway
Dishonesty
Taking a motor vehicle without consent
Rape
Making off without payment
Treason
Kidnapping
Speeding
Indecent assault constituting gross indecency
Causing an explosion likely to endanger life or
-property
Dangerous and/or careless driving/riding
Fencing stolen goods
Hostage taking
Torture
Ship hijacking and Channel Tunnel train hijacking
Publication of obscene matter
Causing death or serious injury to any person
Causing serious financial loss to any person
Abandoning a vehicle
Ticket touting
Driving whilst disqualified
Terrorism
Inciting racial hatred
Blackmail

50 Ways to Communicate

Telephone
Txt
Flyer
e-mail
Braille
Telegram
Morse code
Town crier
Radio
Magazine
Smoke signals
Word
Sign-language
Myspace
Letter
Signal lamp
MSM
Wireless
Announcement
Radar
Advertisement
Flare
Song
Short-wave radio
Instruction manual
TV
Carrier pigeon
Watch-fire
Public address system
Round robin
Poster
Telex
PowerPoint
Window display
Story-telling
Citizen's band radio
Telegraph
Internet
Newspaper
Bugle-call
Leaflet
Mailing list
Narration
Circular
Cablegram
Press release
Messenger
Timetable
Satellite
Semaphore

50 Ways to avoid People

Quickly cross the road
Dodge into a shop doorway
Don't answer the phone
Constantly lick the sole of your shoe
Hood up
Hide behind the settee
Don't reply to text messages
Wear sunglasses after dark
Go out disguised as a road-sweeper
Live in the Himalayas
Always shop at midnight
Buy everything via the internet
Dress like a clown
Walk with a savage dog
Say you've just visited a leper colony
Become famous
Hobble along with your trousers round your ankles
Move to Wales
Develop Tourettes syndrome
Never wash
Get a life sentence in prison
Act drunk
Become a hermit
Introduce yourself as a funeral director at christenings
Dribble when you speak
Avoid walking down the high streets
Move to Grimsby
Announce you've contracted a highly infectious
-disease
Dress as a pantomime cow
Work night shifts
Fall down a hole
Walk down the middle of the road
Never answer the door
Wear a snake around your neck
Always sing in public at the top of your voice
Dress like a giant, pink bunny
Sleep in a coffin
Say you're a marriage guidance counsellor at
-weddings
Develop a nervous tick
Sail around the world, single-handed on a raft
Work in Greenland
Only speak in Andorran
Become a monk
Spend six months in hospital, in traction
Carry an offensive weapon
Live in the jungle
Only communicate via smoke signals
Develop bad breath
Become stranded on a desert island
Introduce yourself as an undertaker at parties

50 Foreign Footballers

Zizinho
Ademir
Jair
Barbosa
Czibor
Kocsis
Hidegkuti
Puskas
Bozsik
Trautmann
Zito
Garrincha
Didi
Beckenbauer
Overath
Eusebio
Carlos-Alberto
Tostao
Pele
Rivelino
Vogts
Muler
Cruyff
Neeskens
Kempes
Ardiles
Passarella
Zoff
Gentile
Rossi
Rummenigge
Maradona
Matthaus
Milla
Baggio
Klinsman
Romano
Ronaldo
Junior
Rivaldo
Barthez
Desailly
Deschamps
Zidane
Suker
Batistuta
Van Nistelrooy
Cantona
Maldini
Gullet

50 Popes	**50 Things to do as an Eskimo**
Benedict XVI	Fish
John Paul II	Wear fur
St. Peter	Look at snow
St. Pius I	Catch fish
St. Anterus	Use a kayak
St. Marcellinus	Freeze
St. Damasus I	Gut fish
St. Sixtus III	Rub noses
John I	Make tents of caribou skin
Pelagius II	Cook fish
Theodore I	Ride a dog sled
St. Gregory III	Build an igloo
Stephen V	Eat fish
Boniface VI	Catch seal
Anastasius	Listen out for polar bears
Formosus	Smell of fish
Sergius III	Build a fire
John XXI	Talk about ice
Leo VIII	Throw fish bones to the huskies
Alexander VII	Burp fish
Lando	Catch cold
Stephen IX	Worship the sea goddess Sedna
Marinus II	Talk about fish
Agapetus II	Try and keep warm
Philip	Talk about snow
St. Martin I	Dream of fish
St. Eugenius I	Dig yourself out
Urban III	Hunt walrus
Innocent III	Catch more fish
St. Vitalian	Gut more fish
Sylvester II	Gut seal
John XIX	Cook more fish
Clement II	Shiver
Victor II	Cut ice into blocks
Calixtus III	Eat more fish
Paschal II	Cook seal
Novatian	Stink of fish
Hippolytus	Catch walrus
St. Miltiades	Have nightmares about fish
Liberius	Wear two layers of fur
St. Zosimus	Eat seal
St. Symmachus	Catch some more fish
Conon	Cook walrus
Paul V	Burp seal
Nicholas IV	Cook some more fish
Pius III	Eat walrus
John XXIII	Carve a walrus tusk
St. Telesphorus	Eat some more fish
St. Sotor	Wear three layers of fur
Dioscorus	Sick of fish

50 Dances	50 Pubs with Silly Names
Foxtrot	586 Ltd.
Samba	Ain't Nothing But
Clog dance	The Pump & Truncheon
Waltz	As Good As It Gets
Ceroc	The Noose & Monkey
Pogo	The Half Time Orange
Tap dance	The Geese Have Gone Over The Water
Two-step	Bag O' Nails
Country dance	The Elusive Camel
Fan dance	The Tipsy Gent
Hula-hula	The Goat & Tricycle
Cancan	Royal Oak & Gas Tavern
Twist	The Couch
Charleston	The Sack of Potatoes
Conga	The Guide Dog Pub
Belly dance	Who'd Have Thought It Inn
Fandango	Goat In Boots
Slam	The Rat & Parrot
Jive	The Leek & Winkle
War dance	The Gypsies Tent
Flamenco	The Fugitive & Firkin
Limbo	The Boy's Head
Morris	The Ribs of Beef
Dance of the seven veils	The Mars
Polka	The Square Pig
Sword dance	Walrus & Carpenter
Quick-step	The Spinning Mule
Barn dance	Ye Olde Cheshire Cheese
Beguine	The Piddle Inn
Hornpipe	The Bald Faced Stag
Cossack dance	The Fighter Pilot
Rumba	The Two Necked Swan
Tango	The Bedroom
Cha-cha	The Dog & Six Stories
Hockey-cokey	The Ferret & Trouser Leg
Lambeth walk	The Mad Bishop & Bear
Square dance	The Jolly Butchers
Soft-shoe shuffle	The Trowel & Telegraph
Irish jig	The Swim Inn
Highland fling	Hop Inn
Cakewalk	In the Fog
Ballet	Ye Olde Reindeer Inn
Mambo	Pig & Whistle
Folk dance	The Ape & Apple
Gay Gordons	The Shovel & Ship
Bolero	Bar Me
Bossa nova	The Goat & Boot
Dashing white sergeant	The Wall Nut Tree Shades
Minuet	The Snooty Fox
Hesitation waltz	The Frying Pan

50 London Theatres

Palladium
Dominion
Shaftesbury
New London
ICA
Astoria
Prince Edward
Piccadilly
Phoenix
Donmar Warehouse
Royalty
Fortune
Drury Lane
Aldwych
Strand
Duchess
Royal National
Cambridge
St. Martins
Arts
Savoy
Adelphi
Vaudeville
Ambassadors
Palace
Albery
Wyndhams
Duke of York's
Royal Festival Hall
Coliseum
Garrick
Queens
Apollo
Globe
Lyric
Sketchley
Prince of Wales
Criterion
Comedy
Haymarket
Her Majesty's
Whitehall
Players
Mermaid
Saddler's Wells
National
Queen Elizabeth Hall
BBC Paris Studios
Bloomsbury
Old Red Lion Theatre

50 Things you could buy from a Victorian Chemist

Milk of sulphur
Farinaceous foods for infants and invalids
Carbonate of soda
Leeches
Tartaric acid
Magnesia
Camphor balls and tablets
Chloroform
Linseed meal
Camomile flowers
Quinine pills
Concentrated essence of ginger
Isinglass
Turkey rhubarb
Saffron
Bear's grease
Violet powder
Pearl powder for the face
Bloom of ninon
Carmine
Black draught
Prepared charcoal
Camphorated plain, rose and violet tooth powders
Sweet spirit nitre
Female and family pills
Scuttle bone
Senna leaves
Teething and worm cakes
Creosote and tooth-ache tinctures
Drops for the ear
Antispasmodic drops
Basilico poppy heads
Opiate pills
Disinfecting solutions of the chlorides of lime
Teething powders for children
Preston and pungent salts
Perfumes for the handkerchief, in variety
Wash for the hair
Oxalic acid
Red and white precipitate of mercury
Camphorated spirits
Anodyne and chilblain liniments
Cold drawn castor oil
Sarsaparilla root
Cod liver oil
Flesh tablets
Aromatic fumigating pastilles
The poor man's plaster
Prepared chalk
Syrups of squills

50 Nuts	**50 Patterns**
Acorn	Paisley
Palm	Polka-dot
Beech	Herringbone
Karaka	Tartan
Madia	Floral
Ngapi	Gingham
Brazil	Fleur-de-lys
Safflower	Arran
Breadnut	Check
Candlenut	Pin-stripe
Java olive	Dogtooth
Chestnut	Criss-cross
Almond	Zig-zag
Gnetum	Patchwork
Coconut	Plaid
Dika	Stripes
Pine	Diamond
Filbert	Tessellation
Hazelnut	Basket-weave
Vabon	Lattice
Gingko	Celtic
Macadamia	Egyptian
Groundnut	Animal print
Kepayang	Zebra skin
Hickory	Leopard skin
Lllipe	Swirly
Calumpang	Turkish
Shea butter	Mottled
Jojoba	Plain
Kedrouvie	Leaf
Kubuli	Crocodile skin
Mankrtti	Wave
Sapucaya	Squares
Naras	Spirals
Yehab	Repeating
Pili	Irregular
Niger seed	Tie-dye
Sandlewood	Tiling
Cobnut	Periodicity
Okari	Cellular Automata
Pecan	Crochet
Souari	Cross-stitch
Pignut	Quilting
Coco de Mer	Psychedelic
Pistachio	Chinese
Sunflower	Rainbow
Walnut	Rose
Peanut	Flower
Sesame	Spotted
Monkeynut	Snakeskin

50 Operas	50 Cockney Rhyming Slang Phrases
Candide	Apples and pears – stairs
The Barber of Seville	Mutt and Jeff – deaf
The Magic Flute	Plates of meat – feet
The Beggar's Opera	Monica Rose – nose
Madame Butterfly	Dog and bone – phone
Don Quixote	Almond rocks – socks
Elektra	Brahms and Liszt – pissed
Tosca	Artful Dodger – lodger
Otello	Ball of chalk – walk
La Traviata	Jam jar – car
The Pirates of Penzance	Barnet Fair – hair
Carmen	Boat race – face
Faust	Boracic lint – skint
Margot la Rouge	Jack and Jill – pill
The Flying Dutchman	Butcher's hook –look
Ivanhoe	China plate – mate
Le Miserables	Daisy roots – boots
The Importance of Being Earnest	Dustbin lids – kids
Tom Jones	Earwigging – listening
Lear	Frog and Toad – road
Macbeth	Jack Jones – alone/on 'is own
HMS Pinafore	Joanna – pianner/piano
Lulu	Loaf of bread – head
Nelson	A pony - £25
Joan of Arc	Mince pies – eyes
Cosi Fan Tutte	Oliver Twist – fist
The Threepenny Opera	Pen and ink – stink
Wat Tyler	Whistle and flute – suit
The Marriage of Figaro	Rosy Lea – cup of tea
Rigoletto	Rabbit and pork – talk
I Pagliacci	Skin and blister – sister
The Pearl Fishers	Stammer and stutter – butter
Salome	Tea leaf – thief
The Valkyrie	Trouble and strife – wife
Where the Wild Things Are	Two and eight – state
Akhnaten	Parky – cold
Wuthering Heights	Rub-a-dub – pub.
A Midsummer Night's Dream	'Apenny dip – ship
Blonde Eckbert	Bacon and eggs – legs
The Doctor of Myddfai	Bat and wicket – ticket
Einstein on the Beach	Bull and cow – row
Gawain	Cherry Hogg – dog
Resurrection	Cain and Abel – table
Porgy and Bess	Dicky dirt – shirt
Yan Tan Tethera	German bands – hands
Twilight of the Gods	Greengages – wages
Electrification of the Soviet Union	Jim Skinner – dinner
The Gamblers	Kate Karney – army
The Happy Prince	A ton - £100
The Mikado	Old pot and pan – old man

50 Things you can buy at the Bakers

Brown loaf
Cornish pastie
White loaf
Saffron cake
Split tin
Scones
Soda bread
Sour dough loaf
Rolls
Custard tart
Plum loaf
Chelsea buns
Bakewell tart
Oatcakes
Wheat loaf
Dundee cake
Shortbread
Muffins
Baps
Almond slice
French bread
Brownie
Baguette
Fudge cake
Jam doughnuts
Cinnamon apple loaf
Mince slice
Granary bread
Cinnamon walnut loaf
Eccles cake
Cheese slice
Bagel
Tea loaf
Apple tart
Mince tart
Cheese loaf
Éclair
Current bun
Danish pastry
Pumpkin bread
Parmesan braid
Banana bread
Carrot cake
Honey wheat loaf
Sticky bun
Cream cheese twist
Apple turnover
Croissant
Sausage roll
Chocolate chip cookie

50 Forms of Therapy

Aromatheraphy
Yoga
Psychotherapy
Counselling
Music therapy
Acupuncture
Physiotherapy
Indian head massage
Reflexology
Hypnotherapy
Alexander technique
Dream analysis
Holistic massage
Reiki healing
Occupational therapy
Beauty therapy
Homeopathy
Chelation therapy
Cognitive behaviour therapy
Balneotherapy
Chiropractice
Laser therapy
Osteopathy
Relaxation therapy
Therapeutic touch
Massage
Hypnosis
Thymus therapy
Neuro linguistic programming
Eye movement desensitisation reprocessing
Ultrasound
Effleurage backrub
Spinal manipulation therapy
Thermo-auricular therapy
Advanced body massage
Phytomer face and body treatments
Meridian energy therapies
E-lybra bio-resonance therapy
Voice technology analysis
Thought field therapy
Emotional freedom therapies
Radiation therapy
Macrobiotic consultations
Acupressure massage
Magnet therapy
Art therapy
Dance movement therapy
Dramatheraphy
Play therapy
Chakra balancing

50 Types of Aircraft	50 Newspapers
50 Types of Aircraft	*50 Newspapers*
Jet fighter	The Sun
Turbo-prop airliner	The Star
Montgolfier hot-air balloon	The Guardian
Fighter	The Daily Courant
Super Hornet	The Hackney Gazette
Spitfire	The Spectator
Gas-filled balloon	Middlesex Journal
Hang glider	South London Press
Doodlebug	Illustrated Times
Sopwith Camel	Loot
Airship	Evening Standard
Harrier Jump jet	The Craftsman
Monoplane	Daily Herald
Concorde	New Camden Journal
Boeing 747	The Daily Telegraph
Swing-wing bomber	The Irish Post
Biplane	The Manchester Guardian
Flying boat	Daily Advertiser
Sea plane	The Globe and Mail
Ground-attack 'Tankbuster'	The Sunday Times
Amphibian plane	The London Journal
De Havilland Mosquito	News of the World
Lockheed U-2	Melody Maker
Executive jet plane	The Times
Airliner	The Sunday Sport
Trainer	The Mafeking Mail
British Aerospace 146	News Chronicle
Freight plane	The Sport
Helicopter	The Daily Mail
Rocket	The Daily Post
Autogyro	Morning Herald
Magic carpet	The Daily Express
Light plane	The Financial Times
Fairchild Metro II	British Workmen
Passenger plane	Times Educational Supplement
Zeppelin	Daily Graphic
Troop-carrier	The Independent
Lancaster bomber	The Daily Mirror
Tiger Moth	Lloyd's Evening Post
Microlight	Record Mirror
Boeing EC-135 Stratotanker	The Observer
Triplane	The Observator
Ballistic missile	Morning Chronicle
Hydroplane	Exchange and Mart
Airbus A380	Evening News
Jumbo jet	The Pictorial
Barrage balloon	Daily Sketch
Messerschmitt 262	The Illustrated London News
Lockheed Electra	The Oxford Gazette
Hawker Tempest Mk. 5	St. James Chronicle

50 Magazines	50 Parts of a Bicycle
GQ	D-lock
Nuts	Freewheel sprocket
Kerrang!	Wheel rim
Woman's Own	Tyre
Vox	Brake block
Here!	Rear brake cable
OK Magazine	Saddle
Best	Seat post
Hello!	Cable guide
Look-in	Inner tube
Woman's Weekly	Seat stay
No. 1	Crossbar
True Romances	Steel frame
Time Out	Down tube
Event	Water bottle
Jackie	Bell
New Woman	Front derailleur
Men Only	Head tube
Loaded	Saddle clamp
Popswop	Pulley bolt
TV Times	Wheels
Cosmopolitan	Spider
Look Now	Tension pulley
Which Car?	Chain
The National Geographical	Mud-guard
Private Eye	Lights
Honey	Chain stay
19	Saddle bag
Bizarre	Crank
NME	Rear derailleur
Exchange & Mart	Pedals
Playboy	Toe clip
Woman	Bicycle pump
That's Life	Spoke
Heat	Valves
Uncut	Hub
Zest	Stem Headset
Vanity Fair	Handlebars
Chat	Brake cables
House and Home	Valve caps
New Scientist	Chain ring
Autosport	Gear shift lever
Tattler	Fork
Zoom	Brake levers
Red	Spoke nipple
Top Gear	Hub quick release lever
TV Weekly	Pannier
Bella	Chain bolt
Take a Break	5-speed gear box
Angling Times	Sprockets

50 Supermodels	50 Armed Forces
Gia	US Marines
Kate Moss	German Infantry
Alex Bardenfleth	Africa Korps
Naomi Campbell	3rd. BN, 75th. Rangers
Bridget Swidrak	Paratroopers
Claudia Shiffer	Royal Navy
Sasha Pivovarova	Ghurkas
Yasmin Le Bon	British Army
Christy Turlington	Royal Air Force
Alek Wek	2nd. Armoured Cavalry Regiment
Nicole Eggert	Royal Field artillery
Cindy Crawford	SAS
Valeria Mazza	Cossacks
Rianne ten Haken	French Foreign Legion
Alessandro Ambrosio	American Armoured Division
Elizabeth Hurley	Vikings
Fernanda Tavares	Australian Infantry
Danni Minogue	French Resistance
Jarolina Kurkova	American Confederates
Twiggy	8th. Army Desert Rats
Elsa Benitez	US Army Pacific
Jean Shrimpton	Japanese Infantry
Heidi Klum	Commandos
Gisele Bundchen	42nd. Infantry Division
Pamela Anderson	Russian Infantry
Kathy Ireland	American Infantry
Colleen Corby	4th. Brigade Combat Team
Carolyn Murphy	British Infantry
Ralph Lauren	Luftwaffe
Adriana Lima	German Desert Troopers
Bridget Hall	17th. Field Artillery Brigade
Daniela Pestova	Infantry Combat Group
Ksenia Konyukhova	US Cavalry
Yasmin Bleeth	Allied Infantry
Eva Herzigova	French Imperial Guard
Christy Turlington	French Hussars
Alicia Silverstone	20th. Special Forces Group
Doutzen Kroes	German Mountain Troops
Karen Mulder	XVIII Airborne Corps
Laetita Casta	German Wehrmacht
Lujan Fernandez	British Foot Guards
Molly Sims	French Grenadier
Patricia Velasquez	British 95th. Riflemen
Jenny McCarthy	English Musketeers
Petra Nemcova	French Line Infantrymen
Yamila Diaz	Bedouins
Suzanne Pots	Roman Army
Renee Bounin	Danes
Vera Zaal	101st. Airborne Division
Le Call	32nd. Army, Air & Missile Defence Command

50 Things we use in the Bathroom

Toothpaste
Towel
Mirror
Toilet-paper
Curling tongs
Razor
Water
Soap
Shampoo
Moisturiser
Contact lens solution
Lipstick
Comb
Cotton wool
Scales
Hairdryer
Straighteners
Toilet
Conditioner
Eye-liner
Nail varnish
Foundation
Talcum powder
Hair dye
Tooth brush
Flannel
Hair brush
Nail clippers
Hair spray
Foam bath
Bath
Light switch
Sponge
Taps
Shaving foam
Nail brush
Candles
Perfume
Hair gel
Mousse
Bathrobe
Slippers
Hair net
Mascara
Nail file
Lip-gloss
Floss
Tweezers
Deodorant
Loo brush

50 Sports Items

Tennis racket
Cricket bat
Bow and arrow
Skates
Football
Canoe
Fishing rod
Shuttlecock
Slalom ski pole
Swimming trunks
Ping-pong ball
Volley ball
Baseball glove
Tennis ball
Shin pads
Riding helmet
Rugby ball
Table-tennis bat
Badminton racket
Golf club
Basketball net
Boxing glove
Bigbore hunting rifle
Javelin
Hurdles
Pole-vault
Hockey stick
Wrestling ring
Racing saddle
Dart
Archery target
Rounders bat
Ice-hockey stick
Corner flag
Rugby boot
Wet fly
American basketball vest
Netball
Wicket
Hurley
Lacrosse net
Discus
Running shoes
Croquet mallet
Tee pegs
Smallbore biathlon rifle
Skies
Show jumping fences
Foil
Judo kit

50 Traditional Children's Toys

Spinning top
Doll
Rocking horse
Teddy
Wooden building blocks
Lego
Picture books
Fuzzy felts
Blanket doll
Rattle
Pushing car
Pick-up-sticks
Marbles
Jester balls
Hobby horse
Bean bags
Hammer and nails
Ludo
Push-up puppet
Yo-yo
Ankle-skip ball
Puzzle
Rag doll
Stacking bricks
Doll's house
Tin soldiers
Kite
Shop till
5 stones
Wooden hoop
Mobile
Plastic money
Snowstorm
Play iron
Play telephone
Wendy house
Teacup set
Face paints
Farm animals
Toy drum
Skittles
Jack-in-the-box
Whip and top
Ball and cup
Kaleidoscope
Skipping rope
Noah's ark
Picnic set
Plastic double-decker bus
Zoo animals

50 Cartoon Characters

Teenage Mutant Hero Turtles
Goofy
Buzz Lightyear
The Little Mermaid
Pluto
Bart Simpson
Samari Pizza Cats
Batman and Robin
Huckleberry Hound
Minnie Mouse
The Ugly Duckling
Mickey Mouse
Bambi
Tweetie Pie
Superman
Donald Duck
Tasmanian Devil
Lady and the Tramp
The Flintstones
Sindbad
The Brave Tin Soldier
Clarabell Cow
Top Cat
Spiderman
Captain Woundwort
Horsecollar Horace
Korky the Cat
Deputy Dawg
The Incredible Hulk
Casper the Friendly Ghost
Roadrunner
Sponge Bob Square Pants
Yogi Bear
Scooby Doo
Henry's Cat
Betty Boo
Homer Simpson
Sylvester
The Joker
Mowgli
Winnie the Pooh
The Pink Panther
Tom and Jerry
Pocahontas
Paddington Bear
Dumbo
Popeye the Sailor Man
Baba Papa
The Mr. Men
The Jetson's

50 Comic Characters

Desperate Dan
Dennis the Menace
Dan Dare
Rupert Bear
Rodger the Dodger
Weary Willie and Tired Tim
Ally Sloper
Jolly Jack
Uncle Oojah
Billy Wizz
Bobby Bear
Japhet and Happy
Teddy Tail
Billy Bunter
Felix the Cat
Biffo the Bear
Big Eggo
Deed-a-Day Danny
Roy of the Rovers
Mickey the Monkey
Superman
Ginger
Susan of St. Bride's
Ken and Joyce on Rainbow Isle
Batman
Tarna – Jungle Boy
Andy Pandy
Spiderman
Captain Condor
Gnasher
Buck Rogers
Ivy the Terrible
Flash Gordon
Joe 90
Mandy
Bunty
Princess Tina
Lord Snooty
Yogi Bear
Sparky
Pippin
Rick Random and the Space Pirates
Kitty Hawke
Whizzer and Chips
Tiger Tim
Pip, Squeak and Wilfred
Plug
Minnie the Minx
The Incredible Hulk
Wolverine

50 Items of Furniture

Settee
Sideboard
Coffee table
Chest of drawers
Dining room table
Radiogram
Occasional table
Trolley
Dress rail
Wardrobe
Double bed
Sofa
Foot stool
Pouffe
Dressing table
Entertainment's unit
Armchair
Shelf unit
Futon
Ottoman
Bedside table
Hi-fi unit
Sofa-bed
Cupboard
Bookcase
Study table
Welsh dresser
Display cabinet
Divan
Storage chest
Bunk beds
Cot
Nest of tables
Chaise longue
Three-piece suite
Dining chairs
Single bed
Computer unit
Swivel chair
Bean bag
Under the bed drawers
Breakfast bar
Bench
Drop-leaf table
Rocking chair
Couch
Four-poster bed
Tallboy
Bureau
Cocktail cabinet

50 Types of Footwear

Platform boots
Slippers
Winklepickers
Brogues
Loafers
Flip-flops
Doctor Martens
Espadrilles
Running shoes
Clodhoppers
Football boots
Toe-ring
Ballet shoes
Clogs
Slingbacks
German Paratrooper boots
Wellington boots
Gym shoes
Sandals
Creepers
Ankle bracelet
Chappals
Ski boots
Mountain boots
Pumps
High-heels
Baseball boots
Hush-Puppies
Slip-ons
Cowboy boots
Tennis shoes
Blue, suede shoes
Oxfords
Waders
Deck shoes
Spats
Mules
Jesus boots
Sneakers
Slipper-socks
Plimsolls
Moccasins
Gum boots
Beetle-crushers
Stilettos
Cuban heels
Thigh boots
Patten shoes
Flippers
Sabots

50 Types of Hat

Fez
Trilby
Stovepipe
Top hat
Fedora
Beaver
Bowler
Derby
Stetson
Ten-gallon hat
Sombrero
Straw hat
Boater
Juliet cap
Slalmon helmet
Skull cap
Turban
Puggaree
Fireman's helmet
Cockernony
Cockscomb
Wimpole
Busby
Bearskin
Crash helmet
Woolly hat
Bobble hat
Rain hat
Sou'wester
Cloth cap
Beret
Tam-o-'-Shanter
Balmoral
Glengarry
Deerstalker
Homburg
Pork-pie hat
Policeman's helmet
Panama
Bush hat
Sunhat
Pith helmet
Bonnet
Pillbox
Cocked hat
Tricorne
Mortar-board
Witch's hat
Sailor's hat
Tin hat

50 Kinds of Coats and Jackets

Frock coat
Raincoat
Cape
Trench coat
Anorak
Crombie
Fur coat
Gaberdine
Cycling cape
Lumber jacket
Overcoat
Gown
Topcoat
Leather jacket
Greatcoat
Oilskins
Poncho
Morning coat
Dressing gown
Redcoat
Bomber jacket
Robes
Windcheater
Garibaldi jacket
Raglan
Coat of mail
Ulster
Car coat
Parka
Duffel coat
Waterproof
Coat of paint
Afghan
Under coat
Mackintosh
Burberry
Redingote
Dress coat
Duster
Housecoat
Donkey jacket
Tail coat
Kagoule
Coat of arms
Mink coat
Sports jacket
Spencer
Leather coat
Chesterfield
Turncoat

50 Electrical Appliances

Fridge
Washing machine
Washer/dryer
Dish washer
Electric can-opener
Electric drill
Food mixer
Hi-fi
Gramophone
Hairdryer
Curling tongs
Sander
Straighteners
Electric blanket
Radio/cassette player
MP3 player
Wallpaper stripper
Photocopier
Video recorder
Computer
Printer
Circular saw
Alarm system
Scanner
CD player
Electric screwdriver
DVD player
Liquidiser
Spin dryer
Guitar amplifier
Jigsaw
Electronic keyboard
Television
Lawnmower
Electric carving knife
Heated rollers
Cooker
Router
Crimpers
iPod
DVD Camcorder
Angle grinder
Toaster
CCTV
Video player
Digital camera
Fax machine
Set top box
Home cinema system
Radio/alarm clock

50 Roman Towns	50 Well-known Films
Lindum	The Jazz Singer
Ratae	Gone with the Wind
Great Casterton	Alien
Venta Icenorum	The Hunchback of Notre Dame
Camulodonum	Taxi Driver
Londinium	Citizen Kane
Verulamium	Pulp Fiction
Durovernum	Star Wars
Portus Dubris	The Maltese Falcon
Noviomagus	Jaws
Venta Belgarum	Casablanca
Sorviodunum	Brief Encounter
Durnovaria	King Kong
Lindinis	Back to the Future
Fishbourne	Saving Private Ryan
Isca Dumnoniorum	The Birds
Aquae Sulis	Psycho
Corinium	Singing in the Rain
Venta Silurum	On the Waterfront
Isca Silurum	Rebel without a Cause
Moridunum	All the President's Men
Glevum	The Bridge on the River Kwai
Viroconium	The 39 Steps
Deva	The Full Monty
Melandra	Bonnie and Clyde
Bignor	One Flew over the Cuckoo's Nest
Mamucium	Four Weddings and a Funeral
Birdoswald	The Matrix
Ribchester	Butch Cassidy and the Sundance Kid
Petvaria	Easy Rider
Eboracum	The Wild Bunch
Isurium	The French Connection
Binchester	Cabaret
Vindolanda	The Godfather
Chesters	Silence of the Lambs
Frampton	Frankenstein
Newport	Rocky
Luguvalium	E.T. The Extra-Terrestrial
Ardoch	The Graduate
Cramond	Billy Elliot
Richborough	Some Like it Hot
Orpington	The Exorcist
Lullingstone	Trainspotting
Portchester	Reservoir Dogs
Chedworth	The Invisible Man
Pevensey	Robocop
Ackling Dyke	Raiders of the Lost Ark
Corbridge	Saturday Night Fever
Roewen	Dirty Harry
Neath	2001: A Space Odyssey

50 Types of Skirts and Dresses

Frock
Sundress
Ball gown
Sari
Mini skirt
Farthingale
Wedding dress
Midi skirt
Kimono
Summer dress
Shift
Maxi skirt
Little black number
A-line skirt
Pannier
Hoop skirt
Sarong
Cocktail dress
Pencil skirt
Cheongsam
Coatdress
Tea gown
Underskirt
Chemise
Pinafore dress
Filibeg
Pleated skirt
Gymslip
Evening dress
Polka-dot skirt
Party dress
Hobble skirt
Dirndl
Kilt
Slit skirt
Culottes
Tutu
Ballet skirt
Crinoline
Pareo
Smock
Kirtle
Straight skirt
Jubbah
Sheath dress
Shirtwaister
Caftan
Petticoat
Bustle
Toga

50 Michael Jackson Songs

Ben
Thriller
Billie Jean
Got to be There
Ease on Down the Road
Don't Stop 'Till You Get Enough
We're Almost There
Beat It
Ain't No Sunshine
Wanna be Startin' Somethin'
Happy (Love Theme from 'Lady Sings the
-Blues')
Say Say Say
I Just Can't Stop Loving You
P. Y. T. (Pretty Young Thing)
Farewell My Summer Love
They Don't Care About Us
Why
Stranger In Moscow
Rockin' Robin
Girl You're so Together
Bad
The Way You Make Me Feel
Man in the Mirror
Get It
Dirty Diana
Another Part Of Me
The Girl is Mine
Smooth Criminal
Leave Me Alone
Liberian Girl
Black or White
Remember the Time
Off the Wall
Rock with You
She's Out of My Life
Girlfriend
One Day in Your Life
In the Closet
Who is It
Jam
Heal the World
Give it to Me
Will You be There
Gone too Soon
Scream
You are Not Alone
Earth Song
Blood on the Dance Floor
History
Ghosts

50 Beatles Songs

Yellow Submarine
I Wanna Hold Your Hand
Yesterday
Something
Help!
She Loves You
Hey Jude
Can't Buy Me Love
I Am the Walrus
Get Back
While My Guitar Gently Weeps
Daytripper
Love Me Do
Please Please Me
The One After 909
From Me to You
A Hard Day's Night
Lucy in the Sky with Diamonds
Dig a Pony
I Feel Fine
Ticket to Ride
Free as a Bird
Maggie Mae
Day Tripper
Across the Universe
When I'm 64
Paperback Writer
Eleanor Rigby
Penny Lane
Strawberry Fields Forever
All You Need is Love
In an Octopussy's Garden
I Me Mine
Dig It
Hello, Goodbye
Lady Madonna
The Long and Winding Road
Real Love
Twist and Shout
I've Got a Feeling
All My Loving
Come Together
Let it Be
We Can Work it Out
Back in the U.S.S.R
Sgt. Pepper's Lonely Hearts Club Band
With a Little Help from My Friends
Magical Mystery Tour
Two of Us
For You Blue

50 Rolling Stones Songs

Honky Tonk Women
Jumpin' Jack Flash
(I Can't Get No) Satisfaction
You Can't Always Get what You Want
Brown Sugar
Not Fade Away
Soul Survivor
Little Red Rooster
The Last Time
Get Off Of My Cloud
19th. Nervous Breakdown
Paint it Black
Have You Seen Your Mother Baby, Standing in
-the Shadows
Let's Spend the Night Together
Ruby Tuesday
We Love You
Let it Rock
Street Fighting Man
Tumbling Dice
Angie
Moonlight Mile
It's Only Rock'N Roll
Out of Time
Fool to Cry
Miss You
Respectable
Emotional Rescue
Casino Boogie
Too Much Blood
She's so Cold
Start Me Up
Waiting on a Friend
Going to a Go Go
Time is on My Side
Undercover of the Night
She Was Hot
Harlem Shuffle
Mixed Emotions
Rock and a Hard Place
Almost Hear You Sigh
Highwire
Love is Strong
You Got Me Rocking
Out of Tears
I Go Wild
Anybody Seen My Baby
Saint of Me
Out of Control
Sister Morphine
Shattered

50 Madonna Songs

Holiday
Like a Virgin
Causing a Commotion
Lucky Star
Borderline
The Look of Love
Material Girl
This Used to be My Playground
Dear Jessie
Crazy for You
Into the Groove
Angel
Gambler
Dress You Up
Live to Tell
Papa Don't Preach
True Blue
Open Your Heart
Express Yourself
Cherish
Don't Cry for Me Argentina
Another Suitcase in Another Hall
Frozen
Hanky Panky
Justify My Love
Rescue Me
Erotica
Deeper and Deeper
Bad Girl
Fever
Drowned World
Rain
I'll Remember (Theme from 'With Honours')
One More Chance
Secret
Take a Bow
Bedtime Story
Human Nature
Vogue
You'll See
La Isla Bonita
Who's that Girl?
Like a Prayer
Oh Father
You Must Love Me
Ray of Light
The Power of Goodbye
Nothing Really Matters
Beautiful Strangers
Little Star

50 Playwrights

John Arden
Christopher Marlowe
Aeschylus
Anton Chekhov
Tom Stoppard
George Bernard Shaw
Noel Coward
Ben Elton
Samuel Beckett
Alan Bleasdale
Jean Cocteau
Arthur Miller
T S Eliot
Henrik Ibsen
Euripides
Ben Jonson
Molière
W H Auden
Bertolt Brecht
Peter Nichols
Sophocles
Oscar Wilde
Eugene O'Neill
John Osborne
Harold Pinter
Simon Grey
Sam Shepard
Jean Racine
Alan Bennett
David Storey
Dylan Thomas
Arnold Wesker
Caryl Churchill
Tennessee Williams
Willy Russell
Pierre Corneille
Georges Feydeau
Alexander Dumas
Christopher Fry
John Godber
Mike Keigh
David Mamet
John Ford
Thomas Middleton
Frank Wedekind
Arthur Wing Pinero
JB Priestley
Neil Simon
Thornton Wilder
Jean Genet

50 London Postal Areas	**50 Circus Acts**
SW1	Juggler
EC4	Knife thrower
N5	Lion-tamer
NW1	Tight-rope walker
E2	Acrobat
SW20	Limbo dancer
W10	Trapeze artist
SE28	Plate spinner
NW9	Clown
N21	Strong man
W8	Fire-eater
N2	Trick-horse rider
SW13	Illusionist
WC2	Quick-change artist
N12	Globe roller
E3	Conjurer
SW5	Chapeaugraphy
E6	Tattooed man
EC3	Sword swallower
SE6	Contortionist
N17	Escapeologist
E16	Weight-lifter
E8	Trick cyclist
N13	Equilibrist
SE22	Elephant rider
E1	Performing dog trainer
N19	Gymnast
E9	Stilt walker
N1	Stuntman
N7	Light dancer
E15	Human cannonball
N10	Magician
E11	Hot coal walker
N16	Hula-hoop dancer
N8	Balancing act
E12	Glass swallower
NW11	Slack ropewalker
E13	Balloon modeller
E7	Ariel silk act
N11	Bullwhip artist
E14	Pick-pocket entertainer
E17	Body music percussionist
N18	Dog trainer
N6	Mime artist
NW4	Angle grinder
SE27	Walkabout actor
E10	Snake handler
E4	Unicyclist
N14	High diver
N20	The ringmaster

50 Popular Zoo Animals	*50 Comedians*
Polar Bear	Harry Hill
Lion	Eric Sykes
Alligator	Charlie Chaplin
Cheetah	Catherine Tate
Spider	Tommy Cooper
Chimpanzee	Benny Hill
Tiger	Jim Carey
Brown Bear	Billy Conolly
Crocodile	Victoria Wood
Camel	Les Dawson
Stick Insect	Bruce Forsythe
Orang-Utan	Phil Silvers
Panther	Dawn French
Elephant	Tommy Trinder
Turtle	Arthur Askey
Owl	Tony Hancock
Penguin	Jennifer Saunders
Hippopotamus	Max Wall
Flamingo	Bob Hope
Ostrich	Matt Lucus
Killer Whale	Sid James
Shark	Joyce Grenfell
Ant-Eater	Max Miller
Snake	Jacky Mason
Rhinoceros	Paul Merton
Eagle	Julie Waters
Puma	Max Bygraves
Lizard	Jimmy Carr
Gorilla	Vic Reeves
Tapir	Hattie Jacques
Giraffe	Max Headroom
Toucan	Freedie 'Parrot-Face' Davis
Koala	Phil Jupitus
Gazelle	Jenny Éclair
Lemur	Jack Benny
Zebra	Groucho Marx
Wolf	Ricky Gervais
Skunk	Lily Savage
Kangaroo	Lee Evans
Panda	Joe Pasquale
Octopus	David Walliams
Seal	Victor Borge
Walrus	Lucille Ball
Bat	Frankie Howard
Sting-Ray	David Jason
Macaw	Russ Abbot
Chameleon	Ronnie Barker
Leopard	Myra Syal
Deer	John Cleese
Dolphin	Frank Carson

50 Places worth a Visit	50 TV Programmes from the 1980's
Big Ben	ER
Eiffel Tower	Brookside
Taj Mahal	Terry and June
Statue of Liberty	Hill Street Blues
The Valley of the Kings	Thirtysomething
St. Paul's Cathedral	St. Elsewhere
Sydney Opera House	'Allo, 'Allo
Grand Canyon	China Beach
Niagara Falls	Cagney & Lacey
The Great Wall of China	Twin Peaks
The Blue Mosque	Moonlighting
The Louvre	Northern Exposure
Acropolis	Blackadder
Notre Dame Cathedral	In Living Colour
Great Barrier Reef	The Cosby Show
Stonehenge	Only Fools and Horses
The Pyramids at Giza	Baywatch
Colosseum	Falcon Crest
Mount Kilimanjaro	Hi-De-Hi
Anne Frank House	The Hitchhikers' Guide to the Galaxy
Abu Simbel Temple	Dallas
Empire State Building	Edd the Duck
The Palace of Versailles	Minder
The Parthenon	Blake's 7
Florida's Coral Reefs	Countdown
Venice	Spitting Image
Pompeii	Max Headroom
The London Eye	Dynasty
Three Gorges of the Yangtze River	Live and Kicking
The Golden Gate Bridge	Benson
The Sydney Bridge	Saturday Super Store
The Leaning Tower of Pisa	Mork and Mindy
Tower of London	The Dukes of Hazard
Miami Beach	The Young Ones
Hofburg Palace	French and Saunders
Flanders Fields	Masters of the Universe
Statue of Christ the Redeemer	Taxi
Sugar Loaf Mountain	Knight Rider
CN Tower	Yes, Minister
Varanasi Ghats	Jim'll Fix It
Easter Island	Fraggle Rock
Forbidden City	The 'A' Team
Charles Bridge	Danger Mouse
Little Mermaid	Magnum P. I.
Geyser	60 Minutes
Dead Sea	Knots Landing
Mount Fuji	Murder, She Wrote
St. Basil's Cathedral	Cheers
Temple of the Reclining Buddha	The Golden Girls
Angel Falls	Roseanne

50 Double-Acts

Canon and Ball
Morecambe and Wise
Little and Large
Laurel and Hardy
Sooty and Sweep
Fry and Laurie
Rowan and Martin
The Two Ronnies
Smith and Jones
Eric Sykes and Hatti Jakes
Badger and Bodger
Allen and Rossi
Bill and Ben
Vic Reeves and Bob Mortimer
Burns and Schreiber
French and Saunders
Abbott and Costello
Martin and Lewis
Derek and Clive
Peter Cook and Dudley Moore
Nichols and May
Hinge and Bracket
Tweedle-Dee and Tweedle-Dum
Flannigan and Allen
Wood and Walters
David Spade and Chris Farley
Wayne and Waynetta Slob
Mork and Mindy
Steptoe and Son
Dastardly and Muttley
Smashie and Nicey
Wheeler and Woolsey
Trev. and Simon
Hale and Pace
Wayne and Shuster
Skinner and Baddiel
Lee and Herring
Penn and Teller
Armstrong and Miller
Chas and Dave
John Fortune and John Bird
Matt Lucas and David Walliams
Gervais and Merchant
Ant and Dec
Terry and June
Ric Mayal and Adi Admondson
Burns and Allen
Cheech and Chong
Bob and Ray
Wallace and Gromit

50 Radio Shows from the 1930's – 1960's

Fibber McGee
Father Knows Best
Sam Spade
Amos and Andy
Nero Wolfe
Lux Radio Theatre
Dr. Kildare
Box 13
Speed Gibson
Sherlock Holmes
Tarzan
You Bet Your Life
Information Please
X Minus 1
Fred Allen
2000 Plus
Suspense
Quiet Please
Life of Riley
Superman
Bing Crosby Variety Show
Gunsmoke
Broadway is My Beat
Six Shooter
Groucho Marx
The Avengers
Beyond Our Ken
I Love a Mystery
The Jack Benny Programme
Dragnet
Life with Luigi
Escape
Couple Next Door
The Halls of Ivy
Boston Blackie
Its Higgins Sir
The Alka Seltzer Show
The Saint
CBS Radio Workshop
The Lone Ranger
Sign of the Four
A Date with Judy
Archie Andrews
Pat Novak – for Hire
Philip Marlowe
Lights Out
A Study in Scarlet
Suspense
Dimension X
The Shadow

50 Characters from the Bible	50 Explorers
God	Marco Polo
Eve	Leif Ericson
Mathew	Bartholomeu Dias
Death	Vasgo De Gama
Adam	Francis Drake
Silas	Edmund Hilary
Titus	Jacques Cousteau
Felix	Robert Scott
Benjamin	Vasco Nùñez de Balboa
The Holy Ghost	Eric the Red
John	Yuri Gagarin
Abraham	Sally Ride
Jacob	David Livingstone
Abel	Saint Brendan
Cain	Neil Armstrong
David	Scylax
Mark	Christopher Columbus
Joseph	Louise A. Boyd
Jesus	Hannu
Moses	Amerigo Vespucci
Mary	John Cabot
Paul	Ferdinand Magellan
Ruben	Hernando Cortez
Simeon	Henry Hudson
King Herrod	Francisco Coronado
Lucius of Cyrene	Mae C. Jemison
Issac	Robert Ballard
Peter	Bjarni Herjulfsson
Ruth	William Beebe
Daniel	Francisco Pizarro
Pontius Pilate	Zhang Quian
Emperor Augustus	Hernando De Soto
Thomas	Abu Abdullah Ibn Battuta
Barnabus	Michael Collins
Damaris	Giovanni da Verranzano
Luke	Jacques Cartier
Nathanael	Edwin Aldrin
Barrabus	Samuel de Champlain
Lazarus	Roald Amundsen
John the Baptist	Father Marquette and Louis Joliet
Kain	Robert LaSalle
Levi	Guion Bluford
Noah	James Cook
Jezebel	Henry the Navigator
Satan	Mary Kingsley
Pestilence	Kit Carson
Judas	Roberta Bondar
Potiphar	Gil Eannes
Elizabeth	Martin Alonzo Pinzon
Samuel	Isabella Eberhardt

50 Traditional Children's Story Characters

Snow White
Cinderella
Dick Whittington
Goldilocks
The Hare and the Tortoise
Rag, Tag and Bobtail
Tom Thumb
The Three Little Pigs
Aladdin
Rupert the Bear
Black Beauty
Peter Rabbit
Rumpelstiltskin
Andy Pandy
The Ugly Duckling
Big Claus and Little Claus
Pinocchio
Bambi
Sleeping Beauty
Janet and John
Puss in Boots
Donald Duck
Sindbad
Grumpy
The Brave Tin Soldier
Thomas the Tank Engine
Jack the Giant Killer
Jermima Puddleduck
Ali Baba
Red Riding Hood
Alice in Wonderland
The Little Match Girl
Sooty and Sweep
Betty Boo
The Owl and the Pussycat
Hansel and Gretel
Winnie the Pooh
Pocahontas
The Goose Girl
The Three Billy-Goats Gruff
Peter Pan
Old Mother Hubbard
Lassie
Paddington Bear
Dumbo
Popeye the Sailor Man
Noddy
The Wizard of Oz
Mickey Mouse
Pip, Squeak and Wilfred

50 Novel Characters

Jane Eyre
Pip
Sherlock Holmes
Joseph K
Dante
Oliver Twist
Winston Smith
Richard Langdon
Harry Potter
Adrian Mole
Dr. Jekyll
Alice
Jim Hawkins
Friar Tuck
Tom Thumb
Mowgli
Lennie Small
Bilbo Baggins
Allen Quartermain
Tom Sawyer
The Invisible Man
Dorian Gray
Robinson Crusoe
Gulliver
Tom Jones
Eliza Doolittle
Miss Marple
Tom Brown
Ivanhoe
Scrooge
Beowulf
Lady Chatterley
Dr. Faustus
Don Quixote
Merlin
Captain Ahab
Moll Flanders
Captain Nemo
Sinbad
Father Brown
Tess Durbeyfield
Ulysses
Heathcliff
Huckleberry Finn
Rip Van Winkle
Cruella De Vil
Fletcher Christian
Madame Bovary
Daisy Miller
Uncle Tom

50 Fictional Detectives	50 Dicken's Characters
Inspector Morse	Oliver Twist
Det. Insp. Frost	David Copperfield
Dixon of Dock Green	Grip
Sherlock Holmes	Ebenezer Scrooge
Inspector Clouseau	Miss Miggs
James Bond	Stagg
Ken Boon	Fagin
Cagney and Lacey	Pip
The Chinese Detective – Det. Sgt. Johnny Ho	Dolly Varden
Dalziel and Pascoe	Inspector Bucket
Don Beech	Mr. Grub
Dempsey and Makepeace	Mrs. Fezziwig
The Equalizer	The Ghost of Christmas Past
DI Maggie Forbes	Uriah Heep
PC Nick Rowan	Conversation Brown
Det. Insp. Roderick Alleyn	Rob the Grinder
Bodie and Doyle	Miss Havisham
Jonathan Creek	Herbert Pocket
Kojak	Uncle Pumblechook
The Lone Ranger	Mr. Bumble
Chief Ironside	M'Choakumchild
Agent Dale Cooper	Merrylegs
Napoleon Solo	Major Hannibal Chollop
Miss Marple	Martin Chuzzlewit
Burnside	Miss Giggles
John Steed	Luke Honeythunder
Perry Mason	The Single Gentleman
Simon Templar alias The Saint	Mr. Slum
April Dancer	Bill Sikes
Starsky and Hutch	Mr. Blogg
Jonathan and Jennifer Hart	Lizzie Hexam
Ilya Kuryakin	Captain Blodwig
Det. Lt. Mike Stone	Sergeant Buzfuz
Det. Insp. Jack Regan	Samuel Pickwick
Taggart	Dr. Slasher
Wycliffe	Jerry Cruncher
Fox Mulder	Madame Thérèse Defarge
Capt. Frank Furillo	Barnaby Rudge
Det. Chief Insp. Barlow	Lady Honoria Dedlock
DCI Jack Meadows	Krook
Emma Peel	Fan
Bergerac	Rosa Dartle
McCloud	Mealy Potatoes
Callan	Jaggers
Randall and Hopkirk (Deceased)	Trabb's boy
The Singing Detective – Phillip E Marlowe	Fanny Dorrit
Rockford	Mr. Edmund Sparkler
Mr. Waverly	La Fayette Kettle
Magnum PI	Miss Twinkleton
Sgt. Suzanne 'Pepper' Anderson	Smike

50 'Ologies	50 Poets
Biology	John Milton
Psychology	Lord Byron
Anthropology	Patti Smith
Pyrology	W H Auden
Cardiology	Robert Burns
Nanotechnology	Virgil
Terminology	William Wordsworth
Zymology	John Cooper-Clarke
Sociology	Siegfried Sassoon
Ethology	Dylan Thomas
Mythology	Robert Browning
Vexillology	Leonard Cohen
Theology	John Donne
Criminology	Wilfred Owen
Paleoanthropology	Sylvia Plath
Symptomatology	Arthur Rimbaud
Ecology	Ogden Nash
Astrology	Dante
Geology	Paul Verlaine
Ichthyology	Don Van Vleit
Lexicology	Ibsen
Apology	W B Yeats
Microbiology	Geoffrey Chaucer
Ontology	John Updike
Reflexology	John Betjeman
Mineralogy	Ted Hughes
Semiology	Lord Tennyson
Petrology	Voltaire
Neurology	Christina Rossetti
Trilogy	Walter de la Mare
Orthopterology	Mathew Arnold
Dendrochronology	Robert Lee Frost
Chronology	John Keats
Pathology	Percy Shelly
Eulogy	Stevie Smith
Teratology	Goethe
Psychophysiology	Ezra Pound
Rheology	Edmund Spencer
Seismology	Bob Dylan
Campanology	Philip Larkin
Xylology	Walt Whitman
Splanchnology	Edward Lear
Archaeology	E E Cummings
Technology	William Blake
Ideology	Homer
Toxicology	Henry Wadsworth Longfellow
Ufology	Edgar Allan Poe
Vermeology	Alexander Pushkin
Zoology	Alan Sillitoe
Onology	Paul Valéry

50 Olympic Events

Shot put
Javelin
100m race
Clay pigeon shooting
Water polo
200m race
Sailing, laser class
400m race
100m relay
High jump
Front crawl
Rowing, double fours
Cycling, 1km sprint
Hockey
Long jump
Weightlifting, one-handed lift
Triple jump
Discus
800m race
Rowing, eights
Back stroke
1,500m race
Yachting, 8m class
Lawn tennis, women's singles
Decathlon
5,000m race
Wrestling, lightweight freestyle
Archery, York round
Boxing, middleweight
10,000m race
Butterfly
Marathon
110m hurdles
Shooting, double trap
Motor boating, 8m class
400m hurdles
Tug-of-war
400m relay
20km walk
Pole vault
Hammer
Heptathion
3,000m steeplechase
50km walk
Equestrian, 3-day event team
Football
Cycling, 5,000 track race
Shooting, running deer (double shot)
Modern pentathion
Rackets, doubles

50 Things to do on a boring Sunday Afternoon

Look out the window
Iron some towels
Clean out the boot of the car
Fiddle with the net-curtains
Polish your shoes
Sew on a button
Look through the 'Yellow Pages'
Dust the pelmets
Re-pot a plant
Cut back the ivy in the garden
Pair up odd socks
Ring your mother
Play Monopoly
Have a look up in the loft
Address a letter
Re-arrange the dinning-room furniture
On the calendar see which day Christmas falls on
De-frost the freezer
Chuck out some old newspapers
Tidy the airing cupboard
Play solitaire on the computer
Bleed the radiators
Clean the bath
Listen to your old Eagles LP's
Look for money down the side of the settee
Wash the windows
Look at your old stamp album
Make some jelly
Re-wind all your old cassettes and videos
Tidy the under-the-sink cupboard
Look through the Argos catalogue
Cut out some washing powder money-off coupons
Chuck out some old clothes
Wash all the dusters and dish cloths
Tighten all the door handles around the house
De-scale the kettle
Throw away out-of-date food tins and packets
Listen to Radio 4
Play 'snap'
Floss
Rummage through old boxes
Have a power-nap
Read the gas meter
Wash all the cushion covers
Check through your insurance papers
Get your clothes ready for work Monday morning
Polish the dinning-room table
Check the water level in the toilet cistern
Write your birthday up on the calendar
Bag up all your loose change

50 Things to Collect

Stamps
Coins
Records
Cigarette packets
Beer mats
Train numbers
First edition books
Spoons
Bookmarks
Pressed flowers
Thimbles
Comics
Cars
Guitars
Cut-glass
Toby jugs
Photographs
Butterflies
Shoes
Animal heads
Hats
Bottle-tops
Ornaments
Pens
Cigarette cards
Games
Fish
Magazines
Drawings
CD's
Newspapers
Stuffed animals
Matchbooks
Beer bottles
Paintings
Bus tickets
Badges
Toys
Postcards
Dolls
Teddies
Sculpture
Maps
Bird's eggs
Jewellery
Letters
Pill boxes
Bubble-gum cards
Medals
Jokes and anecdotes

50 Pets

Cocker Spaniel
Persian cat
Tortoise
Hamster
Goldfish
Tropical fish
Macaw
Snake
Rabbit
Gerbil
English Setter
Siamese cat
Budgie
Guinea Pig
Rat
Mouse
Chameleon
Golden Retriever
Chinchilla
Parakeet
Gecko
Tarantula
Burmese cat
British Shorthaired cat
Labrador
Cockatoo
Horse
Pony
Stick-Insect
Canary
Chipmunk
Homing Pigeon
Frog
Monkey
Terrier
Puppy
Colourpoint cat
Kitten
Terrapin
Finch
Lizard
Basset Hound
German Shepherd dog
Parrot
Toad
Boa
Ferret
Python
Lovebird
Poodle

50 Footballers who have played for England

Tommy Lawton
Wilf Mannion
Ray Clemence
Jimmy Greaves
Brian Robson
Stan Mortenson
Nat Lofthouse
Bobby Moore
Viv Anderson
Jimmy Dickinson
Johnny Haynes
George Hardwick
Bobby Charlton
Martin Peters
Duncan Edwards
Mick Channon
Kevin Keegan
Paul Gascoigne
Alan Ball
Alan Mullery
Stuart Pearce
Tommy Taylor
Alan Shearer
Ian Wright
Francis Lee
David Beckham
John Barnes
Frank Swift
Stanley Matthews
David Platt
Horatio Carter
Geoff Hurst
Peter Shilton
Emile Heskey
Paul Merson
Jack Charlton
Gary Lineker
Ray Wilson
Gordon Banks
Nobby Stiles
Trevor Brooking
Rio Ferdinand
Tony Adams
Jimmy Armfield
Colin Bell
Terry Butcher
Michael Owen
Paul Ince
Trevor Francis
Norman Hunter

50 Bottled Waters

Evian
Perrier
Vittel
Malvern
Pampara
Volvic
Scottish Spring
Natural Springs
Eva
Deep Rock
Vivendi
Alasika
Vals
Aqua Pura
Kirkland
Aquafina
Penta
Brecon Carreg
Ashbourne
Highland Spring
Cwm Dale Spring
Aqua Parmalat
Uliveto
Propel Fitness water
Dasani
Valvert
Buxton
Tŷ Nant
Contrex
Pure Blue
Contrexéville
Deja Blue
San Pellegrino
Santa Maria
Abbey Well
Aqua
Gleneagles
Aquana
Bonaqua
Lakeside Spring
Radnor Hills
Spadel
Cerist
Cotswold Spring
Orchard Fruits
Mountain Spring
Sasal
Spa
Ramlösa
Fiji

50 Cricketers who have played for England

David Gower
Tony Greig
Graham Thorpe
Alec Bedser
Basil D'Oliveira
Godfrey Evans
Alec Stewart
Michael Atherton
Colin Cowdrey
Geoff Pullar
Graham Hick
Derek Underwood
Ian Botham
Tony Lock
Phil Tufnell
Tom Graveney
Keith Fletcher
Mike Smith
Michael Vaughan
John Snow
Geoff Boycott
Robin Hobbs
Ashley Giles
Len Hutton
Alan Knott
Freddie Trueman
Jim Laker
Bob Taylor
Darren Gough
Ken Barrington
Alan Lamb
Mike Brearley
Brian Luckhurst
Trevor Bailey
Robin Smith
Bob Willis
Graham Gooch
Chris Old
Peter May
John Lever
Andrew Flintoff
Derek Randal
John Emburey
Denis Compton
Reg Simpson
Ray Illingworth
Nick Knight
Andy Caddick
Brian Statham
Dominic Cork

50 Forms of Small-Talk

Chat
Chin wag
Chew the fat
Natter
Gossip
Rant
Rabbit
Tongue wag
Converse
Repartee
Banter
Badinage
Slanging
Verbal intercourse
Duologue
Tête-à-tête
Causerie
Table talk
Prattle
Tattle
Jabber
Tittle-tattle
Spiel
Fireside chat
Chatter
Heart-to-heart
Pow-wow
Cozy chat
Gab
Parley
Bandy
Buzz
Whisper
Rhubarb rhubarb
Tommyrot
Mumbo jumbo
Gibberish
Gabble
Babble
Gibber-jabber
Drivel
Twaddle
Chitchat
Fiddle-faddle
Bosh
Tosh
Verbiage
Blah-blah-blah
Flimflam
Yak yak

50 Shakespeare Insults

Thou crusty botch of nature!
Thou surly shard-borne devil-mon!
Thou bootless doghearted moldwarp!
Peace, ye fat guts!
Thou venomed tardy-gaited lout!
Thou mewling ill-nurtured foot-licker!
Thou art ... a fusty nut with no kernal!
Thou goatish unwash'd codpiece!
Thine horrid image doth unfix my hair
Thou fawning fly-bitten mumble-news!
...Marry a fool; for wise men know well enough
-what monsters you make of them
Thou art a fool, a coward, ...an ass, a madman
Thou jarring swag-bellied malcontent!
Thou puny knotty-pated baggage!
I think thou wast created for men to breath
-themselves upon thee
Thou art the rudeliest welcome to this world
Thou slander of thy heavy mother's womb!
Thou goatish folly-fallen gudgeon!
Would thou wert clean enough to spit upon!
Thou froward shard-borne ratsbane!
Thou craven dread-bolted moldwarp!
Thou loggerheaded scurvy-valiant bum-bailey!
Thou elvish-mark'd, abortive, rooting hog!
Thou spongy half-baked foot-licker!
Confusion now have made his masterpiece!
What, you egg! Young fry of treachery!
Degenerate and base art thou
Thou frothy rampallian knave!
You are a fishmonger
You are as a candle, the better burnt out
Thou cockered swag-bellied clack-dish!
Thou fobbing knotty-pated death-token!
Thou art ... spacious in the possesion of dirt
Thou art a superficial, ignorant, unweighing fellow
Your virginity breeds mites, much like a cheese
Thou bawdy folly-fallen malt-worm!
Thou cullionly unchin-snouted maggot-pie!
Idol of idiot-worshippers!
Thou venomed full-gorged dewberry!
You ... speak an infinite deal of nothing
Thou mountain of mad flesh!
Thou wayward hedge-born ratsbane!
Thou paunchy fool-born bugbear!
Sell your face for five pence and 'tis dear
Out of my sight! Thou dost infect my eyes
Thine ... breath stinks with eating toasted cheese
I think thou never was where grace was said
Thou currish malmsey-nosed bugbear!
Thou burly-boned, beetle-headed coxcomb!
Thou lumpish beetle-headed mammet!

50 Outdoor Leisure Pursuits

Walking
Rock climbing
Fishing
Ballooning
Yachting
Horse riding
Skiing
Fencing
Running
Caving
Swimming
Quad biking
Off-roading
Archery
Clay pigeon shooting
White water rafting
Abseiling
Diving
Sky-diving
Go-karting
Surfing
Snow-boarding
Karate
Tobogganing
Cycling
Mountain biking
Canoeing
Pot-holing
Boxing
Hurdling
Shot-putting
Jogging
Snorkelling
Judo
Kayaking
Mountaineering
Fell running
Gliding
Golf
Paragliding
Orienteering
Paintballing
Polo
Wind surfing
Rowing
Hiking
Pony trekking
Sail boarding
Hunting
Parachute jumping

50 Things to use in the Gym

Cushion mat
Parallel bars
Bench
Treadmill
Elliptical trainer
Rack
Rowing machine
Exercise bike
Climbing frame
Weights
Horse
Bullworker
Floor
Cross trainer
Dumbbells
Multi gym
Rope ladder
Running machine
Barbells
Punch bag
Vault
Cones
Step
Ab roller
Crunch trainer
Tumble mat
Heart-rate monitor
Hand weights
Mini trampoline
Body ball
Climbing rope
Hoop
Speedball
Trapeze bar
Rings
Bean bag
Soft ball
Tyre swing
Buck
Wrist weights
Form
Skipping rope
Ankle weights
Play parachute
Scooter boards
Foam shapes
Tug-of-war rope
Weight plates
Balance beam
Horizontal bars

50 Counties in Britain and Ireland

Kent
Fife
Essex
Powys
Suffolk
Norfolk
Clwyd
Bedfordshire
Strathclyde
Dumfries and Galloway
Cambridgeshire
Cheshire
Kerry
Northamptonshire
Cornwall
Limerick
Somerset
Dorset
Londonderry
Devon
East Sussex
Wiltshire
Cumbria
Derbyshire
Leicestershire
Kildare
Durham
North Yorkshire
Gloucestershire
Hampshire
Hertfordshire
Cork
Lancashire
Wexford
Gwent
Northumberland
Grampian
West Sussex
Nottinghamshire
Oxfordshire
Highland
Shropshire
Lincolnshire
Surrey
Warwickshire
Buckinghamshire
Down
Worcestershire
Clare
Armagh

50 Things to do at the Seaside	50 Castles

Swim	Arundel
Paddle	Dover
Collect shells	Castel del Monte
Forget to put on suntan lotion	Edinburgh
Throw a beachball	Bran
Sunbathe	Hever
Build sandcastles	Huniazi
Have a packed lunch	Leeds
Look for crabs	Bratislava
Go caving	Peles
Pose in a deckchair	Rochester
Wear a hankie on your head	Krasna Horka
Read a good book	Beckov
Change into swimwear	Tower of London
Get sand in your shoes	Colditz
Listen to your Walkman	Budatin
Play frisbee	Slovenska Lupca
Look through a pair of binoculars	Fagaras
Dig a hole	Heidelberg
Put up a wind-breaker	Eltz
Keep the blanket clear of sand	Ooidonk
Get stung by a wasp	Windsor
Feel your shoulders starting to burn	Bojnice
Look for dead fish washed up along the shore	Spiš
Walk along the promenade	York
Eat an ice-lolly	Bolingbroke
Snorkel	Begur
Find interesting pebbles and stones	Cachtice
Cut your toe on a piece of glass	Devín
Have a nice, cold drink	Hricov
Wear sunglasses	Kežmarok
Wear a sun hat	Lietava
Play bat and ball	Modrý Kameň
Get stung by a jellyfish	Kremnica
Walk out to meet the sea	Orava
Watch fishermen dig for lugworms	Stará L'ubovňa
Dry off in the sun	Burg Stahleck
Visit the beach shop	Strečno
Write messages in the sand	Castle Cerveny Kamen
Swat away flies	Trencin
Look up at the cliffs	Zvolen
Play in the sand dunes	Neuschwanstein
Nap in the shade	Versailles
Listen to the seagulls	Carcassonne
Ride on a donkey	Blair
Walk to the end of the pier	Beltiar
Play run away from the waves	Parma
Watch a Punch & Judy show	Wand Chaumont
Wear shorts and flip-flops	Chatsworth
Burn	Mont Saint Michel

50 Prime Numbers	50 Musical Terms
2	Adagio – slow
61	Lontana – as from a distance
149	Affrettando – hurrying onwards
239	Lusingando – caressingly
347	Agitati – agitated
443	Ma non troppo - but not too much
563	Allargando – getting slower
659	Mancando – dying away
773	Allegro – fast, lively
887	Martellato – hammered out
3	Andante – walking pace
67	Morendo – slowly dying away
151	Animato – animated
241	Nobilmente – nobly
349	Appassionato – passionately
449	Parlante – sung as spoken
569	Arpeggiare – like a harp
661	Patètico – with great feeling
787	Bravura – boldness and spirit
907	Brio – vigour
5	Piacevole – agreeably
71	Con anima – with feeling
157	Pizzicato – plucked, picked
251	Deciso – decisively, firmly
353	Prestissimo – as fast as possible
457	Dolce – sweetly, tenderly
571	Rallendando – gradually slower
673	Dolente – sadly
797	Rigoroso – strictly, rigorous
911	Risvegliato – increasingly animated
7	Energico – with energy
11	Ritardando – gradually held back
59	Forte-piano – loud, then soft
139	Scherzando – playful
233	Forzando – sudden emphasis
337	Capriccio – quick and spirited
439	Fugato – in fugal style
557	Impromptu – to improvise
653	Grave – slow and solemn
769	Staccato – detached
883	Impetuoso – impetuously
1013	Strepitoso – boisterously
1009	Lacrimoso – sadly, tearfully
881	Suave – gentle, smooth
877	Largo – slow and stately
17	Tacet – silent
89	Legato – smoothly
179	Tempo primo – at original speed
733	Leggiero – nimble and delicate
313	Tranquillo - calmly

50 Sails	50 Parts of the Ear
Main sail	Helix
Mizzen gaff topsail	Upper crux of antihelix
Jibsail	Scaphoid fossa
Mizzen sail	Antihelix
Main gaff topsail	Antitragus
Fore staysail	External auditory meatus
Dipping lug foresail	Triangular fossa
Tabling	Lower crux of antihelix
Mizzen yard topsail	Concha
Standing lug mizzen	Tragus
Fore topmast staysail	Intertragic notch
Fore sail	Lobule
Main topsail	Malleus (hammer)
Velum	Incus (anvil)
Fore upper topsail	Stapes (stirrup)
Upper topsail brace	Auricle
Outer jib halyard	Auditory canal
Su-wei	Cartilaginous part of meatus
Fore peak halyard	Cartilage of auuricle
Lower topsail clewline	Temporal bone
Fore yard lift	Vestibular membrane
Fore lower topsail	Osseous
Inner jib halyard	Tympanic membrane
Fore throat halyard	Semicircular canal
Lug sail	Cochlea
Fore staysail halyard	Vestibulocochlear nerve
Damaged sail	Tensor tympani muscle
Foot	Mastoid process
Inner jib downhaul	Internal carotid artery
Outer jib downhaul	Eustachian tube
Outer jib sheet	Styloid process
Flying jib sheet	Cupula
Inner jib sheet	Membranous portion
Flying jib downhaul	Osseous portion
Flying jib	Crista
Outer jib	Hair cell of crista
Reef point	Ampullar nerve
Inner jib	Utricle
Fore staysail sheet	Saccule
Mizzen course	Vestibular nerve
Mizzen topgallant sail	Common crus
Main topgallant sail	Posterior seicircular canal
Fore mast topgallant sail	Organ of corti
Sprit topsail	Median canal
Spritsail course	Spiral ganglion
Artemon	Basilar membrane
Jib halyard	Oval window
Main course	Cochlea nerve
Main sheet	Vestibule canal
Luff	Tympanic canal

50 Famous Deaths

King Harold – arrow in the eye
Isadora Duncan – strangled by own scarf caught
-around car wheel
Joan of Arc – burnt at the stake for heresy and
-witchcraft
Princess Diana – car crash
John F. Kennedy – assassination
Cleopatra – suicide via snake bite
Guy Fawkes – hung, drawn and quartered for
-conspiracy
General Custer – shot at Little Big Horn
Amy Johnson – drowned after parachuting jump
Yuri Gagarin – aeroplane crash
Karen Carpenter – anorexia nervosa
Che Guevara – assassinated
William the Conqueror – died after fall from horse
Anne Bolyn – beheaded for adultery
Louis XVI – decapitated for treason
Adolf Hitler – suicide
Claudius –poisoned by his wife
Edmund I – stabbed at a banquet
Attila the Hun – nosebleed leading to choking
Virginia Woolf – suicide by drowning
Robert Maxwell – disappearance
W. C. Fields – drug overdose
Glenn Miller – aeroplane crash
Charles I – executed
Jesus of Nazareth – crucified for sedition
Adolf Eichmann – executed for war crimes
Catherine Howard – beheaded for adultery
Dick Turpin – hung for robbery
Ghengis Khan – died after fall from horse
Jill Dando – murdered
Sharon Tate – murdered by Manson family
Malcolm X – murdered
Steve Biko – killed by police
Fred West – suicide in prison
Leon Trotsky – assassinated with ice axe
Tommy Cooper – heart attack on stage
Francis Bacon – pneumonia
Sonny Bono – skiing accident
Lord Byron – malaria
James Dean – car crash
Marty Feldman – shellfish poisoning
Marilyn Munroe – overdose
Mata Hari – firing squad
Rock Hudson – AIDS
T. E. Lawrence – motorcycle accident
Marie Antoinette – guillotined
Percy Shelly – drowned
Mary, Queen of Scots - beheaded
Tennessee Williams – choked on bottle cap
Natalie Wood – drowned

50 Bank and Building Society Names

Midlands
Abbey National
Turkish Bank
TSB
Dime Savings Bank of Williamsburgh
Halifax
First Fedral Savings Bank of Indiana
Chelsea Building Society
Lloyds
Bradford and Bingley
Georgia State Bank
Nat West
Alliance and Leicester
Royal Bank of Scotland
Cheltenham and Gloucester
Hudson National Bank
IWA and Commercial Credit Union
HSBC
Woolwich
Yorkshire Bank
Kingfield Bank
First Direct
Barclays
Chase Manhattan Corporation
Coutts
Allied Irish Bank
Marine National Trust
Glacier Bank
Britannia Building Society
Capital One Bank
Bank of Cyprus
Nevada First Holdings Inc.
Co-Operative Bank
Nationwide
Laiki Bank
Oxford Bank
People's Bank
University Federal Credit Union
State Bank of India
ING Direct
Cahoot
First State Bank of California
Citibank
Vermont National Bank
Smile
The One Account
Clydesdale Bank
Irish Permanent International Bank
Bank of Elk River
Northern Rock

50 Knots

Bowline
Round, turn and two half hitches
Sheepshank
Thumb knot
Clove hitch
Slip knot
Granny knot
Running knot
Reef knot
Half hitch
Turk's head
True-love knot
Gordian knot
Double loop bowline
Angler's loop
The Angler's knot
Common tie knot
Sailor's knot
Figure of eight stopper
Rolling hitch
Hangman's knot
Sheet bend
Anchor hitch
Splice
Adjustable jamming
Eye splice
The dolly
Windsor tie knot
Flemish knot
Cow hitch
Savoy knot
Square knot
The Weaver's eight
Lark's head
Water knot
Magnus hitch
Flag bend
Double sheet bend
Midshipman's tautline
Halibut knot
Thief knot
Timber hitch
Overhand knot
Englishman's bend
Lanyard hitch
Carrick bend
The Monkey fist
The Cowboy bowline
The Artillery loop
Buntline

50 Easy DIY Jobs

Changing a fuse
Putting up a shelf
Wiring a plug
Painting a wall
Bleeding a radiator
Changing a lightbulb
Dusting
Hanging a picture
Adjusting the hot-water cylinder thermostat
Stripping wallpaper
Filling small holes and cracks
Plugging in a kettle
Rewiring a table lamp
Replacing a broken downpipe
Changing a toilet seat
Bedding in garden plants
Hanging a door
Making a cushion
Replacing a broken tile
Dealing with a blocked sink
Putting up a flat-pack chest-of-drawers
Patching damaged plaster
Vacuuming
Lagging a boiler
Insulating hot and cold water pipes
Adding security bolts to doors
Laying cork tiles
Replacing a one-way switch with a dimmer switch
Re-lighting the pilot-light
Shampooing a carpet
Positioning a new rug
Fitting a door knob
Fixing a creaky floorboard
Fitting a new flex to an iron
Replacing a broken window pane
Fitting a door chain
Unblocking guttering
Fitting draught-proofing
Repairing a dripping tap
Putting up a bird table
Fitting a loft ladder
Dealing with a blocked toilet
Adjusting the cistern water level
Reading a meter
Replacing a wall socket
Connecting a light flex to a ceiling rose
Installing telephone extensions
Hanging curtains
Clearing out a drain
Ironing

50 Cheeses

Caboc
Edam
Brie
Camembert
Sage Derby
Red Windsor
Lancashire
Caerphilly
Emmental
Gruyère
Cheddar
Bel paese
Parmesan
Gouda
Gudbransdalsost
Cheshire
Double Gloucester
Stilton
Red Leicester
Wensleydale
Feta
Mozzarella
Leicestershire
Goat's cheese
Leerdammer
Gorgonzola
Danish blue
Venezuelan Beaver cheese
Norwegian Jarlsberg
Cottage cheese
Limburger
Queso Fresco
Crackerbarrel
Danbo
Orkney
Mycella
Port-salut
Tôme au Raisin
Dunlop
Havarti
Austrian smoked cheese
Dolce Latte
New Zealand Cheddar
Bousin
Demi-set
Bleu de Bresse
Petit Suisse
Cream cheese
Irish Cheddar
Roquefort

50 Bacteria and Viruses

Borrelia burgdorferi
Human immunodeficiency virus
West Nile virus
Measles
Escherichia coli
Streptococcus
Common cold
Staphylococci
Bacterial meningitis
Salmonella typhi
Bacterial conjunctivitis
Poliomyelitis
Mumps
Treponema pallidumcholera
Bronchiolitis
Hanta virus
Influenza
Thermotoga maritima
Tumor virus
Pseudomonad bacteria
Tuberculosis
Cyanobacteria
Acaciella australica
Hepatitis A
Chickenpox
Rhizobia
Spirochetes
Lactobacillus acidophillus
Leukemia virus
Prochloron bacteria
Oligochaete
Anthrax
Yersinia pestis
Ebola virus
Herpes simplex
Rabies virus
T-4 Bacteriophage
Mycobacterium tuberculosis
Pneumococcus
Scarlet fever
Rhumatic fever
Tetanus
Diphtheria
Small pox
Coliform bacteria
Bacteriophages
Capripox virus
Rift Valley fever virus
Russian spring-summer encephalitis virus
Rubella

50 Types of Weather

Cloudy
Windy
Stormy
Heatwave
Sunny
Freezing
Rainy
Indian summer
Blustery
Cold
Dreary
Warm
Cold snap
Chilly
Thunder and lightening
Rough weather
Inclement
Squall
Rainstorm
Humid
Sunny periods
Blue skies
Balmy
Close
Like a summer's day
Wintry
Fair
Glorious
Wet and windy
Foul weather
Overcast
Icy
Showery
Snowy
Mild
Sleety
Hot
Changeable
Summery
Hail
Misty
Drizzly
Gusty
Foggy
Calm
Breezy
Below freezing
Dirty weather
Dry spell
Fine

50 Well-known 'Sayings' from the Cinema

"You talking to me? You talking to me?"
"Go ahead, make my day."
"Frankly my dear, I don't give a damn!"
"Why don't you come up sometime 'n see me?"
"The horror, the horror…"
"You can't handle the truth!"
"Keep watching the skies…"
"They're here."
"Is it safe?"
"What's a girl like you doing in a place like this?"
"Fasten your seatbelts, you're in for a bumpy -ride."
"Take that, you dirty rat!"
"The name's Bond; James Bond."
"Please Sir; can I have some more?"
"There's no place like home."
"Elementary, my dear Watson."
"Houston, we have a problem."
"It's the bells you know… they made me deaf."
"What you rebelling against?" "-What you got?"
"I ate his liver with some fava beans and a nice -Chianti."
"I'll have some of what she's having."
"Get off of your horse and drink your milk."
"I guess you're wondering; did he fire 6 shots or -only 5?"
"Here's… Johnny!"
"Beetlejuice, Beetlejuice, Beetlejuice!"
"I am not an animal! I am not an animal!"
"Here's looking at you kid."
"Good morning Miss Moneypenny."
"Marty! We've got to go …back to the future!"
"E.T. …phone home…"
"Will ya take a look at that; like jello on springs."
"…Practically perfect in every way."
"We are not worthy, we are not worthy…"
"Hi ho, hi ho, it's off to work we go…"
"We got rats in the cellar you know…"
"Made it Ma! Top of the world!"
"I see dead people."
"May the force be with you."
"You're gonna need a bigger boat."
"I'll be back."
"Play 'Misty' for me."
"We rob banks."
"Hasta la vista, baby."
"Goodbye, Mr. Bond."
"It's alive!"
"I want to be alone."
"Play it Sam. Play, 'As Time Goes By.' "
"We have ways of making men talk."
"My precious."
"Whaddya hear? Whaddya say?"

50 Breeds of Pig

Large White
Landrace
Ba Xuyen
Duroc
Kele
Fengjing
Berkshire
Mulefoot
Pietrain
Middle White
Bantu
Tamworth
Welsh
Gloucester Old Spots
Red Wattle
Jinhua
Meishan
Saddleback
Dermantsi Pied
Tibetan
Large Black
Vietnam Potbelly
Hezuo
Small Yorkshire
Lithuanian Native
Mangalitsa
Krskopolje
Black Slavonian
Wessex Saddleback
Minzhu
Poland-China
Essex Saddleback
Turopolje
Chester White
Hampshire
Arapawa Island
Czech Improved White
Mora Romagnola
Danish Landrace
Guinea Hog
Lacombe
Hertford
Iberian
Kunekune
Mong Dai
Norwegian Landrace
Oxford Sandy and Black
Wuzhishan
American Yorkshire
British Lop

50 Breeds of Cattle

Beef Shorthorn
Galican Blond
Dexter
Chinampo
Ayrshire
Finnish
Holando-Argentino
Sussex
Belted Galloway
Africander
Dairy Shorthorn
Brahman
Aberdeen Angus
Charolais
Philippine Native
Galloway
Hereford
Evolène
Antaloian Black
South Devon
Simmental
Friesian
Dajal
Guernsey
Norwegian Red
American White Park
Fighting Bull
Lincoln Red
Groningen Whiteheaded
Highland
Costeño Con Cuernos
Devon
Irish Moiled
Red Poll
Welsh Black
Normande
Jamaica Hope
Kerry
Limpurger
Madagascar Zebu
Karan Swiss
Jersey
Auroch
Texas Longhorn
Belarus Red
Dulong
Russian Black Pied
Hungarian Grey
Montbéliard
Ovambo

50 Pieces of Armour	50 Chain-Stores
Aiguilette	Debenhams
Pauldron	Selbys
Breastplate	Pronto-Print
Hundskul	Sainsbury
Sallet	British Home Stores
Backplate	McDonalds
Cervellaire	Comet
Pavaise	Esprit
Visor	Virgin
Sabaton	Books etc.
Bevor	Top Shop
Rerebrace	Littlewoods
Greaves	Burger King
Spaulder	Pollards
Heaulm	Primark
Casque	Marks & Spencer
Chamfron	Subway
Spangen	Do It All
Epaule de Mouton	Ryman's
Faulds	Somerfields
Barbute	Co-op
Gauntlet	Jones Brothers
Targe	Boots
Hauberk	Tesco
Mail	Argos
Chapel de Fer	Safeway
Ailettes	C & A
Lames	Burton's
Shynbalds	Homebase
Spur	Dixon's
Vamplate	Allied Carpets
Poleyns	IKEA
Rondel	Carphone Warehouse
Buckle	Habitat
Plate collar	New Look
Armet	H & M
Coif	Tie Rack
Rivets	Woolworth's
Shield	Sketchley's
Vambrace	Ingam's
Besagews	Kwik-Fit
Ventail	Curry's
Stechtarsche	Shelly's
Tasset	Angus Steak House
Gatlings	Pizza Express
Vervelles	Dillons
Wing	J D Sport
Couter	Next
Gorge	Gap
Aketon	Specsavers

50 Words to describe 'Hot'

Warm
Burning
Ardent
Searing
Fiery
Scorching
Blazing
Flaming
Sizzling
Smouldering
Flushing
Stifling
Sweating
Heated
Sweltering
Boiling
Roasting
Braising
Melting
Singed
Furnace
Torrid
Tropical
Fireball
Inflamed
Overheated
Fervent
Fervid
Glowing
Fuming
Oppressive
Sudorific
Perspiring
Fevering
Steaming
Smoking
Ebullient
Scalding
Grilling
Broiling
Seething
Blistering
Baking
Toasting
Flaring
Ablaze
Afire
Molten
Balmy
Sultry

50 Words to use instead of 'Nice'

Good
Ok
Alright
Fine
Easy
Acceptable
Pleasing
Pleasant
Not bad
Amiable
Congenial
Palatable
Agreeable
Interesting
Satisfactory
Affable
Genial
Welcoming
Delightfull
Gratifying
Cordial
Considerate
Helpful
Thoughtful
Mindful
Heedful
Great
Swell
Dandy
Capital
Wholesome
Salutary
Edifying
Tolerable
Passable
Respectable
Standard
Adequate
Fair
Sufficient
Unobjectionable
Unexceptionable
Indifferent
Middling
Mediocre
Ordinary
Fifty-fifty
Average
So-so
Safe

50 Names of Stars	50 Books of the Bible
Sun	Amos
Proxima Centuri	Corinthians
Alpha Centauri A	John
Bernard's Star	Obadiah
Wolf 359	Hebrews
Sirius A (The Dog star)	Lamentations
UV Ceti B	Jonah
Ross 248	Matthew
Epsilon Eridani	Peter
Sirius B	Deuteronomy
Lutyen 789-6	Psalms
Procyon B	Joel
Lalande 21185	Kings
Mintaka	Judges
Tau Ceti	Revelations
Ross 154	Titus
Altair	Tobit
Rta Cassiopeiae	Exodus
Alpha Centauri B	Zephaniah
Beta Hydri	Genesis
Fomalhaut	Micah
Pi-3 Orionis	Samuel
El Nath	Maccabees
Vega	Job
Mu Herculis	Ruth
Zeta Herculis	Chronicles
Deneb Algedi	Habbakuk
Antares	Isaiah
Alpha Hydri	Leviticus
UV Ceti A	Daniel
Muphrid	Numbers
Beta TrA	Philemon
Arcturus	Ecclesiastes
Pollux	Philippians
Porrima	Joshua
Capella	Proverbs
Castor	Jeremiah
Alderbaran	Thessalonians
Procyon A	Ezekiel
Spica	Zechariah
Tania Borealis	Mark
Wezen	Hosea
Enif	Colossians
Cor Caroli	James
Omega Centauri	Solomon
Zubenelgenubi	Song of Songs
Ras Alhague	Luke
Miaplacidus	Ezra
Gamma Velorum	Romans
Acrux	Timothy

50 Dr. Who Monsters	50 Vampire Films
The Daleks	Kiss of Evil
Abzorbaloffs	Daughters of Darkness
Cybermen	Blood for Dracula
Argolins	Incense of the Damned
Bandrils	Blood is my Heritage
Ice Warriors	Nosferatu the Vampyre
Cheetah People	Blood of the Demon
Chelonians	House of Dark Shadows
Hy-Bractors	Dracula
Fenrics	The Blood Demon
Cryons	Vamp
Dominators	Blood of the Vampire
Sea Devils	Kiss of the Vampire
Moroks	Blood on Satan's Claw
The Graske	The Legend of the Seven Golden Vampires
Quarks	Blood and Roses
Kitlings	The Return of Dracula
Mox of Balhoon	Billy the Kid and the Green Baize Vampire
Krynoids	House of Dracula
Drahvins	The Living Dead Girl
Forest of Cheem	Vampire Circus
Dulcians	Dance of the Vampires
Foamasi	Dracula: Dead and Loving It
The Gelth	The Fearless Vampire Killers
Menoptras	The Hunger
Ogrons	Blacula
Animus	The Brides of Dracula
Gundans	Bram Stoker's Count Dracula
Haemovores	Vampire in Brooklyn
The Horda	Count Yorga Vampire
The Sisters of Plentitude	Countess Dracula
Jagaroths	Dead Men Walk
Krillitanes	Devil Bat's Daughter
Lurmans	Vampires in Venice
The Macra	Devils of Darkness
Zarbi	The Vampire Bat
Monoids	Dracula 71
Autons	Dracula AD 1972
Movellan	Dracula Has Risen from the Grave
The Ogri	Dracula is Alive and Well and Living in London
Draconians	Vampire Cop
The Face of Boe	Dracula Prince of Darkness
Reapers	Requiem for a Vampire
New Humans	Dracula versus Frankenstein
The Pakhar	Vampire's Kiss
Naglons	Dracula's Daughter
The Kaled	Dracula's Dog
Opteras	Dracula 2000
Rills	The Lost Boys
Pimords	Lesbian Vampires

50 Cowboy Films	50 Things to do at 'Camp'
Fort Apache	Pitch a tent
How the West was Won	Gather wood for the fire
High Noon	Draw food from the Quartermaster's store
Frontier Marshal	Abseil
Gunsmoke	Orienteering
My Darling Clementine	Check the map
Cattle King	Prepare a meal
The Bride wasn't Willing	Dig a cesspit
The Great Sioux Massacre	Wide game
Bandit Ranger	Kit inspection
Ride the High Country	Light a fire
The Magnificent Seven	Hoist the flag
West of the Pecos	Cook a meal
Hangman's Knot	Dig a trench
Gunpoint	Mushroom hunting
Cattle Annie and Little Britches	Blow up the air mattress
Guns of the Timberland	Use a flashlight at night
Fort Massacre	Put up a clothesline
Cattle Empire	Use a Dutch oven
The Good, the Bad and the Ugly	Hike
The Bandit Queen	Air your sleeping bag
Bandolero!	Bird-watch
The Cowboys	Sing campfire songs
The Guns of Fort Petticoat	Tracking
Western Union	Rock climbing
The Shooting	Use a compass
The Hanging Tree	Build a bivouac
Randy Rides Alone	Fan the fire
Six Black Horses	Fish
Cattle Queen of Montana	Draw water from the pump
A Fist Full of Dollars	Find a tear in the groundsheet
West of the Divide	Trek
Hang 'em High	Get stung by a hornet
The Horse Soldiers	Learn to read the clouds for rain
Horizons West	Play rounders
The Outlaw	Drink beer
The Hangman	Split logs with an axe for the fire
Rangers of Fortune	Tie knots
The Shootist	Wash up
Westward Ho the Wagons	Heat up water in a 'billy'
The Outlaw Josey Wales	Make tea over the fire
Shootout at Medicine Bend	Have a barbecue
Wagonmaster	Whittle
Sitting Bull	Use the chemical toilet
Smoke Signal	Swim
Westward the Women	Rock climb
Shootout	Canoe
Gold is where You Find It	Wash in the open
Westbound	Collect leaves
Shotgun	Strike camp

50 Phobias

Barophobia – (fear of) gravity
Merinthophobia – being tied up
Epistemophobia - knowledge
Cainolophobia - novelty
Harpagophobia - theft
Ophthalmophobia – being stared at
Optophobia – opening one's eyes
Aphenphosmphobia – being touched
Xenophobia – strangers or foreigners
Ereuthophobia - blushing
Pnigerophobia - choking
Coulrophobia - clowns
Chromatophobia - colours
Medomalacupphobia - detumescence
Gephyrophobia – crossing bridges
Pteronophobia – tickling with feathers
Selachophobia - sharks
Arachnophobia - spiders
Enochlophobia - crowds
Agoraphobia – large open spaces
Kakorrhiaphobia – failure or defeat
Catgelophobia – being ridiculed
Xenoglossophobia – foreign languages
Hippopotomonstrosesquippedaliophobia – long
-words
Ranidaphobia - frogs
Doraphobia – the skins of animals
Cymobphobia – sea swell
Trichopathophobia - hair
Stygiophobia - hell
Kenophobia - voids
Atelophobia - imperfection
Acarophobia - itching
Scorodophobia - garlic
Rhytidophobia – getting wrinkles
Tapinophobia – being contagious
Pogonophobia - beards
Teratophobia - deformity
Anthropophobia - people or society
Keraunothnetrophobia – fall of satellites
Phasmophobia - ghosts
Didaskaleinophobia – going to school
Iatrophobia - doctors
Aurophobia - breezes
Barophobia - gravity
Philematophobia - kissing
Chionophobia – snow
Spheksophobia – wasps
Claustrophobia – small, confined spaces
Bathmophobia – stairs or steep slopes
Zoophobia – animals

50 Common Medicines

Paracetamol
Gavescon
Rennie
Nurofen
Strepsils
Milk of magnesium
Night nurse
Rinstead pastels
Bazuka gel
Karvol
Solpadeine
Resolve extra
Beecham's powders
Andrew's liver salts
Lemsip max
Setlers
Oxy 5
Germoline
Anusol
Prozac
Vicks vaporub
Blistex
Deep heat
Gripe water
Pro plus
Calms
Wind-eze
Optrex
Bonjela
Ex-lax
Eno's
Sudafed
Zovirax
Vaseline
Radian B cream
Amoxil
E 45 cream
Pepto-bismol
Dexedrine
Ventolin
Diocalm
Panadol
Calmine lotion
Disprin
TCP liquid antiseptic
Lipsyl cold sore cream
Asilone antacid liquid
Alka-seltzer
Calpol
Hedex

50 Words beginning with 'X'	**50 Films starring John Wayne**
Xanthate	True Grit
Xyster	The Sons of Katie Elder
Xenolith	The Man Who Shot Liberty Valence
Xiphisternum	Stagecoach
Xenomorphic	El Dorado
Xanthous	The Green Berets
X-axis	Hellfighters
Xerography	The Shootist
Xe	Rider's of Destiny
Xanthochroid	Sands of Iwo Jima
Xenon	The Spoilers
Xebec	The Searchers
Xenakis	The Lucky Texan
Xenia	Blue Steel
Xenogenesis	West of the Divide
Xerophilous	McLintock
Xenopus	The Long Voyage Home
Xeric	The Alamo
Xerophyte	Red River
Xerosis	The Horse Soldiers
Xanthippe	Flying Tigers
Xiphosuran	The Fighting Seabees
Xeroderma	The Dawn Rider
Xenophon	Hell Town
Xylan	Randy Rides Alone
Xerophthalmia	The Desert Trail
Xenograft	The Undefeated
Xylem	Hatari
Xerosere	Donovan's Reef
Xerox	Fort Apache
Xerxes	She Wore a Yellow Ribbon
Xhosa	They were Expendable
Xi	Back to Bataan
Xian	Lawless Range
Xiang	His Private Secretary
Xinjiang	Wake of the Red Witch
Xenophobe	The Conqueror
Xanthine	The Magnificent Showman
Xiamen	The Star Packer
Xenocryst	Pot of Gold
Xanthoma	Lawless Frontier
Xiphoid	Man from Utah
Xizang	'Neath the Arizona Skies
X-ray	Hurricane Express
Xanthophyll	Great Guy
Xenogamy	Rainbow Valley
Xylene	Paradise Canyon
Xylidine	Public Cowboy No. 1
Xylograph	Angel and the Badman
Xylophone	The Old Corral

50 TV Catchphrases

Turned out nice again
Ooh Tommy, you got my skin
Nice to see ya, to see ya… nice!
I'll 'ave 'alf
I'll get you Blakey
Hi-de-hi
Ooh, shut that door
And it's good night from me. And it's good night
-from him
Bernie; the bolt
Good game, good game
What are the scores, George Doors
Ooh you are awful, but I like you
It's all done in the best, poss-ible taste!
What do you think of it so far? –Rubbish!
Beam me up Scotty
Who lives in a house like this?
…And I mean that most sincerely really I do
D'oh!
You cannot be serious!
T. T. F. N.
I have a cunning plan
Keep 'em peeled
Nanu, nanu
Nobody expects the Spanish Inquisition
I'll have a 'P' Bob
Stupid boy, Pike
What you see is what you get
Engage!
Points mean prizes
Yeah but, no but, yeah but…
I du-no!
You are the weakest link. Goodbye
I don't be-lieve it!
Are you sitting comfortably? Then I'll begin…
Come on down
Evening all
Surprise surprise!
And now for something completely different
Hello, good evening and welcome…
Here's one I made earlier…
I wanna tell you a sto-ry
Didn't he do well?
I'm free!
I've started so I'll finish
Loadsamoney!
Gizza job
Hello John, got a new motor?
Know wot I mean 'Arry?
Who loves ya, baby?
Nudge nudge, wink wink, say no more…

50 Record Labels

EMI
RCA
Geffen
Charisma
Parlaphone
London
Virgin
4 A.D.
Do It
Chrysalis
Beggar's Banquet
Columbia
Fresh
Island
Factory
Popscene
One Little Indian
Fly
Food
Mercury
A&M
Harvest
Chapter 22
CBS
MCA
United Artists
MGM
Warner Brothers
Sony
Arista
Electra
Top Rank
Reprise
Epic
His Master's Voice
Tamla Motown
Polydor
RAK
Rough Trade
Stiff
Riva
Atlantic
Sire
Decca
Pye International
Ensign
Telstar
Mute
WEA
Capitol

50 Book Publishers

Allison & Busby
Seker & Warburg
John Brown Publishing Ltd.
Cassell
Jonathan Cape Ltd.
Octopus Publishing Group
André Deutsch Ltd.
Dorling Kindersley Ltd.
Faber & Faber Ltd.
Flamingo
Picador
Granada Books
Chatto & Windus Ltd.
Granta Books
Anderson Press Ltd.
Hamish Hamilton
Bloomsbury Publishing Plc.
HarperCollins Publishers Ltd.
Lion Publishing
The Lutterworth Press
Macmillan Publishers Ltd.
Bodley Head
Puffin
Vintage
Scholastic Ltd.
Hippo
Corgi
Blackwell Publishers Ltd.
Ladybird Books
Random House UK Ltd.
New English Library
Reinhardt Books Ltd.
Omnibus Press
Penguin UK
William Heinemann
Arrow
Lawrence & Wishart Ltd.
Little, Brown & Co. (UK)
Virago
Pan
Minerva Press Ltd.
Everyman
Isis Publishing Limited
Kingfisher Publications Plc.
The Watts Publishing Group Ltd.
Dedalus Ltd.
A & C Black Publishers Ltd.
The Orion Publishing Group Limited
Queen Anne Press
The X Press

50 Football Grounds

Arsenal Emirates Stadium
Old Trafford
Villa Park
Stamford Bridge
Selhurst Park
Craven Cottage
Victoria Park
Elland Road
Leyton Stadium, Brisbane Road
Kenilworth Road
City Ground
Hillsborough
The Stadium of Light
Vetch Field
County Ground
White Hart Lane
Prenton Park, Birkenhead
The Hawthorns
JJB Stadium
Huish Park
Molineux
Layer Road
Alexandra Stadium, Gresty Road
Williamson Motors Stadium
Shay Stadium
Underhill
Oakwell
St. James' Park
Fitness First Stadium, Dean Court
Recreational Ground, Saltergate
Kingston Communications Stadium
Alfred McAlpine Stadium, Leeds Road
Vale Park
Deepdale
Moss Rose
New Den, Bermondsey
Bootham Crescent
The Britannia Stadium
Roots Hall, Southend
Belle Vue
Goodison Park
Anfield
Rangers Stadium, Loftus Road
St. Mary's Stadium
Boleyn Ground, Upton Park
The Reebok Stadium
Ninian Park
Whaddon Road
National Hockey Stadium, Milton Keynes
Spotland

50 Designer Labels

Lee Cooper
Adidas
DKNY
Benneton
Helmut Lang
Jean Paul Gautier
Ben Sherman
Brutus
Levi Strauss
Fendi
Puma
John Galliano
Reebok
Gap
FCUK
Nike
Yves Saint Laurent
Moschino
Gucci
Head
Jimmy Choo
Converse
Pierre Cardin
Warehouse
Burberry
Umbro
Hogan
Kookai
River Island
Punky Fish
Chelsea Girl
Links of London
Section 60
Armani
Prada
Evisu
Laura Ashley
Etro
Diesel
Dolce & Gabbana
Alexander McQueen
Versace
Stone Island
Calvin Klein collection
Lacoste
Fila
Timberland
Wrangler
Balenciaga
Hugo Boss

50 Perfumes

Chanel No. 5
Aramis
Brut 33
White Linen
CKOne
Pagan Man
Eternity
Obsession
Dior
Old Spice
Poême
Armani
Joy
Hugo Boss
Cossack
Opium
Lou Lou
Charlie
Tabac Origional
Dune
Poison
Hai Karate
Trésor
Escape
Chlöe
Fahrenheit
Knowing
Miss You Nights
So Pretty
Le Jardin
Forbidden
Cheap and Chic
Aqua Manda
Must
Ultraviolet
Polo
Shocking
Chanel No. 19
Red
Special No. 127
Tweed
Vent Vent
Eau de Bonpoint
Imperial Leather
L'interdit
Only
Paco Rabanne
Anaïs Anaïs
Chypre
Drakkar Noir

50 Electrical Brand Names	50 Words for 'Dirt'
Sony	Silt
Pioneer	Mud
Philips	Earth
Sanyo	Sludge
Olympus	Quagmire
Sharp	Filth
Dyson	Clay
Bush	Scum
Morphy Richards	Crud
Panasonic	Soil
Electrolux	Peat
Bosch	Sewage
Black & Decker	Effusion
Daewoo	Clod
LG	Dust
Hinari	Bog
Russell Hobbs	Grime
Breville	Mire
Kenwood	Slime
Moulinex	Grease
Tefal	Discharge
Cookworks	Waste
Braun	Dung
Goblin	Manure
Rowenta	Muck
Indesit	Guano
Hoover	Trash
Hotpoint	Refuse
Servis	Spoilage
Zanussi	Offal
Candy	Debris
Tricity Bendix	Slag
Beko	Faeces
Samsung	Smut
Alba	Grouts
Belling	Shit
AEG	Dregs
BaByliss	Sediment
Remington	Must
Revlon	Residuum
Hitachi	Dross
Goodmans	Effluence
Technics	Slough
JVC	Scurf
Grundig	Plaque
Wharfdale	Soot
Toshiba	Foul
Mikomi	Sleaze
Worx	Fust
Ryobi	Yuk

50 Words for 'Dark'

Noir
Ebony
Black
Sooty
Night
Gloomy
Murky
Inky
Dusky
Umbra
Shadowy
Funereal
Dreary
Swarthy
Dismal
Pitchy
Louring
Shady
Nocturnal
Clandestine
Noctivagant
Grubby
Jet
Silhouetted
Veiled
Unlit
Subfuse
Lightless
Overcast
Befogged
Sombre
Brown
Clouded
Dim
Grey
Leaden
Swart
Smoky
Wan
Dun
Muddy
Dingy
Grimy
Sable
Fuliginous
Dirty
Nigritude
Livid
Bruised
Smirched

50 Words for 'White'

Pale
Creamy
Blanc
Clear
Ivory
Albescent
Albino
Pearl
Alabaster
Marble
Sallow
Magnolia
Frost
Chalky
Flaxen
Champagne
Neutral
Ecru
Lucid
Ashen
Milky
Blonde
Flour
Faded
Snow
Light
Bleached
Transparent
Waxen
Wan
Unpigmented
Blanched
Ghostly
Ice
Etiolate
Lactescence
Hoar
Bright
Crystal
Translucent
Opalescent
Buff
Uncoloured
Wine
Faint
Anaemic
Pallid
Whey
Pasty
Fair

50 2nd. World War Films

Saving Private Ryan
The Boat
Schlinder's List
The Battle of Bloody Beach
The Eagle has Landed
Bridge on the River Kwai
The Great Escape
The Dambusters
The Bridge
Battle Cry
The Colditz Story
Don't Look Now…We're Being Shot At
A Bridge too Far
Big Red One
The Guns of Navarone
The Longest Day
Where Eagles Dare
The Dirty Dozen
Ice Cold in Alex
Battle of Britain
Kelly's Heroes
The Pianist
Tora! Tora! Tora!
Cross of Iron
633 Squadron
Patton
Empire of the Sun
Catch 22
The Cruel Sea
Carve Her Name with Pride
A Matter of Life and Death
Master and Commander
From Here to Eternity
Hope and Glory
A Town Like Alice
Reach for the Sky
Stalingrad
In Which We Serve
The Battle of Algiers
Oh! What a Lovely War
Went the Day Well
Von Ryan's Express
Memphis Belle
Europa, Europa
Hell in the Pacific
The First of the Few
The Way to the Stars
One of Our Aircraft is Missing
Desert Victory
The True Glory

50 'Space' Films

Dark Star
Alien
Star Wars Episode IV: A New Hope
Star Trek: First Contact
Lost in Space
Dr. Who and the Daleks
Mars Attacks!
Space Raiders
Apollo 13
Star Wars Episode V: The Empire Strikes Back
Mission to Mars
War of the Worlds
Silent Running
Moon 44
Star Trek III: The Search for Spock
Moon Pilot
Close Encounters of the Third Kind
Star Wars Episode VI: Return of the Jedi
Space Jam Alien 3
2001: A Space Odyssey
Moon Zero Two
Star Trek VI: The Undiscovered Country
Moonraker
Aliens
Starship Troopers
Rocketman
Star Trek: Insurrection
Solar Crisis
Star Wars Episode I: The Phantom Menace
Space Cowboys
Cat Women of the Moon
Space Master X-7
Space Truckers
Dune
Star Trek IV: The Voyage Home
Stargate
The Black Hole
Spaceballs
Rocketship X-M
Battlestar Galactica
Space Camp
Star Wars Episode III: Revenge of the Sith
Spaced Invaders
Spacehunter: Adventures in the Hidden Zone
Star Trek V: The Final Frontier
Alien Resurrection
Plan Nine from Outer Space
Conquest of Space
U.F.O
Alienator

50 Songs with the word 'Love' in the Title

The Power of Love
Love Will Tear Us Apart
I Love You Love Me Love
Do You Love Me
She Loves You
I Can't Give You Anything (But My Love)
Love Me Do
Love on Your Side
Love Me Two Times
I Love to Love (But My Baby Just Loves to Dance)
Love Me Tender
Secret Love
I Want to Know What Love Is
Can't Buy Me Love
Hot Love
When You're in Love with a Beautiful Woman
Puppy Love
Young Love
(I Can't Help) Falling in Love with You
I'm Not in Love
Give a Little Love
I'll Never Fall in Love Again
Under the Moon of Love
Love is All Around
I Feel Love
Feels Like I'm in Love
Woman in Love
Saving All My Love for You
Tainted Love
Save Your Love
You Can't Hurry Love
Love Grows (Where My Rosemary Goes)
All You Need is Love
I Just Called to Say I Love You
Caravan of Love
How Deep is Your Love
I Just Can't Stop Loving You
A Groovy Kind of Love
I Will Always Love You
Falling in Love Again
I'd do Anything for Love (But I Won't do That)
Love Can Build a Bridge
Forever Love
Love Won't Wait
I Love You, You Big Dummy
Never Knew Love Like This
Where is the Love
Love Don't Live Here Anymore
Burning Love
Too Much Love Will Kill You

50 Songs with the word 'Boy' or 'Girl' in the Title

Oh Boy
Girls on Film
Bachelor Boy
My Girl
The Boys of Summer
Who's that Girl?
London Boys
Hey Boy Hey Girl
The Boys are Back in Town
Young Girl
Boys Keep Swinging
Oh Girl
Boy You Knock Me Out
Sulky Girl
Tomboy
My Little Girl
Boys Don't Cry
The Girl is Mine
Boy
Girl
The Boy Done Good
The Girl Can't Help It
The Boy from New York City
Girl Crazy
A Boy from Nowhere
Girls Just Wanna have Fun
The Boy in the Bubble
The Girl from Ipanema
The Boy is Mine
Girl from Mars
A Boy Named Sue
Girls, Girls, Girls
Boy Oh Boy
The Girl I Used to Know
The Boy Racer
Girl I'm Gonna Miss You
The Boy Who Came Back
The Girl in the Wood
The Boy with the Thorn in his Side
Girl, I've Been Hurt
The Boy with the X-Ray Eyes
A Girl Like You
Boy Wonder
The Girl of My Best Friend
Boys
Girl of My Dreams
Boys and Girls
Girl Power
Boys Better
The Girl Sang the Blues

50 Boys Names

Paul
John
Nigel
Edward
Luke
Mark
William
Gary
Dave
Jake
Charlie
Roger
Neil
Colin
Tony
Jim
Pete
Rob
Larry
Graham
Adam
Tom
Bert
Tim
Andy
Ben
Bob
Fred
Dan
Steve
Michael
Harry
Ian
Joshua
Terry
Vince
Frank
Matt
Henry
Martin
George
Eric
Robin
Jerry
Ken
Leslie
Rick
Nick
Chris
Roy

50 Girls Names

Carol
Mary
Daisy
Veronica
Jane
Tracey
Sharon
Ivy
Linda
Julie
Sarah
Eileen
Maud
Jill
Beth
Heather
Jackie
Hazel
Natalie
Ruth
Cindy
Charlotte
Gemma
Tina
Kim
Vera
Wendy
Angie
Catherine
Elizabeth
Sylvia
Justine
Gwen
Gladys
Jennifer
Emma
Melanie
Kate
Victoria
Dawn
Edith
Jean
Vanessa
Clare
Maggie
Penelope
Pauline
Jessica
Deborah
Karen

50 Well-known Surnames

Jones
Williams
Wood
Banks
Wheeler
Thompson
Clark
Smith
Townsend
Fisher
Cooper
Green
Black
Brown
Watson
Carter
Thatcher
Johnson
Russell
Biggs
Walker
Fox
Waterman
Stewart
Kent
Watt
Scott
Cross
Wells
Major
Harris
Field
Walton
Ross
Potter
Foster
Hill
Miller
Bishop
Castle
Turner
Farmer
Butler
Harvey
Burton
Shepherd
Blake
White
Newman
Morris

50 Pet Names

Spot
Patch
Rex
Rover
King
Rocky
Billy
Lassie
Tiger
Caesar
Toby
Lady
Hooch
Fang
Fluffy
Bobby
Buck
Kip
Blackie
Charlie
Fred
Lucky
Goldie
Spud
Bruno
Jasper
Harry
Chuck
Penny
Sandy
Sparky
Twinky
Barney
Tommy
Spotty
Whitie
Sukie
Tats
Seamus
Chewy
Jack
Nipper
Petra
Pickles
Dickie
Buddy
Millie
Skip
Ginger
Susie

50 Beers and Lagers

Kronenbourg 1664
Boddington's draught
Grolsch
John Smith's bitter
Fosters
Kilkenny
Red Stripe
Smithwicks
Holst
Brains bitter
Guinness
Young's bitter
Tusker
Skol
Carlsberg Export
Carling
Fiddler's Elbow
Badger beer
Budweiser Budvar
Abbot ale
Miller Light
Pure Corsica Colomba
Tennant's Super
Pils
Harp
Ruddles County
Heineken
Worthington Creamflow bitter
Caffrey's
Stella Artois
Beck's
Cooper's pale ale
Amstel
Murphy's
Cobra
Corona Extra
Hoegaarden
Tiger beer
Erdinger Weissbier
Newcastle Brown ale
Bud Ice
Tetley's Smoothflow
Hobgoblin
Bishop's Finger
Carlsberg Special Brew
Miller Genuine draft
Carling Premier
Castlemaine XXXX
Kaliber lager
Foster's Ice

50 Whiskeys

Canadian Club
Chivas Regal
Bell's extra special whiskey
Claymore Scotch whiskey
Drambuie
Macallan single highland malt
Mellow Corn
Glayva
J & B Rare
Talisker Isle of Skye malt
Johnnie Walker Black Label
Teacher's
The Famous Grouse
Whyte & Mackay
Tullibardine vintage malt
William Grant's Family Reserve
Jack Daniel's
Jim Beam
Glenfiddich Special Reserve highland malt
Tallamore Dew
Green Spot
Aberlour single highland malt
Heaven Hill Kentucky bourbon
Pikesville
Black Bush
Balvenie single highland malt
Bushmills Original
Paddy Old Irish whiskey
Dalwhinnie single highland malt
John Powers
Locke's Irish whiskey
Rittenhouse Rye
Glenmorangie single highland malt
Jameson's
Cabin Still Kentucky bourbon
Echo Spring
Highland Park Orkney single malt
Johnny Drum
Bulleit bourbon
Isle of Jura Islands single malt
JTS Brown
Old Fitzgerald
Wild Turkey
Laphroaig Islay single malt
Maker's Mark
Fighting Cock
Woodford Reserve
Bushmills single malt
Buffalo Trace
Knob Creek

50 Green things to Eat

Pea
Runner bean
Broad bean
Lettuce
Cabbage
Leek
Sprout
Broccoli
Green pepper
Lime
Apple
Mint
Rocket
Greengage
Gooseberry
Chives
Olive
Grape
Chicory
Asparagus
Parsley
Cress
Cucumber
Marrow
Celery
Watermelon
Chilli
Watercress
Spinach
Sage
Gherkin
Seaweed
Avocado
Pear
Green salad
Greens
Artichoke
Calabrese
Kale
Petit pois
Mangetout
Sugarsnap peas
Crab apple
Okra
Spring onion
Split peas
Fennel
Pippin
Sorrel
Endive

50 Types of Bags and Cases

Handbag
Shoebag
Holdall
Swimbag
Backpack
Paper bag
Pannier
Carrier bag
Wheeled holdall
Gymbag
Sports bag
Shoulder bag
Briefcase
String bag
Pilot case
Beach bag
Rucksack
Kit bag
Sling bag
Gasmask bag
Suitcase
Despatch bag
Satchel
Saddlebag
Book bag
Trunk
Wash bag
Document case
Duffel bag
Vanity case
Bum bag
Garment carrier
Messenger bag
Shopping bag
Attaché case
School bag
Laptop case
Sandwich bag
Flight case
Knapsack
Overnight bag
Plastic bag
Daysac
Cool bag
Gladstone bag
Carpet bag
Guitar case
Sponge bag
Wicker basket
Sleeping bag

50 Different Ages

Childhood
Stone age
Medieval
Jurassic period
Roaring 20's
Tudor
Middle ages
Bronze age
Victorian
Age of Exploration
Air age
Jacobean
Proterozoic period
Swinging 60's
Age of Reason
Elizabethan
Queen Anne
Teenage
Golden age
Car age
Age of Invention
Triassic period
Iron age
Cretaceous period
Technological age
Georgian
Middle age
Age of Enlightenment
Renaissance
Carboniferous period
Age of Discovery
Space age
Silurian period
Steam age
Roman
Computer age
Phanerozoic period
Mechanical age
Copper age
Industrial age
Miocene period
Age of Science
Modern age
Age of Medicine
Paleoproterzoic period
Dark ages
Reformation
Viking age
Silver age
Old age

50 Things to do on a Summer Holiday

Get delayed at the airport
Complain about your room
Write loads of postcards
Have a row with the waiter
Hire a car
Lose your suntan lotion
Read in the hotel lobby
Spend most of your time in the games room
Buy cheap sunglasses
Fall off a donkey
Read the local newspaper
Eat out
Get drunk by the pool
Go to a disco
Enter the fancy dress competition
Visit old churches
Make a mess in the hotel
Lose you shorts in the pool
Eat too much pasta
Play bingo
Play volleyball
Buy lurid, lime-green flip-flops
Ride on a camel
Befriend a stray dog
Watch very poor singers mime to backing tapes
Sit on your sunglasses
Join in with the poolside games
Eat too many ice creams
Chat with the locals
Throw someone in the pool
Ballroom dancing
Get a frisbee in the eye
Lose your room key
Listen to your iPod
Go out in a boat
Get addicted to the pinball machine
Wear big, baggy Bermuda shorts
Grow a beard
Go topless
Spend too much money
Play crazy golf
Forget to post your postcards
Lose a flip-flop
Swim in the sea
Buy rubbish in the gift shop
Sample the local food
Get a stomach bug
Meet a couple from your home village
Snog the waitress
Miss your flight home

50 Things to do in the Town

Spend half an hour looking for a parking space
Go shopping
Take a jumper back to a clothes store
Buy some stamps
Meet a friend for coffee
Visit the library
Look on the market stalls
Buy early Christmas presents
Pop into the bank
Nearly buy a new three-piece suite
Buy some new socks
Answer an obscure charity questionnaire
Wait for ages at the lights to cross the road
Bump into an old friend from school
Admire the old church
Get a coffee
Bump into old ladies
Buy a CD
Purchase some underwear
Get caught in the rain without your umbrella
Drink from the old fountain
Avoid an old teacher from school
Buy a new kettle on a whim
Narrowly avoid being run over by a car
Remember you've forgotten to bring your inside leg
-measurements along again
Wish it wasn't so cold
Worry about getting home to put out the 'recycling'
-rubbish
Buy a magazine with a free make-up bag
Get pooped on by a pigeon
Get chewing gum stuck on your shoe
Get lost in the arcade
Visit the toilets
Stare at a couple having a row in the street
Buy a book from a charity shop
See a penny, pick it up
Get pestered for spare change
Stare in shop windows where you can't afford
Go for a swift 'half'
Avoid some demonstration
Nearly give blood
Look in the 'crafty' shop
Squirm for a while on a new, shiny, unsittable bench
Lunch
Tread in dog's mess
Have a free 'tipple' of whiskey in the supermarket
Get your hat blown off
Get called Sir in the clothing stores
Buy some mints
Have to carry all the bags
Come back to the car to find you've been clamped

50 Obscure Words beginning with 'Q'

Quiche
Quagga
Quinary
Quelea
Quahog
Quango
Quarrion
Quartile
Quassia
Quaestor
Quarerninon
Quebracho
Quercetin
Quadrennium
Querulous
Quetzal
Quiddity
Quartziferous
Quidnunc
Quillet
Quinate
Quinque
Quartan
Quisling
Quivive
Quindecennially
Quixotic
Quodlibet
Quoin
Quokka
Qoutha
Quotient
Qwaqwa
Quadrate
Quadriplegia
Quenelle
Quaich
Quamash
Quantasome
Quartic
Quinquagenarian
Quaternary
Quatage
Quondam
Querist
Quiescent
Quietus
Quitrent
Quotidian
Quack

50 Words beginning with 'Zoo…'	**50 Estate Agents**
Zoo	Shaw & Co.
Zoos	ASK Property Consultants
Zoology	Bairstow Eves Ltd.
Zoometry	Stickley & Kent
Zoological	Copping Joyce
Zoogeography	Philip Phillips Estates
Zooid	Drivers & Norris
Zoophobia	Stattons
Zoochemistry	Foxtons
Zoom	Granvilles
Zoolatries	Camden Bus
Zoophilism	Hayes & Wilson
Zoomorphic	Saffron
Zoochore	Home
Zoogeographic	Shogun Realty
Zoonoses	Hotblack Desiato
Zoogeographer	ibuyhomes.co.uk
Zoogloea	In London Properties
Zoophilic	Keatons Estate Agents Ltd.
Zoosporangium	Frank Knight
Zooidal	Douglas Allen Spiro
Zool	Martyn Gerrard Estate Agents
Zoolatry	Next Move
Zoolater	Oakwood
Zoolatrous	Castles Estate Agents
Zoologist	Live & Lets Live Property Service
Zoologies	Hetheringtons Countrywide Town & Country
Zoomed	-House Agents
Zoogeographically	Parkheath Estates
Zooming	Myspace
Zooms	Location Location
Zootaxy	Behr & Butchoff
Zoometric	Hunters
Zoometrically	Salter Rex
Zooplankton	Hobarts
Zoomorphism	One Stop Home Shop Ltd.
Zoomorphy	Smart Move
Zoonosis	Kinleigh Folkard & Hayward
Zoophyte	Epad
Zoophagous	Space
Zoophile	Wayne & Silver
Zoophilous	Prickett & Ellis
Zoophobous	Winkworth
Zoophytic	Dutch & Dutch
Zoometrical	Holden Mathews
Zoophytical	Monopoly Estates
Zooplasty	1st. Class Estates
Zooplastic	Absolute Property
Zoospore	Olivers
Zootechny	Bunch & Duke
	EZ2 Estates

50 Things not to say in an Interview

I've just got out of prison
I don't believe in exams and GCSE's
My hobbies are; drinking, watching TV and graffiti
I've been unemployed for ten years
I tend to get sick a lot
I get bored easily
Sorry I'm late; traffic geez
I got kicked out of school when I was thirteen
I can't think of anyone who'd give me a reference
I suffer from poor concentration
I've a history of violence
I have trouble getting up in the mornings
I don't get on with other people
I'm a bit of a pyromaniac
I always carry a knife in case of any trouble
Any GCS... what?
Erm... I've got no home address
I suffer from Tourettes syndrome
Wot? A? ...I'm hard of hearing mate
I don't respond well to authority
Do you mind if I lay on the floor... it's my back
My English? It's blinding, init!
I can't work on a Monday... it's my religion
I'm extremely dyslexic
Sorry, can you repeat the question a fourth time
A character reference? No, no I'm not an actor
Hobbies? Would you like to see my tattoos?
I've got no qualifications
I'm just sleeping on a mate's floor at the moment
My social worker refuses to give me a reference
I don't posses an alarm clock
I'm still working off my community service; so if I
-can leave early on a Tuesday?
You couldn't spare us 50p so I can get a beer?
I'll need an afternoon doze if that's not a problem?
Can I bring my dog into work; he's ever so quiet?
I've no previous jobs –only previous convictions
No, I don't know how old I am... I can't remember
-my date of birth
These are false teeth by the way
Oh, I'm really sorry! ...I suffer from incontinence
Further education? -What a stupid question!
Do you do 'duvet days' here?
I've never held a job down for longer than 3 months
The rubber ring? –Oh, I suffer from piles
Before we start, have you got change for the coffee
-machine? I'm parched!
Do you mind if I smoke a joint?... it relaxes me
Would you like to see my holiday snaps first
Sorry, it's the girlfriend; I must take this call
Do I get my own office?
I'll need at least eight weeks holiday
I can't hold a pen or pencil... I'm allergic to them!

50 Good People

Bob Geldof
Abraham Lincoln
Elizabeth Fry
Princess Diana
Mother Teresa
Baha'u'llah
Leo Tolstoy
Socrates
Benjamin Franklin
Prophet Muhammad
Rosa Luxemburg
St. Francis of Assisi
Copernicus
Charles Darwin
Isaac Newton
Galileo
Elizabeth I
Horatio Nelson
Florence Nightingale
Robert Baden Powell
Alfred the Great
Ken Livingston
Queen Victoria
William Booth
Dr. Thomas Barnardo
J. P. Morgan
Jane Addams
Henry Ford
Charles Dickens
Alexander Fleming
Michael Faraday
Stephen Hawking
William Tyndale
Albert Einstein
Emmeline Pankhurst
St. Peter
Sir Francis Drake
René Descartes
Joan of Arc
Douglas Badar
Desmond Tutu
David Lloyd George
Sir Christopher Wren
Robert the Bruce
Francis Bacon
Che Guevara
William Shakespeare
William Caxton
Sir Walter Raleigh
Paraoh Ramasses II

50 Tastes	50 Swords
Sweet	Rapier
Sour	Egyptian Sickle sword
Bitter	Cavalry sword
Creamy	Butterfly sword
Salty	Cutlass
Spicy	Japanese sword
Fruity	Falchion
Greasy	Grossmesser
Peppery	Mortuary sword
Minty	Flamberge
Tangy	Smallsword
Mouldy	Ancient Greek double-edged stabbing sword
Oily	Foil
Sharp	Sabre
Bland	Stormbringer
Nutty	Shordsword
Fizzy	Claymore
Meaty	Spadone
Doughy	Philippine Talibon
Crisp	Japanese Nodachi
Crumbly	Lightsabertooth
Fresh	Scimitar
Sticky	Greatsword
Tart	Campilan
Acidic	South Asian Pulwar
Ripe	Excalibur
Bad	Galatine
Savoury	Umbrella sword
Aromatic	Tizona
Mellow	Polish Szczerbiec
Juicy	Joyeuse
Succulent	Longsword
Rich	Viking Legbiter
Gamy	African Flyssa
Gingery	Glamdring
Tasteless	Broadsword
Burnt	Mediterranean Gladius
Stale	Anlace
Milky	Arming sword
Melliferous	Cinquedea
Mulled	Dirk
Rancid	Espada Ropera
Uncooked	Épée
Overdone	Mameluke
Chocolatey	Seax
Watery	Shashka
Alcoholic	Japanese Bokken
Dry	Dha
Seasoned	Macana
Smokey	Kaskara

50 Sounds

Ding
Click
Bang
Crash
Ping
Donk
Bash
Boing
Chime
Thud
Rustle
Creak
Crack
Sigh
Quack
Grunt
Squelch
Slash
Plop
Plip
Plonk
Scrape
Shuffle
Huff
Puff
Sizzle
Twitter
Trumpet
Boom
Peal
Groan
Ring
Whistle
Drone
Dirge
Hoot
Jeer
Pop
Roar
Screech
Squeal
Slosh
Gurgle
Gargle
Growl
Howl
Hiss
Clack
Crunck
Squawk

50 Smells

Stink
Stench
Odour
Whiff
Honk
Fragrance
Fetid
Aroma
Bouquet
Essence
Foulness
Myrrh
Fume
Emanation
Effluvium
Reek
Waft
Redolence
Tang
Trail
Pungence
Perfume
Niff
Balm
Fetor
Thurification
Malodour
Incense
Pong
Pen and ink
Spicery
Mephitis
Eau-de-cologne
Miasma
Ambrosia
Scent
Taint
Musk
Putrification
Fumigation
Must
Fust
Staleness
Frowst
Fug
Nidorous
Ponk
Humming
Hircine
Rancid

50 Touchy/Feely Words

Soft
Silky
Velvety
Woolly
Rough
Bumpy
Bubbly
Wet
Dry
Clammy
Smooth
Oily
Rubbery
Warm
Cold
Cool
Hot
Slippery
Furry
Leathery
Textured
Plasticy
Icy
Burning
Papery
Crumbly
Sticky
Sweaty
Damp
Metallic
Rusty
Slithery
Itchy
Sharp
Blunt
Hard
Delicate
Gentle
Strong
Wispy
Wooden
Glassy
Cottony
Waxy
Dirty
Alive
Earthy
Curvaceous
Hairy
Grainy

50 Things you'd find on the Dinner Table

Salt and pepper pots
Butter knife
Plate
Serviette
Fork
Cold meat platter
Bowl of fruit
Soup spoon
Table cloth
Pot of potatoes
Coffee pot
Candelabra
Bottle of salad cream
Mustard
Gravy stains
Dinner plate
Tea spoon
Steak knife
Sugar tongs
Drinking glasses
Vegetable platters
Cookie jar
Wine
Gravy boat
Cheese board
Dessert spoon
Mug
Lazy Susan
Pickle
Side plates
Soup cauldron
Serviette ring
Fish knife
Butter dish
Name place card
Teapot
Jug of water
Toothpicks
Hotplate
Ketchup bottle
Wine glasses
Elbows
Finger bowl
Serving spoons
Salad bowl
Jar of pickles
Napkins
Sugar bowl
Cup and saucer
Cake stand

50 Things the Seven Dwarfs might have done if Snow White hadn't woken Up

Gone back to work
Done the washing-up
Cried
Darned their own socks
Sighed
Advertised for another live-in maid
Bought a washing machine, dishwasher, cooker etc.
Made their own beds
-Laid in them
Shaved
Worked without whistling
Drew up a housework rota
Given up work and become hermits
Dressed Sleepy up as an au pair
Cooked their own dinner
Muttered, "good riddance."
Started buying TV dinners
Tried to sell their story to the local Gazette
Starved
Walked around in rags
Rang in sick the next day
Got up a posse to hunt down the witch
Sobbed
Went back to living in squalor
Decided not to rent 'Snow White' on DVD
Shrugged
Grew their beards even longer
Gave up eating apples
Had a big fight on Snow White's old bed
Tried to sell some of her clothes on eBay
Visited her glass coffin every day
Thought about moving
Ranted to the king
Got drunk at the castle
Went on the rampage
Got into debt with the funeral director
Designed a nice obituary
Took to wearing flip-flops rather than boots
Begged their sisters to come and clean up after them
Sat in mourning around the coffin
Smashed the cottage up
Formed a band and went off on tour
Lamented to the moon
Blamed Doc.
Punched the next door-to-door salesman
Went witch hunting in the middle of the night
Overslept every morning
Bought Windoline to clean the coffin with
Tried to employ Rose Red
Sold up and went west

50 Infamous People

Adolf Hitler
Genghis Khan
Osama Bin Laden
Ian Brady and Myra Hindley
Joseph Göbbels
Attila the Hun
King Herod
Pontius Pilate
Michael Jackson
Reginald and Ronnie Kray
Emperor Hirohito
John Profumo
Jesse James
King Herod
Gary Glitter
Adolf Eichmann
Charles Manson
Ivan the Terrible
Sid Vicious
Bonnie And Clyde
George W. Bush
Fred and Rosemary West
Pisistratus
Jeffrey Archer
Richard III
Caligula
Al Capone
Marquis de Sade
Robin Hood
Saddam Hussein
General George Custer
Fidel Castro
Ronnie Biggs
Lee Harvey Oswald
Benito Mussolini
Henry VIII
Joseph Stalin
Napoleon Bonaparte
Billy The Kid
Slobodan Milosevic
Ned Kelly
Oswald Mosley
Jack the Ripper
Emilano Zapata
Juan Perón
Ayatollah Ruhollah Khomeini
Pharaoh Ramesses II
Guy Fawkes
Che Guevara
Ted Bundy

50 Things Cinderella might have done if the Glass Slipper hadn't Fit

Swore
Carried on sweeping out the fireplace
Gone on a diet
Flirted with the Prince's men
Ran away
Shown the Prince phone pix of them both dancing
E-mailed her fairy godmother for another night out
Cried
Demanded to see the King
Got her solicitor involved
Punched the shoe-fitter
Stood gobsmacked
Desperately txt the Prince
Walked off in a huff
Flung up her arms in horror
Begged
Shot the Prince
Declared the fitting as 'rigged'
Screamed
Demanded a re-fit
Got the first horse out of town
Batted her eyelids
Attempted to ask the Prince out anyway
Phoned her lawyer
Picked up her brush and dustpan and shuffled off
Spat
Proffered video evidence
Rang the palace to see when the next disco was
Shown her ticket stub
Shot herself
Dragged the DJ forward as a witness
Complained to the 'Fairy Tales Fair Trading
-Commission'
Flashed her ankles
Declared the Prince to have 'bad breath' anyway
Slagged off her fairy godmother
Looked at her ugly sisters with renewed disdain
Plotted revenge
Shrugged in defeat and went back to her ironing
Declared the shoe as bogus
Wrote to her MP
Threw on a disguise and re-joined the fitting queue
Recited all songs played at the ball
Began proceedings to sue the King for stress
Strangled the shoe-fitter
Flashed her latest bank statement
Buried her head in a pumpkin
Called the Prince a 'lily-livered-slime-bag'
Fainted
Kicked the King's men
Declared the shoe too 'chav' to be seen dead in
-anyway

50 Comedy Films

Airplane
Tootsie
Police Academy
Big
Blazing Saddles
Young Frankenstein
Bridget Jones' Diary
National Lampoon's Animal House
Monty Python and the Holy Grail
Safety Last
Dr. Strangelove or: How I Learned to Stop
-Worrying and Love the Bomb
The War of the Roses
It's a Mad, Mad, Mad, Mad World
The Graduate
Back to the Future
Toy Story 2
Wallace & Gromit in The Curse of the Were
-Rabbit
Home Alone
American Pie
There's Something About Mary
A Night at the Opera
Dumb and Dumber
Simon
Four Weddings and a Funeral
The Seven Year Itch
Ace Ventura, Pet Detective
Bringing Up Baby
The Kid
What's Up, Doc?
Carry on Camping
I Was a Male War Bride
Love Actually
Notting Hill
Beetlejuice
Duck Soup
Murder by Death
Some Like it Hot
Forrest Gump
Finding Nemo
Annie Hall
The Butcher Boy
A Fish Called Wanda
The Naked Gun
Scream
Men in Black
This is Spinal Tap
The Tramp
Sons of the Desert
Monster in Law
In Her Shoes

50 Disaster Movies

Volcano
The Towering Inferno
Airport
The Poseidon Adventure
The Abyss
Earthquake
The Hindenburg
A Night to Remember
Outbreak
The Day the Earth Caught Fire
Runaway Train
San Francisco
Twister
Old Chicago
When Worlds Collide
Cyclone
Testament
The High and the Mighty
The Swarm
Meteor
Independence Day
Daylight
Dante's Peak
Deep Impact
Armageddon
The Core
The Day After Tomorrow
Virus
Asteroid
Aftershock: Earthquake in New York
Airport '77
Two-Minute Warning
Panic in the Skies
On the Beach
When the Wind Blows
Category 6: Day of Destruction
Category 7: The End of the World
Night of the Comet
Without Warning
Doomsday Rock
Avalanche
Storm
Crack in the World
The Night the World Exploded
The Last Wave
Devil Winds
Epidemic
When Time Ran Out
The Rains Came
The Titanic

50 Films starring Bette Davis

The Star
Dark Victory
Of Human Bondage
Jezebel
The Petrified Forest
Hush, Hush, Sweet Charlotte
All About Eve
The Letter
Whatever Happened to Baby Jane?
Marked Woman
The Little Foxes
Now Voyager
Corn is Green
Pocketful of Miracles
Phone Call from a Stranger
Kid Galahad
Death on the Nile
Mr. Skeffington
Bureau of Missing Persons
Where Love has Gone
Watch on the Rhine
Satan Met a Lady
Juarez
The Virgin Queen
Nanny
The Great Lie
Watcher in the Woods
All This and Heaven Too
Stolen Life
The Anniversary
The Whales of August
Old Maid
Dangerous
Old Acquaintance
Hell's House
The Bride Came C.O.D.
Beyond the Forest
The Man Who Came to Dinner
Fog Over Frisco
Front Page Girl
Special Agent
The Golden Arrow
That Certain Woman
It's Love I'm After
The Sisters
The Private Lives of Elizabeth and Essex
Shinning Victory
In This Our Life
Deception
June Bride

50 Anglers	50 Films starring Jack Nicholson
Robert Tesse	One Flew Over the Cuckoo's Nest
Steve Curtin	The Shinning
Raimondo Tedasco	Easy Rider
Dave Roper	Five Easy Pieces
Joseph Fontanet	The Postman Always Rings Twice
Dennis Flack	As Good as it Gets
Jacques Isenbaert	A Few Good Men
Gunter Grebenstein	Chinatown
Mark Neal	The Crossing Guard
Jean Mainil	The Pledge
Marcel Van den Eynde	Something's Gotta Give
Jean-Pierre Fourgeat	About Schmidt
Jonathan Pack	Mars Attack!
Gérard Huelard	Batman Returns
Ramon Legogue	The Two Jakes
Martin Bowler	The Witches of Eastwick
William Lane	Heartburn
Arlbert Richter	Prizzi's Honor
Ian Heaps	Terms of Endearment
Derek Smith	The Shooting
Wolf-Rudiger Kremkus	Ride in the Whirlwind
Henri Guiheneuf	The Wild Ride
Dave Thomas	Flight Of Fury
Rob Garner	Studs Lonigan
Kevin Ashurst	Hell's Angels on Wheels
Hubert Levels	The St. Valentine's Day Massacre
Peter Smith	Head
J. Gasson	Rebel Rousers
Pierre Michiels	On A Clear Day You Can See Forever
Bobby Smithers	Carnal Knowledge
Lud Wever	The King of Marvin Gardens
Steve Terry	The Last Detail
Clive Branson	The Last Tycoon
Tom Pickering	The Missouri Breaks
Bob Nudd	Goin' South
Mick Pardoe	The Border
David Wesson	Broadcast News
Dino Bassi	Man Trouble
Mario Barros	Hoffa
John Shayler	Wolf
Ray Lewis	The Evening Star
Paul Jean	Blood and Wine
Alan Scotthorne	Anger Management
Jacopo Falsini	Little Shop of Horrors
Umberto Balabeni	The Terror
Georgina Ballatine	Back Door to Hell
Ray Clarke	Psych-Out
G. Blasco	The Trip
Robin Harris	The Guns of Will Sonnett: Season One
Tamas Walter	Tommy

50 Films starring Katherine Hepburn	**50 Baby Items**
The African Queen	Cot
This Can't be Love	Dummy
Laura Lansing Slept Here	Nappies
Grace Quigley	Baby wipes
On Golden Pond	Bib
A Delicate Balance	Highchair
The Trojan Women	Changing mat
The Madwoman of Chaillot	Rattle
The Lion in Winter	Baby food
Guess Who's Coming to Dinner	Calpol
Long Days Journey Into Night	Teething ring
Stage Door	Plug socket covers
A Woman Rebels	Baby bouncer
The Philadelphia Story	Booties
Summertime	Pushchair
Suddenly, Last Summer	Babygrow
Desk Set	Sudo cream
The Iron Petticoat	Play mat
The Rainmaker	Stair gate
Alice Adams	Teddy
Dragon Seed	Baby carrier
Pat and Mike	Cupboard/drawer locks
Adam's Rib	Alphabet books
The Man Upstairs	Height chart
The Corn is Green	Feeding bottle
Rooster Cogburn	Nappy pins
Love Among the Ruins	E45 cream
The Glass Menagerie	Sterilising unit
Little Women	Powdered formula milk
State of the Union	Baby walker
Song of Love	Hand-knitted cardigan
The Sea of Grass	Mobile
Undercurrent	Baby chair harness
American Creed	Building bricks
Without Love	Balloon wallpaper
Keeper of the Flame	Mittens
Woman of the Year	Car seat
Holiday	Pram
Bringing Up Baby	Playpen
Spitfire	Fridge/freezer lock
Quality Street	Twin buggy
Mary of Scotland	Crib
Sylvia Scarlet	Changing unit
Break of Hearts	Baby bath
Mrs. Delafield Wants to Marry	Step
The Little Minister	Baby monitors
Morning Glory	Sleepsuit
Christopher Strong	Rain cover
A Bill of Divorcement	Potty
Olly, Olly, Oxen Green	Comfort blanket

50 Cleaning Implements

Mop
Sponge
Tissue
Cloth
Clothes brush
Broom
Dustpan and brush
Vacuum cleaner
Swab
Flannel
Hair brush
Scourer
Toothbrush
Loofah
Duster
Nail brush
Feather duster
Toothpick
Dental floss
Comb
Carpet sweeper
Doormat
Shoe brush
Scrubbing brush
Foot-scrapper
Pipe cleaner
Windscreen wiper
Air-filter
Washing-up brush
Brillo pad
Eraser
Dishwasher
Washing machine
J cloth
Dishcloth
Tea towel
Chamois leather
Facecloth
Towel
Handkerchief
Serviette
Wire brush
Carpet beater
Pumice stone
Besom
Strigil
Squeegee
Rag
Washboard
Toilet brush

50 Wedding Gifts

Toaster
Sheets
Towels
Iron
Ironing board
Linen basket
Kettle
Duvet set
Lamp standard
Bread bin
Set of kitchen knives
Glassware
Microwave
Coffee maker
Set of cutlery
Egg timer
Kitchen clock
DVD player
His and hers bathrobes
Set of crockery
Electric toothbrushes
Coffee table
Coat stand
Under the bed drawers
Cooker
Tea, coffee and sugar containers
Chopping board
Fridge-freezer
Dishwasher
Biscuit barrel
Set of drinking glasses
Matching bedside cupboards
TV
Computer
Car
House
Double bed
Wardrobes
Chest of drawers
Bedside lamps
Set of place mats and coasters
Pouffe
Settee
Rug
Living room clock
Flannels
Electric blanket
Weighing scales
Dinning room table
Washing up bowl

50 Reality TV Shows

Big Brother
Fantasy Island
I'm a Celebrity get me out of Here
Top Chef
Party Party
Extreme Makeover: Home Edition
The Real World
Survivor
Challenge Anneka
The Apprentice
A Victorian House
Starting Over
Colonial House
Combat
Ghost Hunters
What not to Wear
Fame Academy
Dragon's Den
Wife Swap
Boot Camp
The Salon
Faking It
999
The Apprentice
Hell's Kitchen
Popstars
The Edwardian Country House
Queer Eye for the Straight Guy
Suppernanny
Totally Outrageous Behaviour
The Restaurant
While you were Out
Groundforce
Candid Camera
You've been Framed
Fear Factor
Endurance
Renovate my Family
The Osbourne's
Maximum Exposure
I want a Famous Face
Rich Girls
Tough Enough
The Family
Danger Island
Pimp my Ride
Most Extreme Elimination Challenge
Children's Hospital
Showdog Moms and Dads
Beg, Borrow and Deal

50 Names not to call your Funeral Service

Death.com
Dead & Buried
Stiffs-R-Us
Diggers & Co.
Grave & Grave
Corpse Hill & Sons
The Fire Brigade
All Bodies
At Death's Door
Out Of Luck
Don T. Careless Funeral Director
Dead Right
Bereaved Yet Relieved
About Time Funeral Services
Weep In Peace
For A Few Dollars More
U. Bury Funerals
His & Hearse
Good Grief
Sympathy for the Devil
A. Death & Sons
B4 They Go
Funerals.co.ffin
Get Cross Funeral Services
A. Grave Funeral Director
Coffins, Caskets & Crypts
We Undertake
Grief & Wreath
U. R. Dead & I. Bury Funerals
Dust 2 Dust
Will Dig
Cremate Yer Mate
One Stop Coffin Shop
Drive-By Funeral Parlour
A. Grave Situation
Shovel & Spade Funeral Care
Cemetery Blues
Death Become Us
Graves A Go Go
Deadly Nightgrave
Poppin Coffins
Non-Stop Funerals Ltd.
The Pallbearers Funeral Planners
Bury Good Funeral Directors
Community & Communal Graves Services
Coffins Limited
Come into our Parlour
Long Time Dead Funeral Care
A. Grave & Sons
Rest Assured

50 Funeral Items

Coffin
Hearse
Gravestone
Grave plot
Cemetery
Undertaker
Casket
Flowers
Wreath
Embalming sheet
Embalming oil
Obituary notice
Funeral director
Pallbearers
Clergy honoraria
Vault
Cremation urn
Grave excavator/digger
Crypt
Coffin key
Casket shipping order
Bottles of embalming fluid
Cross
Silk memorial flower arrangement
Bereavement remembrance gift rose
Funeral photographs
Antique mourning box
Cemetery marker stone
Solar cross
Sympathy cards
Cremation jewellery
Engraved plaque
Grave marker
Casket trolley, wheeled
Bouquet
Casket spray
Posy
Kosher Shiva basket
Butterfly release
Mourning suit
Funeral plan
Hymn books
Funeral register book
Funeral poems
Keychain urn
Vicar
Grave flower vase
Embalming instrument case
Casket handles
Cremation urn name plate

50 Things to 'Catch'

A cold
A train
A disease
A cricket ball
The 'jist' of something
A man
A fish
A rabbit
A poacher
A virus
A basketball
An infection
The last ten minutes of a TV programme
A bus
A movie
The postman
The shops before they shut
The last post
The ferry
Something in the wind
The wedding bouquet
5 jacks
The late show
An escaped convict
A 'whiff'
A volleyball
A thief
Someone's drift
A plane
A taxi
Some sun
The tide
Your finger in the door
Your breath
A butterfly
A mouse
A falling star
Your death of cold
A rugby ball
Someone with their hands in the till
A frisbee
The leader
Flies
A little action
The news
Someone 'at it'
A smuggler
A runaway horse
The milkman
A rat

50 Archers	50 Things to 'Throw'
M. Sawicki	A cricket ball
J. Kurkowska	A party
L. Reith	A wobbly
D. .McKenzie	A boomerang
H. Kjellson	A frisbee
Ina Catani	A line
A. van Kohlen	A lasso
E. Heilborn	A soft ball
G. de Rons	One's head back
Ingo Simon	Bread to the ducks
F. Hades	A grenade
N. Weston Martyr	Stones
R. Beday	The baby out with the bathwater
E. T. Holbek	A fish back in the water
N. de Wharton Burr	Out some old clothes
H. Deutgen	Your voice
B. Waterhouse	A spear
Jean Lee	A javelin
S. Andersson	A shot-put
B. Lundgren	A Molotov cocktail
Jean Richards	A throw rug
N. Andersson	Someone off guard
K. Wisniowska	Up
O. Smathers	Open
C. Meinhart	In the towel
S. Thysell	On some clothes
S. Johansson	A fit
J. Caspers	One's money around
Ann Corby	A spanner in the works
J. Thornton	Cold water on an idea
N. Vanderheide	Down the gauntlet
C. Sandlin	Good money after bad
V. Cook	Ashes to the wind
M. Haikonen	In one's hand
M. Lindholm	Off the scent
Ray Rogers	Light on the subject
Hardy Ward	One's weight about
M. Maczynska	The book at
D. Lidstone	Overboard
J. Williams	Back
E. Gapchenko	Sand in one's face
M. Frangilli	In
Yun Mi-Jin	The dice
J. K. Yeon	A snowball
S. H. Park	A dart
Chil Hong Sung	A caber
Lee Eun Kyung	Off guard
Kim Du-Ri	Off course
Linda Myers	To the lions
Darrell Pace	Caution to the wind

50 Chores	50 Parts of the Body
Washing-up	Head
Dusting	Nose
Emptying the rubbish	Fingernails
Vacuuming	Wrists
Polishing	Teeth
Washing clothes	Legs
Weeding	Lips
Ironing	Shoulders
Drying-up	Eyes
Brushing the dog	Knees
Cleaning the bathroom	Cheeks
Decorating	Hair
Tidying	Arms
Sweeping	Elbows
Washing floors	Fingers
Hoeing	Ears
Cleaning the windows	Hands
Changing a light bulb	Chest
Putting away	Waist
Hanging out washing	Navel
Worming the cat	Hips
Answering the front door	Bottom
Making the dinner	Neck
Pruning	Eyelashes
Sewing on a button	Feet
Darning socks	Kneecaps
Changing a fuse	Toenails
Wiring a plug	Tongue
Removing stains	Chin
Straightening ornaments	Forehead
Cleaning out the pet cage	Nape
Arranging CD's in alphabetical order	Back
Changing the beds	Torso
Washing the windows	Ankles
Cleaning the toilet	Heels
Cooking	Brow
Shopping	Nipples
Opening mail	Genitals
Cleaning the kitchen	Sides
Walking the dog	Palms
Answering the phone	Calves
Washing the car	Armpits
Mowing the lawn	Knuckles
Making a packed lunch	Thighs
Preparing meals	Forearms
Altering the clocks	Eyebrows
Cleaning the cooker	Shins
Collecting dry-cleaning	Throat
Mending clothes	Stomach
De-frosting the freezer	Toes

50 Parts of the outside of a House

Roof
Guttering
Chimney stack
Cavity wall
Finial
Foundations
Garden path
Front door
Damp-proof
Cladding
Bricks
Windows
Downpipes
Roof slates
Roof tiles
Garage
Garden gate
Front garden
Gable
Porch
Hip tiles
Doorbell
Driveway
Bay windows
House alarm box
TV ariel
Satellite dish
Window sills
Chimney pots
Ridge tiles
Flashing
Apron
Drains
Parapet
Hopper
Window frames
Overflow
Outdoor stopcock
Weather-vane
Bargeboard
Soffit
Fascia
Pebbledashing
Patio
House number
Railings
Outside tap
Letter-box
Flower beds
Ventilation grills

50 Things we do with our Bodies

Eat
Talk
Hug
Walk
Recline
Drink
Jump
Clap
Sing
Sit
Stand
Twist
Drive
Jog
Run
Stride
Lie
Smile
Skip
Shuffle
Turn
Swim
Spring
Laugh
Fall
Shiver
See
Love
Shake
Hear
Act
Climb
Dive
Squat
Fight
Kiss
Mime
Roll
Doze
Kneel
Hop
Stretch
Reach
Cry
Embrace
Think
Dance
Cycle
Listen
Sleep

50 Days out with the Kids

Chessington World of Adventures
London Zoo
Walt Disney World Amusement Park
Longleat House and Safari Park
Fantasy World
Legoland
Alton Towers
Abbotsbury Children's Farm
American Adventure Theme Park
Camelot Theme Park
London Dungeon
Flamingo Land Theme Park and Zoo
Folly Farm
Gulliver's Kingdom
Lightwater Valley Theme Park
Sea World
Pleasure Beach Blackpool
Pleasure Island Theme Park
Colchester Zoo
Robin Hill Adventure Park
Storybook Glen
Tales of Robin Hood
Thorpe Park
Edinburgh Dungeon
Brighton Pier
Watermouth Castle
Wicksteed Park
Peter Pan's Playground
Alice in Wonderland Park
Battersea Funfair
Billing Aquadrome
Brean Leisure Park
Dreamland
Frontierland
Funland Amusement Park
Glasgow Zoo Park
Great Yarmouth Pleasure Beach
Joyland
Hastings Pier
King Alfred's Wonder Land
Wookie Hole
Marine Lake Amusement Park
Merlin's Magic Land
Milky Way Adventure Park
Paradise Park
Pleasurewood Hills
Teenage Mutant Hero Turtle Park
Toon Town
World in Miniature
Wonderland

50 Popular Sayings and Phrases

"All mouth and no trousers."
"Push the boat out."
"Let your hair down."
"Back to square one."
"Get it off your chest."
"It's no bed of roses."
"Run rings round 'im."
"Below the belt."
"The bee's knees."
"Bit down in the mouth."
"Bunny boiler."
"All dressed up like a dog's dinner."
"A flash in the pan."
"The full monty."
"Got out the wrong side of the bed."
"Bless his cotton socks."
"Give a dog a bad name."
"Let the cat out of the bag."
"There's not enough room to swing a cat."
"Don't pass the buck."
"The real McCoy."
"Now the tables are turned."
"Chuck in the towel."
"Now the boot is on the other foot."
"Too slow to catch a cold."
"Butter-fingers."
"Bob's your uncle."
"Slow-coach."
"Bit of a catch 22 situation."
"Don't cry wolf."
"In a tiz."
"On his last legs."
"Bushed."
"Don't get a bee in your bonnet."
"A waste of space."
"It doesn't float my boat."
"Hot under the collar."
"Out of the frying pan, into the fire."
"Cut off your nose to spite your face."
"Chomping at the bit."
"It's the early bird that catches the worm."
"Gone for Burton."
"-You want jam on it?"
"Mind your 'P's and 'Q's."
"On tenterhooks."
"Sorted!"
"Give him a grilling."
"Give us a shout."
"You are what you eat."
"Pain in the arse."

50 Skip Hire Firms	50 Ways to shout 'Run'
A & R	Let's go
A1 Skips	Scarper
Skiphire	Skidaddle
Wicksy's Skips	23 skiddoo
HW Howard Waste	On yer bike
Select A Skip	Beat it
Brewsters	Let's get out of here
Wisewaste Skip Hire	Leg it
Danny's Skips	Go like the wind
NSM	You won't see me for dust
Lynch	Get your skates on
Able Skips	Let's move on out
Brown Skips	Let's roll
Ace Skip Hire	Ride 'em cowboy
LH Express Skips	Quick march
Glynn's Skips	Forward
Olympic Skips Ltd.	Like a shot
M & K Skip Hire	Eat my dust
Oak Tree Skips	Let's scoot
O'Donovan	Zoom
London Skips & Containers	Rock on
W. Peck (Haulage) Ltd.	Race
Winters	Jog
Ashley Two Men & A Tipper	Canter
Angel Road Skips Ltd.	Gallop
C. P. L.	Zip
Donnellan Skip Hire	Let's fly
D. O'Sullivan	Like a bullet from a gun
Bywaters	Let's make like a tree and leaf
Tosca Waste	I'll get my coat
Enfield Skips Ltd.	I'm outta here
Express Skip & Waste Co.	See yer later
Topskips	Better make ourselves scarce
Simpson	Move it
Skipy	Better split
Boulton's	Up and running
Collins	Race yer
Paxton Skips	Sprint
SkipHireUk	Take a hike
Rent-A-Skip	Go climb a mountain
Tin Bins	Saddle up
Bugg	Dash
Colne Skips	Scram
Prettygate Skips	Like a bat out of hell
Badgers Skips	Better take-off
Bexley Miniskips	Hot-rod it
Chalton Speedy Skips	Whoosh
Easyload Ltd.	Shoot
Wicked Waste Ltd.	Go, go, go
McGrath Bros.	Flee

50 World Record Holders

100m - Tim Montgomery - 9.78
Pole vault - Yuliya Pechonkina – 4.92
100m hurdles – Yoedanka Donkova – 12.21
200m – Michael Johnson – 19.32
800m – Wilson Kipketer – 1:41.11
Hammer – Mihaela Melinte – 76.07
Mile – Hicham El Guerrouj – 3:43.13
5,000m – Elvan Abeylegasse – 14:24.68
1 hour – Arturo Barrios – 21,101m
Half marathon – Paul Tergat – 59:17
1,000m – Svetlana Masterkova – 2:28.98
25,000m (road) – Paul Kosgel – 1:12.45
1,000m – Noah Ngeny – 2:11.96
Marathon – Paula Radcliffe – 2:15.25
2 miles – Daniel Komen – 7:58.61
Long jump – Galina Chistyakova – 7.52
5,000m – Kenenisa Bekele – 12:37.37
Javelin (post 1999) – Osleidys Menéndez – 71.54
30,000m (road) – Takayuki Matsumiya – 1:28.36
100m – Florence Griffith-Joyner – 10.49
3,000m s/chase – Saif Saeed Shaheen – 7:53.63
110m hurdles – Colin Jackson – 12.91
2,000m – Sonia O'Sullivan – 5:25.36
400m hurdles – Kevin Young – 46.78
Mile - Svetlana Masterkova – 4:12.56
Pole vault – Sergey Bubka – 6.14
High jump – Javier Solomayor – 2.45
Long jump – Mike Powell – 8.95
Triple jump – Jonathan Edwards – 18.29
Shot put - Randy Barnes – 23.12
400m hurdles – Yuliya Pechonkina – 52.34
Marathon – Paul Tergat – 2:04:55
High jump – Stefka Kostadinova – 2.09
Triple jump – Inessa Kravets – 15.50
Discus – Jürgen Shult – 74.08
Hammer – Yury Sedykh – 86.74
Javelin – Jan Zelezny – 98.48
Decathlon – Roman Sebrie – 9026
200m – Florence Griffith-Joyner – 21.34
400m – Marita Koch – 47.60
800m – Jamila Kratochvilova – 1:53.28
1,500m – Qu Yunxia – 3:50.46
20,000m – Tegla Loroupe – 1:05:26.06
3,000m s/chase – Gulnara Samitova – 9:01.59
1 hour - Tegla Loroupe – 18,304m
Half marathon – I. Kristiansen – 1:06.40
Shot put – Natalya Lisovskaya – 22.63
Discus – Gabriele Reinsch – 76.80
Heptathlon – Jackie Joyner-Kersee – 7291
300m - Michael Johnson – 30.85

50 Things not to do on a First Date

Query the bill
French kiss
Look embarrassed
Discuss your bowel problems
Fart
Forget your wallet
Burp
Suggest meeting outside a porn shop
Say, 'I'll be wearing my 'Ted Bundy' T-shirt.'
Discuss politics
Have a row
Enquire if she's wearing false teeth
Show her your genital piercing
Do your John Travolta dance
Spit in the street
Ask if she's into threesomes
Mention you've been unemployed for 20 years
Pick money up off the pavement
Drive like a maniac
Drink like a fish
Show her your monkey impression
Arrive with a banjo
Wear that pink '70's satin suit
Say you didn't have time for a bath
Mention you suffer from halitosis
Say you've arranged to take her bungy jumping
Say you're technically still married, but…
Chain smoke
Arrive with your ex-girlfriend
Pick a fight with the waiter
Grope her
Take her to see a sex film
Bite her
Talk incessantly about football
Develop a nervous tick
Cough in her face
Take her to a talk on Marxism
Pick your nose
Arrive an hour late
Say you can't stay too long as you've got a
-colonic irrigation appointment
Wear flip-flops in winter
Show her your live hamster juggling skills
Arrive dressed as a banana, even if it is your day
-job
Offer to do her laundry
Make crude remarks about her cleavage
Clean out your ears
Sleep
Get down on one knee
Look up her skirt
Read

50 Medals and Awards

Victoria Cross
George Cross
Order of the Garter
Medal of Honour
Order of the Whistle
Order of St. Patrick
Hero of the Russian Federation
Order of the Bath
Brevet Medal
Order of Merit
Order of the Star of India
Navy Cross
Order of St. Michael & St. George
Royal Guelphic Order
Air Force Cross
Silver Star
Order of the Indian Empire
Order of Leopold II
Royal Order of Victoria & Albert
Royal Victorian Order
Order of the Civil
Royal Order of the Lion
Order of the KDPR Gold Star Medal
Legion of Honour
Order of the White Eagle
Cross of Valour
British Empire Military
Companion of Honour
Distinguished Service Order
Order of Propitious Clouds
Ministry of Defence Medal Brotherhood in Arms
Khemara Pateka Medal of Cambodian Recognition
Bharat Ratna
Order of the Rising Sun
Royal Victorian Chain
Royal Norwegian Order of St. Olaf
Baronet's Badge
Police Heroism Order
War Cross 1914 – 18
Order of St. John
Medal of Merit in Agriculture
Conspicuous Gallantry Cross
Ribbon of the Three Orders
Order of the Tower and the Sword
Star of Courage
Distinguished Service Cross
Military Cross
Air Crew Europe Star
UNEF Medal
Chief of Staff Citation

50 Cubs and Scouts Badges

Angler
Camper
Circus Skills
Hiker
Athletics
Fire Safety
Canoeist
Forester
Photographer
Hill Walker
Sewing
Knots
Hobbies
Librarian
DIY
Life Saver
Orienteer
Equestrian
My Faith
Climber
Quartermaster
The Country Code
Radio Communicator
Skater
Survival Skills
Water Sports
Animal Care
Book Reader
Artist
Trekking and Trailing
Cyclist
First Aid
Astronomer
Home Help
Martial Arts
Global Conservation
Naturalist
Home Safety
Local Knowledge
Cooking
Navigator
Physical Recreation
Road Safety
Collector
Water Activities
Administrator
Caver
Entertainer
Adventure
Knitting

50 Hobbies	50 Kid's Programmes
DIY	Byker Grove
Trainspotting	Grange Hill
Watching TV	The Adventures of Black Beauty
Painting model soldiers	Little House on the Prairie
Playing an instrument	Animal Magic
Fixing cars	Swapshop
Photography	Tiswas
Drawing	The Munsters
Painting	The A-Team
Jewellery making	Worzel Gummidge
Keeping pets	The Waltons
Dog breeding	Space: 1999
Crochet	The Banana Splits
Pottery	Captain Scarlet and the Mysterons
Wood carving	Vision On
Computer games	Blue Peter
Designing and building electronic circuits	Dr. Who
Model engineering	Magpie
Reading	Flipper
Board games	Lassie
Homebrewing	Daktari
Blogging	Happy Days
Learning a foreign language	Crackerjack
Silk screen	Metal Mickey
Upholstery	Six Million Dollar Man
Collecting stamps	Tarzan
Matchstick models	Zoo Time
Model railways	Bewitched
Radio-controlled cars	Jackanory
Kite flying	Thunderbirds
Singing	Junior Criss Cross Quiz
Gardening	Mister Ed
Dancing	Knight Rider
Collecting coins	The Lone Ranger
Magic tricks	Circus Boy
Amateur theatre	The Monkees
Bee keeping	The Saint
Calligraphy	The Time Tunnel
Embroidery	Mork and Mindy
Origami	Buffy the Vampire Slayer
Stained glass making	The Muppet Show
TV and FM Dxing	The Partridge Family
Amateur film making	Rawhide
Wargaming	Secret Diary of Adrian Mole, Aged 13¾
Writing	Randall and Hopkirk (Deceased)
Sewing	Catweazle
Sculpture	Lost in Space
Musical composition	Stingray
Restoring old furniture	The Phil Silvers Show
Amateur astronomy	Voyage to the Bottom of the Sea

50 Things you might find in a Castle	50 Types of Tea
King	English Breakfast
Drawbridge	Earl Grey
Portcullis	Lady Grey
Loophole	Peppermint
Lord	Lemon
Moat	Darjeeling
Turret	Arctic Raspberry
Round-arched window	Assam
Servants	Green
Quoin	Oolong
Battlements	Rooibos
Merlon	Honeybush
The Great hall	Rosehip
Arrow slits	Black
Outer ward	Cherry Rose Sencha
Prison tower	Blackcurrant
Crenel	Blueberry
Soldiers	Mango Mist
King's tower	Peach and Apricot
Tetrahedral spire	Strawberry
Cornice	Lady Londonderry
Buttress	Buckingham Palace Garden Party
Curtain wall	Lapsang
Parapet	Jasmine
Dungeon	Berry of Yorkshire
Chapel	Silver Wips White
Inner ward	Masala Chai
Stockhouse tower	Peaches and Cream
Machicolations	Capetown Red Bush
Barbican	White Chocolate Toffee Red Bush
Lookout tower	Golden Yunnan Supreme
Keep	Jade Oolong
Storerooms	Fruits de Bois
Gatehouse	Vintage Ceylon
Kitchens	Almond Cookie Green
Bailey	Snow Flake
Courtyard	Men's
Palisade	Stress Blocker Herbal
Mural towers	Mexican Winter
Gun loop	Orange
Stone walls	Hot Cinnamon Spice
Conical towers	Bavarian Chocolate Crème
Chemise	Twig
Donjons	Georgian Village
Passageways	Texas Blend
Squinch	Bamboo Sprouts Green
Flying buttresses	Organic Black Golden Pu-Erh Tuo Cha
Fireplaces	White Monkey Green
Stone staircases	Silver Needles Bai Hao
Queen	C. S. Lewis Blend

50 Things you might say when arriving at the Gates of Hell

Where's the doorbell?
Oh, I thought it would be bigger than this
You got a light mate?
Have you got a pass in case I wanna get out again?
What the devil!
No St. Peter?
I'll be bad, honest
So where's all the action?
When do we get to meet Satan?
I'm only passing through
This must be the place
It's showtime!
At last!
But I repented!
Is there a hairdressers?
Do you need to see ID?
I didn't need to bring a jumper, is that right?
For eternity you say?
I've bought my own firelighters just in case
Bring on the dancing girls!
Fire in the disco!
Where do we sleep?
Do we get two weeks holiday in heaven?
Toilets?
Party time!
No, I'll keep my clothes on if you don't mind
I'd like to set up an amateur dramatics group?
Actually, …I've changed my mind
Wow, it's hot down here!
Is that Hitler?
Can I get a glass of water?
I think I booked a single room?
Where do I hang my coat?
Is the big boss about?
So I'm really dead then?
This can't be right; I returned all my library books
Can I keep my pocket bible please?
Forever seems a bit too long
Complaints box?
I'd like to keep my umbrella for when it rains
Do I get to jab people with a pitchfork as well?
I'm certainly not running around naked!
Is that Judas?
Looks a bit crowded
Pay to get in? You are joking!
Do I come back here to pick up my mail?
Is there a back gate?
The nearest chemist?
Map?
Still open?

50 Yellow things to Eat

Parsnip
Banana
Apple
Swede
Lemon
Sherbet
Vanilla
Yam
Custard
Egg
Yellow pepper
Salad cream
Mayonnaise
Lemon curd
Cheese
Pineapple
Sweet corn
Grapefruit
Water melon
Potato
Butter bean
Onion
Garlic
Bamboo shoots
Lentils
Chick peas
Wheat
Maize
Corn
Cornflakes
Butter
Margarine
Vegetable fat
Batter
Pita bread
French stick
Scone
Waffle
Cracker
Crisp
Cheesecake
Shortbread
Rich tea biscuit
Custard cream
Cream
Natural yoghurt
Honey
Syrup
Cream cheese
Haddock

50 Things not to say on your Wedding Night

I'm just popping out to get a kebab
Now you get to see me in my pyjamas
That wedding cake's given me the runs
Hell! I forgot to bring condoms
Your parents were so drunk
D'you mind if I say my prayers first?
Hey! This is the same hotel room I stayed in with
-my first wife
Let's watch telly
Oh, I'm so tired
OK straight to sleep, got to get to the airport by six
Can't wait to get on that toilet
I think I'm gonna be sick
Let's just read
I think I'll just listen to my iPod
I'll just ring the children
Your mother's a bit of a flirt
My dad said you look cross-eyed in all the photos
Next time we'll skip the reception
Did you see my dad kissing your mum?
Well that was boring
I used to be a woman
Let's get a divorce —only kidding
500 press-ups first
Back to work tomorrow
Married. Who'd have thought; after all those rows?
Your brother's fat
It'll take us years to pay off that wedding
That's a hat trick for me
I've forgotten my passport
…And I was only an hour and a half late
I'm sorry I got your name wrong in my speech
Give me 20 minutes to get into my rubber gear?
Let's order in a pizza
Hot chocolate?
Just texting mother, let her know what room I'm in
I've left my top hat at the reception
Did you think the vicar looked gay?
Now that we're married, shall we wee together?
Finally, I get to see your knockers!
Did you see my dad kissing your dad?
Thank God that's all over
I think I'll have a bath and go to bed
What a waste of money
Your sister's really attractive isn't she?
I'm going down to reception to get a pot noodle
My nan said she'd look in on us, tuck us in…
I guess we can sell most of the gifts on eBay
Shame you don't take a good photo
Hitched at last
Now for the baby bit

50 Things a man shouldn't say when present at the Birth of his Child

I can't stay long
Can I smoke in here?
Move over a bit love, I need to lie down
Dr., could ya just take a few snaps of us together?
Do you mind if I set the video up in here?
I must be getting back to the office now dear
Just finishing my book; I'm on the last chapter
Do I get to dress up in a white gown as well?
I really didn't want another one
I think I've seen enough
What if it's not a boy or a girl?
I'm on a meter so don't be long love
You could have picked a better-looking midwife
You're pushing for two remember
Hurry it up a bit honey; Emmerdale's on soon
Special delivery!
It's going to come out of where!
Cover yourself up for goodness sake!
I had nothing to do with it
I'm beginning to regret this now
I think I'm going to be sick
If you wait a bit, it'll be born on the 1st. Feb.
-rather than the 31st. Jan
How dare you spank my baby!
Can you make less noise dear; it's so
-embarrassing
Are you sure I'm the father?
Are you sure you're the mother?
Hope it's triplets
Really, this is most inconvenient
I thought you were picking the kids up!?
I've bought my packed-lunch to eat while I watch
No, I'm sorry, I never switch my mobile off
Where can I plug in my laptop?
I won't take my coat off
I'm just passing
…Turn the baby's head; it'll make a better photo
What does this button do…?
Push it-Push it real good! Push it-Push it real
-good!
I've had to interrupt a round of golf for this
You're looking a bit flushed honey
You want me to rub oil into her perine-what?
Stitches!?
-Ok, but sew it up nice and tight please
Traffic was awful… oh; you're all done here
I've brought my own midwife
Well, who'd have thought it would lead to all this
I can't get over the fact you're lying there naked!
No, don't worry; I'll be back in an hour
I've bought some DVD's for us to watch
Should I take all my clothes off as well doctor?
That's no son of mine!

50 Darts Players

Phil Taylor
Ray Barneveld
Tommy Gibbons
Martin Adams
Kevin Painter
Andy Foedham
John Part
Mark Dudbridge
Tony David
John Walton
Eddie Brown
Tom Barrett
Dixie Newberry
Mervyn King
Richie Davies
Rod Harrington
Marshall James
Ronnie Baxter
Peter Manley
Paul Lim
Paul Cook
Ted Hankey
Harry Leadbetter
Dennis Priestley
Les Wallace
Steve Beaton
Richie Burnett
Wally Seaton
John Lowe
Jocky Wilson
Bob Anderson
Eric Bristow
Keith Deller
Leighton Rees
Bobby George
Ivor Hodgkinson
Dave Whitcombe
Mike Gregory
Alan Warriner
Dave Lee
Roy Morgan
Stefan Lord
Mick Norris
Bill Lennard
Derek White
Peter Chapman
Dennis Filkins
Henry Barney
Barry Twomlow
Bill Duddy

50 Things not to say when you first meet your Girlfriend's Parents

Oh, you both look younger in the photos
I can see now where she gets her stupidity from
So you live in a council flat?
Your Mother's much fatter now
I'll need to know both your incomes
She must get her looks from the grandparents then
You're both tone deaf I hear
She's right, you can't see your colostomy bag
You got any photos of her as a baby I could have?
Your Father's a bit thick
Do we have to stay long?
Before you ask; yes, we have protected sex
You've got your Mother's hips
I am looking for a job
I'm like a Father to her
We've met before
Jean and Bob? Oh sorry, that was the last parents
You've got your Father's bald patch
So, you're the ones to blame
I've got a bone to pick with you old man
How do I know you've got a scar there? We came
-across some of your old bedroom photos
…That's why she's so clumsy
I must say you don't look like an alcoholic
We've been together a year, though we've been
-split-up for 9 mths.
I'm giving her all the things she never had as a
-child
Could I borrow money from you?
We're emigrating
Gosh, you're both looking old!
…Thank God, that's over. They were so boring!
No, I've been unemployed for years
Alright geezers!
We need to talk about how you bring up children
Oh yeah, your bedroom's so cool by the way
This is where she gets her motormouth from!
She's good in bed, your daughter
Which one's your mum
I've got cheap porn in my bag if your interested?
How's the breakdown going?
Oh, we've just eaten
Fancy going on to a club
I used to be gay
Here's our holiday snaps… oops, I thought I'd
-taken those ones out!
Who's the one who can't control their temper?
Are you working class?
I'm getting used to meeting all you parents now
So neither of you are creative in any way?
You're a dead ringer for your father
Are those false teeth?
I'll just buy my own; I can't afford a whole round
She said you were both well educated

50 Words beginning with 'Sun…'

Sunhat
Sunspot
Sunday
Sunshine
Sunshade
Sunglasses
Sunkissed
Sunket
Suntrap
Sunny
Sunk
Sunbathe
Sunbeam
Sunbed
Sunburn
Sundae
Sunder
Sunderland
Sundial
Sundog
Sundown
Sundress
Sundries
Sunflower
Sungod
Sunken
Sunless
Sunray
Sunrise
Sunseeker
Sunset
Sunshade
Sunstone
Sunstroke
Suntan
Sunward
Sunbird
Sungrebe
Sunlit
Sunlight
Sunstar
Sunup
Sunwise
Sunfish
Sunbaked
Sunglow
Sunblind
Sunbonnet
Sunbow
Sundew

50 Things the Queen might say when Waking

What a night!
I slept through the alarm again
I can't even ring in sick
Is that a Corgi I've got my feet on
Philip, it's your turn to make the tea
What day is it?
At least I don't have to get up and sign on
God; I've got such a hangover
Who put that bucket by the bed?
Yes Jeeves, you can put away the PVC gear now
The Prime Minister here already!
Hell, I think I've wet the bed again
Hello? What! We're out of milk!
First I must see how my items are selling on eBay
The President! –Tell him I've got diarrhoea
Jeeves; one biscuit! Is that's too much to ask for!
Postman ma'am; he needs you to sign for a parcel
Philip; I'm sorry but I want a divorce
Holmes? Bring the lilac-coloured jet round
They've got my emblem on the label, why can't I
-have free jam!
Is it the colonic irrigation woman today dear?
I'm never eating kebab again
Hello? I beg your pardon! Run my own bath!
Don't let me drink so much beer next time Phil
Slam, slam! If I hear another door slam!
Let's go for a jog!
-Changing of the Guard? No, I'll keep the old one
No, I haven't got money to pay the milkman!
Which handbag shall I take to the toilet with me?
Engaged! Who's using my personal toilet!
Must change this Simpson's duvet
Er? Why are my pants hanging off the lampshade?
Breakfast and telly in bed; this is the life!
No I don't have 50p for the meter; that's your job!
Yes, can I have Coco-pops again?
Bring the post up, I'm expecting a Premium
-Bond!
No, I'm too ill today; get that look-a-like in again
There's no bread to make toast? -Let me eat cake
Shall we watch my Coronation again Phil?
Oops I mustn't forget to close the curtains
I'll be bathing in cow's milk this morning
I don't care if it's lunchtime; I want breakfast!
Hello? No this isn't the stable girl! It's the
-bloody Queen!
Do I have to clean my own teeth again!
100 sit-ups first
Philip do you have to wear socks in bed?
I am not drinking out of a Queen Victoria cup!
Oh, I can't keep staying up to watch the late film
What do you mean it's my turn to walk the dogs?!
Hello? Is anyone there?

50 Religious Festivals around the World

3rd. Jan. Pueblo Deer Dances – Native American
13th. Jan. Mitvintersblot – Norse
16th. Jan. Festival of Ganisha – Hindu
31st. Jan. Hecate's Feast – Ancient Greek
2nd. Feb. Imbolc – Wiccan
18th. Feb. Spenta Armaiti – Zoroastrian
25th. Feb. Day of Nut – Ancient Egypt
28th. Feb. Buddha's Conception – Tibet
2nd. Mar. Mother's March – Bulgarian
3rd. Mar. Doll Festival – Japanese
8th. Mar. Birthday of Mother Earth – Chinese
26th. Mar. Plowing Day – Slavic
1st. Apr. April Fool's Day – Secular
6th. Apr. Tomb Weeping Day – Chinese
25th. Apr. Holocaust Remembrance Day - Jewish
26th. Apr. Flower Parades – Dutch/Secular
30th. Apr. Walpurgisnacht – German
8th. May White Lotus Day – Theosophy
11th. May Rain Ceremony – Guatemalen
13th. May Our Lady of Fatima – Portuguese
23rd. May Declaration of the Bab – Baha'I
5th Jun. Sheena-Na-Gig – Irish
16th. Jun. Night of the Drop – Ancient Egypt
20th. Jun. Day of Ix Chel – Mayan
24th. Jun. Feast of the Sun – Aztec
7th. Jul. Tanabata, Star Festival – Japan
10th. Jul. Lady Godiva Day – Old England
15th. Jul. Festival of the Dead – China
20th. Jul. Binding of the Wreaths – Lithuania
3rd. Aug. Tisha B'av, Day of Mourning - Jewish
11th. Aug. Puck Fair – Ancient Ireland
13th. -15th. Aug. Our Lady of Good Death - Brazil
18th. Aug. Festival of Hungry Ghosts – China
15th. Sept. Independence Day - Guatemala
19th. Sep. Annual Feast for Gula – Ancient Babylon
28th. Sep. Birthday of Confucious – Confucianism
10th. Oct. Festival of Light begins – Brazil
15th. Oct. Festival of Mars, God of War – Roman
19th. Oct. Trang Vegitarian Festival - Thailand
29th. Oct. Feast of the Dead – Iroquois
2nd. Nov. Day of the Dead - Mexico
3rd. Nov. New Year – Gaelic
10th. Nov. Goddess of Reason Festival – French
13th. Nov. Jupiter Festival – Roman
18th. Nov. Day of Ardvi Sura – Persian
26th. Nov. Light Festival – Tibetan
2nd. Dec. Festival of Shiva – Hindu
8th. Dec. Festival of Neith – Ancient Egypt
14th. Dec. Festival of Nostradamus – French
26th. Dec. Death of Prophet Zarathustra - Zoroastrian

50 Fashion Accessories

Handbag
Scarf
Straw hat
iPod
Footballer boyfriend
Sports car
Prada carrier bag
Designer jewellery
Gucci wrap
Tattoo
Rolex watch
Pierced belly button
Bracelet
Versace cufflinks
Anklet
Police sunglasses
Armani belt
Hair extensions
Diamante evening gloves
Kenzo earrings
Poodle
Calvin Klein waistcoat
Minder
Saville Row suit
Cigarette
D & G lingerie
Tie pin
Givenchy tie
Belly clip
Mary Quant powder compact
Therapist
Yves Saint Laurent perfume
Film star girlfriend
Fendi wallet
MP3 player
Celine shoes
Digital camera
Gaultier bikini
Pop star escort
Tommy Hilfiger purse
Wedding dress
Valentino jeans
Diamante costume jewellery
Tongue piercing
Funky mobile
Ralph Lauren fan
Shawl
Dior fancy hat
Walking stick
Umbrella

50 Different 'Balls'	*50 Mathematical Terms*
Tennis ball	Equals
Football	Add
Ping-pong ball	Takeaway
Rugby ball	Divide
Bowling ball	Subtract
Golf ball	Length
Ball gown	Capacity
Ball and chain	Multiply
Billiard ball	Times
Cannonball	Plus
Musket ball	Minus
Ball bearing	Order
Marble	Equate
Ballcock	Symmetry
Cricket ball	Estimate
Ball point pen	Approximate
Pinball	Round-up
Masked ball	Round-down
Ball and socket joint	Tessellation
Ball lightning	Work-out
Ball pein hammer	Halve
Chinese exercise balls	Quarter
Rubber ball	Comparing
Pool ball	Place value
Mirror ball	Sort
'Freshers' ball	Plot
Beach ball	Measure
Hi-ball	Weigh
Ball park	Investigate
Volley ball	Test
Soft ball	Apply
Rounders ball	Mass
Squash ball	Infer
Puffball	Sequencing
Snowball	Double
Bouncing ball	Treble
Ball of wool	Handling data
Fireball	Calculate
Netball	Check-back
Ballroom	Analyse
Balloon	Pay-back
Lacrosse ball	Numbering
Medicine ball	Carry-over
Exercise ball	Less than
Hockey ball	More than
Soccer ball	Remainder
Crystal ball	Fraction
Basket ball	Decimal
Kick ball	Ratio
Cue ball	Average

50 Scientific Terms

Acceleration
Boiling point
Combustion
Deformation
Eclipse
Permutation
Erosion
Sublimation
Filtration
Genetic engineering
Natural selection
Yield point
Refraction
Quantum jump
Humidity
Oscillation
Vacuum distillation
Impermeable
Chain reaction
Adaption
Kinesis
Germination
Temperature
Magnitude
Luminosity
Fission
Solubility
Neutralisation
Radiation
Velocity
Occlusion
Metabolism
Incandescence
Osmosis
Petrifaction
Biosynthesis
Wavelength
Qualitative analysis
Diffraction
Regeneration
Speed of light
Terminal velocity
Nuclear fusion
Photosynthesis
Hydrolysis
Vaporisation
Titration
Malleability
Conduction
Evaporation

50 Geological Terms

Erosion
Filtration
Weathering
Mountainous
Tributary
Visibility
Absorption
Rainfall
Calcification
Shoreline
Temperature
Wind speed
Declination
Wave trough
Igneous
Ablation
Base flow
Fossilisation
Rock formation
Bifurcation ratio
Meandering
Ecosystems
Sediment
Topography
Feedback loop
Epicentre
Strata
Faultline
Matric force
Moraine
Porous
Habitat
Elastic rebound theory
Facilitation
Plateau
Exfoliation
Volcanic
Laminar flow
Formation
Anticline
Decomposition
Rock strata
Cartography
Gelifluction
Metamorphic
Mineral
Waterfall
Fossil fuel
Terrace
Crust

50 Historical Terms	**50 London Underground Stations**
Era	Camden Town
Archive	Marble Arch
Baroque	Liverpool Street
Medieval	Kings Cross/St. Pancras
Rebellion	Woodside Park
Bourgeoisie	Notting Hill Gate
Opinion	Mordon
Judgement	Waterloo
Epoch	Piccadilly Circus
Dictatorship	Aldgate East
Etymology	Bakerloo
Feudal	Oxford Circus
Vikings	Angel
Fiefdom	Tottenham Court Road
Treason	West Ham
Primary source	Hyde Park Corner
Succession	Hornchurch
Roman	Old Street
Renaissance	Kentish Town
Classical	Mornington Crescent
Bloodline	Archway
Monarchy	Euston
Artefacts	Goodge Street
Economics	Brixton
Trade	Paddington
Peasants	Amersham
Century	Ladbroke Grove
Slavery	Crossharbour & London Arena
Christianity	Mudchute
Ancient	White City
Non-conformist	Cyprus
Relic	Bond Street
Remains	Dagenham Heathway
Evidence	Whitechapel
Reform	Ravenscourt Park
Parliament	Pinner
Saxon	Bank
Exploration	Turnham Green
Colonise	St. Paul's
Knights	Perivale
Treaty	King George V
Tudor	Oval
Timeline	Cutty Sark
Secondary source	Harrow & Wealdstone
Democracy	Croxley
Bolshevism	Manor House
Chronology	Heathrow Terminals 1, 2 and 3
Interpretation	Fairlop
Contemporary	Shepherd's Bush
Empire	Upminster

50 Satellite TV Channels

Sky One
Discovery Kids
Livingtv
Artsworld
Paramount Comedy 1
Sky Sports 1
E4
UKTV Drama
Bravo
Challenge
Animal Planet +1
Fashion TV
Discovery Channel
Hallmark
Sky Two
Channel 4
Sky News
BBC1
Boomerang
Sky Movies Screen 1
TV5
DW-TV
More4
RTE One
Sci-Fi
TCM
Sky Three
Sky Movies Screen 2
MTV 2
BBC News 24
Sky Vegas Live
Adventure One
History Channel +1
Star Plus
Discovery Travel & Living
Sky Movies Screen 3
Nickelodeon
BBC 2
CNN
National Geographical Channel +1
Sky Sports 2
Trouble
Sky Cinema Screen 1
Biography Channel
Discovery Home & Health
UKTV People
Sky Movies Screen 7
Cartoon Network
Kerrang!
Magic

50 Playstation Games

Grano Heat
Super Magical Hat Turbo Flying Adventure
Space Channel Circus Fever
Woodruff and the Schnibble of Azimuth
Virtua Fighter Cyber Generation Ambition of the
-Judgement Six
Furious Karting
Alpha Black Zero; Intrepid Protocol
Dominion: Storm Over Gift 3
Arcanum – of Steamworks and Magik Obscura
Peanut Butter Monkey
Thingy and the Doodahs
Puppy Helmet
Cabella's Dangerous Hunts
Rainbow Six 2
Jim Bob and the Locked Thread
Ring of Red
Driving Emotion Type-S
A Train 6
O Story
Permanent Expert IV
Mechsmith
Gungriffon Blaze
Grappler Avenger
I am Captain
Beatmania II DX 3rd. Style
Crazy Bumps
Angle Story
Happy! Happy! Boarders
Dog of Bay
Super; Starring Morning Girl
Lunatic Dawn Tempest
Tokyo Bus Guide: You are the Driver Today
Remococonon
Farm Story 6
Hotel Giant
Horse Breaker
Guilty Gear X Plus
Hippa Linda
Simple 2000 – The Bus Edition
Jet Go 2
I am Superior Base Ball 2
Strange Adventure of Jojo Golden Sensation
Money Soup
I am Small
Bad Officer
Metal Slug
Egg Mania
Space Fisherman
Sprout Sword
Waku Waku Volley 2

50 Moon Crater Names	50 Jobs, Trades and Professions A-L
De la Rue	Accountant
Hercules	Advertising executive
Atlas	Ambulance driver
Montes Apenninus	Architect
Cleomedes	Attorney
Macrobius	Babysitter
Julius Caesar	Baker
Langrenus	Banker
Vendelinus	Barman
Cyrillus	Barber
Petavius	Beautician
Fracastorius	Bookkeeper
Furnerius	Bricklayer
Catharina	Builder
Rupes Altai	Bus driver
Albategnius	Butcher
Ptolemaeus	Car mechanic
Arzachel	Car salesman
Walter	Carpenter
Deslandres	Cashier
Stöfler	Chef
Maginus	Chemist
Clavius	Chiropractor
Tycho	Civil engineer
Bailly	Clerk
Alphonsus	College professor
Schickard	Computer programmer
Milne	Computer repairer
Apollo	Construction worker
Doppler	Cook
Hilbert	Counsellor
Pasteur	Dentist
Fleming	Detective
Joliot	Dietician
Compton	Director
Montes Cordillera	Doctor
Jules Verne	Editor
Van de Graaff	Electrician
Gargarin	Estate agent
Plato	Farmer
Sinus Iridum	Funeral director
Archimedes	Glazier
Mach	Grocer
Avogardro	Handyman
D'Alembert	Horticulturist
Campbell	Insurance salesman
Roche	Janitor
Copernicus	Judge
Fra Mauro	Lawyer
Encke	Librarian

50 Jobs, Trades and Professions M-Z

Medical technician
Midwife
Miner
Minister
Model
Mortician
Newsreader
Newspaper reporter
Nurse
Nursery worker
Occupational therapist
Painter and decorator
Paramedic
Pharmacist
Photographer
Physicist
Physiotherapist
Plumber
Police officer
Postal worker
Producer
Publicist
Public relations specialist
Radio announcer
Receptionist
Roofer
Sales clerk
Scientist
Secretary
Security guard
Ski instructor
Shop assistant
Sports trainer
Statistician
Stewardess
Street cleaner
Stockbroker
Surveyor
Swimming instructor
Taxi driver
Teacher
Tour guide
Traffic warden
Undertaker
Veterinarian
Waitress
Weatherman
Webmaster
Writer
Zoologist

50 Bands and Singers from the 1950's

Al Martino
Vera Lynn
Kay Starr
Eddie Fisher
Pere Como
Guy Mitchell
Stargazers
Lita Roza
Frankie Lane
Mantovani and his Orchestra
David Whitfield
Eddie Calvert
Doris Day
Johnnie Ray
Kitty Kallen
Frank Sinatra
Don Cornell
Rosemary Clooney
Winifred Arwell
Ruby Murray
Tony Bennett
Jimmy Young
Alma Cogan
Slim Whitman
Johnston Brothers
Bill Haley and his Comets
Dean Martin
Dream Weavers
Pat Boone
The Teenagers
Tommy Steele and the Steelmen
Frankie Vaughan
Tab Hunter
Lonnie Donegan and his Skiffle Group
Andy Williams
Elvis Presley and the Jordanaires
Paul Anka
The Crickets
Harry Belafonte
Jerry Lee Lewis
Michael Holliday
Marvin Rainwater
Connie Francis
Vic Damone
Everley Brothers
Kalin Twins
Tommy Edwards
Conway Twitty
Shirley Bassey
The Platters

50 Bands and Groups from the 1970's

Slade
Edison Lighthouse
Simon & Garfunkel
The Sweet
Christie
Smokey Robinson and the Miracles
Freda Payne
Dave Edmunds Rockpile
Mungo Jerry
Dawn
Middle of the Road
T. Rex
Diana Ross
The Tams
Suzi Quatro
Rod Stewart
The New Seekers
Nilsson
Wizzard
Don McLean
Mud
Donny Osmond
David Cassidy
Lieutenant Pigeon
Rubettes
Gilbert O'Sullivan
Alvin Stardust
10cc
Peters & Lee
Alice Cooper
Gary Glitter
Elton John
Paper Lace
Terry Jacks
Abba
The Three Degrees
Carl Douglas
Sweet Sensation
David Essex
Barry White
Status Quo
Pilot
Bay City Rollers
Typically Tropical
The Stylistics
Queen
The Four Seasons
Brootherhood of Man
The Real Thing
Hot Chocolate

50 Scottish Football Teams

Aberdeen
Berwick Rangers
Celtic
Airdrie United
Dumbarton
East Fife
Vale of Leven
St. Mirren
Airdrieonians
Raith Rovers
Falkirk
Lochgelly Albert
Greenock Morton
Clyde
Dumfermline Athletic
Gretna
Hamilton Academical
Albion Rovers
Inverness Caledonian Thistle
Kilmarnock
Third Lanark
Livingston
Stenhousemuir
Ross County
Montrose
Alloa Athletic
East Sterling
Partick Thistle
Heart of Midlothian
Clydebank
Peterhead
Queen of the South
Brechin City
Dundee
Forfar Athletic
Queen's Park
Rangers
Arbroath
St. Johnstone
Dundee United
Cowdenbeath
Stirling Albion
Elgin City
Motherwell
Stranraer
Renton
Hibernian
Ayr United
Saltcoats Victoria
Cove Rangers

50 Bands and Groups from the 1990's	50 TV Presenters and Personalities
New Kids on the Block	Russell Harty
Kylie Minogue	Michael Parkinson
Sinead O'Conner	Jeremy Clarkson
Snap!	Ant & Dec
Madonna	Cheryl Baker
Adamski	Judith Charmers
The Beautiful South	Bruce Forsythe
Vanilla Ice	Danny Baker
Phil Collins	Barry Norman
Cher	Ann Diamond
Jason Donavan	Noel Edmonds
Bryan Adams	David Frost
Colour Me Badd	Terry Wogan
U2	Esther Rantzen
Michael Jackson	Gloria Hunniford
George Michael	Clive Anderson
Wet, Wet, Wet	Chris Tarrant
Right Said Fred	Jonathon Ross
Erasure	Ulrika Jonsson
Shamen	Sarah Kennedy
Boyz II Men	David Dimbleby
Whitney Houston	Ruby Wax
2 Unlimited	Magnus Magnusson
Shaggy	Keith Chegwin
The Bluebells	Alan Whicker
Ace of Base	John Noakes
UB40	Andi Peters
Take That	Anneka Rice
Meat Loaf	Lily Savage
D:Ream	Jeremy Beadle
Mariah Carey	Angus Deayton
Whigfield	Philip Schofield
East 17	Anne Robinson
Celine Dion	Magie Clarke
Outhere Brothers	Carol Smillie
Oasis	Lisa Tarbuck
Blur	Dale Winton
Simply Red	Zoe Ball
Prodigy	Anthea Turner
Gina G	Dani Behr
Fugees	Roger Cook
Spice Girls	Peter Duncan
Peter Andre	Lloyd Grossman
Boyzone	Richard Madeley
LL Cool J	Graham Norton
No Doubt	Angela Rippon
R. Kelly	Cilla Black
Olive	Patrick Kielty
Eternal	Robert Kilroy-Silk
Aqua	Des Lynam

50 Sports Personalities

Steve Davis
Robin Cousins
Virginia Wade
Henry Cooper
Jonny Wilkinson
Stirling Moss
Frank Bruno
Jackie Stewart
Brendan Foster
Chris Chataway
John Curry
Martina Navratilova
Bobby Moore
Steve Ovett
Sebastian Coe
Ian Botham
Daley Thompson
Gordon Banks
Ann Jones
David Beckham
Mary Peters
Dorothy Hyman
Linford Christie
Damon Hill
David Steele
Vladimir Kuts
Jonathan Edwards
Greg Rusedski
Gordon Pirie
Michael Owen
Lennox Lewis
Steven Redgrave
Jim Laker
Paula Radcliffe
Steve Cram
Barry McGuigan
David Hemery
Roger Bannister
Nigel Mansell
Fatima Whitbread
David Broome
Nick Faldo
Paul Gascoigne
Liz McColgan
George Best
Anita Lonsbrough
Mary Rand
Muhammad Ali
Gary Lineker
Dai Rees

50 Silent Movie Stars

Constance Talmadge
Lon Chaney
Lillian Gish
Bela Lugosi
Mary Pickford
Charlie Chaplin
Lorna Doone
Douglas Fairbanks Sr.
Theda Bara
John Gilbert
Clara Bow
Rudolph Valentino
Louise Brooks
Fatty Arbuckle
Greta Garbo
W. C. Fields
Gloria Swanson
Buster Keaton
Blanche Sweet
Laurel and Hardy
Pearl White
Harold Lloyd
Baby Peggy
John Barrymore
Renée Adorée
Monte Blue
Vilma Banky
Richard Dix
Enid Bennett
William Haines
Florence Vidor
Betty Compson
Lars Hanson
Dolores Costello
Rod La Rocque
Viola Dana
Adolphe Menjou
Mildred Davis
Owen Moore
Billie Dove
Conrad Nagel
Leatrice Joy
Ramon Navarro
Doris Kenyon
Theodore Roberts
Laura La Plante
Gilbert Roland
Lila Lee
Henry B. Walthall
Bessie Love

50 Film Stars from the 1960's

Julie Christie
Catherine Deneuve
Donald Sutherland
Mia Farrow
Michael Caine
Sean Connery
Jane Fonda
Bruce Dern
Raquel Welch
Julie Andrews
Peter O' Toole
Elizabeth Taylor
Peter Sellers
Clint Eastwood
Jack Nicholson
Barbra Streisand
Faye Dunaway
Dustin Hoffman
Lana Turner
Judy Garland
Joanne Woodward
Elizabeth Taylor
Richard Burton
Katherine Hepburn
Audrey Hepburn
Omar Sharif
Rod Steiger
Charlton Heston
Ava Gardner
Anthony Perkins
Janet Leigh
Paul Newman
Marilyn Monroe
Clark Gable
Marlon Brando
Alec Guinness
Anthony Quinn
James Mason
Bette Davis
Joan Crawford
Rex Harrison
Vanessa Redgrave
David Hemmings
George Segal
Warren Beatty
Gene Hackman
Anne Bancroft
Sidney Poitier
Robert Redford
Steve McQueen

50 Contemporary Film Stars

Uma Thurman
Ben Affleck
Brittany Murphy
Brad Pitt
Angelina Jolie
Johnny Depp
Helena Bonham Carter
Zac Efron
Kate Beckinsale
Daniel Radcliffe
Sandra Bullock
Vin Diesel
Jennifer Aniston
Jim Carrey
Carmen Electra
Tom Hanks
Cameron Diaz
Samuel L. Jackson
Julia Roberts
Ben Stiller
Gweneth Paltrow
Keanu Reeves
Catherine Zeta-Jones
Tom Cruise
Christina Appleton
Orlando Bloom
Drew Barrymore
Jude Law
Elizabeth Hurley
Matt Damon
Eva Herzigova
Macaulay Cualkin
Halle Berry
Leonardo DiCaprio
Vanessa Paradis
Colin Farrell
Julianne Moore
Val Kilmer
Kate Winslet
Ewan McGregor
Keira Knightley
David Owen
Kirsten Dunst
Joaquin Phoenix
Nicole Kidman
Christian Slater
Penelope Cruz
Elijah Wood
Reese Witherspoon
Renee Zellweger

50 Things not to say when stopped by the Police

I smell bacon
Accompany yourself to the bloody station
No; you can't fool me! You're in fancy dress
I didn't know I needed car insurance
Only if you give me your name first
Ok, ok… Mr. Donald… Duck
Oh, not again!
I'm minding my own business… unlike you
Is that a truncheon in your pocket or are you just
-pleased to see me?
My address; it's written on the side of the van mate
I can drink and drive; I'm a registered alcoholic
Sorry, I thought you were a traffic warden
Have you people got nothing better to do?!
No, it's not my car at all… it's nicked
Can I try your hat on mate?
It's Michael… Mouse –honestly!
Disturbing the peace? –Peace off!
Address? No, I'm wearing trousers lol! Get it?!
Sorry I'm on an important call, give me 15 minutes
So I'm not allowed to wear a black & white stripy
-top and carry a 'swag' bag?
Why do they call you pigs anyway?
So they're letting midgets into the Police these days
What's an M O T?
I don't have a name… I am only a number
If I'm loitering then what are you doing?!
Can I use yer radio, I've out of credit on my phone?
Why is your helmet shaped like a tit!
Address? No. 1, Park Bench, Any City Square
Sorry, I can't stop; it's too cold
A dirty old raincoat is all I can afford…
The tree suddenly came at me, it crashed into me!
If I was speeding then so were you!
I'm making a citizen's arrest. Yes, on an old woman
His wallet just fell out of his bag and into my hand!
-These electrical goods?! Am I not still in the shop?
Yes, of course. Can you hold my burger for me?
I think you guys are wonderful
I've got an alibi
I was singing out loud, 'Give me all your money'
No I aint (hiccup) been (hiccup) drinking offisheeer
Is it true you're all failed parking attendants?
I don't care for your tone detective inspector gadget
D'you do this for a living
A warren for my arrest? Do I look like a rabbit!
God's truth now. It's Henry; …the Eighth. I am! I am!
You know, I just hate being stopped by the Police
It was a good evening 'til you clowns showed up
What happened to the, 'Hello, hello, hello.'
It's Sir to you
On yer bike mate

50 Types of Biscuit

Ginger Nuts
Digestives
Hob Nobs
Custard Creams
Garibaldi's
Rich Tea
Chocolate Hob Nobs
Jammy Dodgers
Bourbons
Jaffa Cakes
Nice
Coconut Cookies
Chocolate Digestive
Shortbread
Penguin
Ginger Snaps
Crunch Crinkles
Sport
Trio
Malted Milk
Wagon Wheel
Fig Roll
Time Out
Rocky
Gold Bar
Homewheat
Blue Riband
Breakaway
Coconut Rings
Chocolate Chip Cookies
Fruit Shortcake
Boasters
Hazelnut Choc Chip
Chocolate Caramel Digestives
Butter Crunch
Echo
Brandy Snaps
Sport
Crunch Creams
Classic Bar
Pink Wafer Biscuit
Fortune Cookies
Choco Leibniz
Yoyos
Lady Fingers
Chocolate Fingers
Petit Beurre
Mello Moment
Almond Tea
Extra

50 Tinned Items	50 Fonts
Baked beans	Times New Roman
Processed peas	Ariel
Tinned tomatoes	Baskerville Old Face
Sliced peaches	Century
Spaghetti hoops	Desdemona
Pineapple slices	Eras Bold ITC
Mushy peas	Placard Condensed
Chicken soup	Lucida Sans Typewriter
Butter beans	Felix Titling
Rice pudding	Bauhaus 93
Macaroni cheese	Frankling Gothic Book
Carrots	Verdana Ref
New potatoes	Modern No. 20
Pear halves	Garamond
Tomato soup	Haettenschweiler
Kidney beans	Directions MT
Ratatouille	Rockwell Extra Bold
Asparagus	Impact
Meatballs	Onyx
Caviar	Juice ITC
Stewed prunes	Kino MT
Sardines	Adadi Condensed MT Extra Bold
Tuna	Westminster
Condensed milk	SimSun
Lentil soup	Lucida Blackletter
Semolina	Comic Sans MS
Sweetcorn	Mead Bold
Chick peas	Keystrokes MT
Blackcurrants	News Gothic MT
Broad beans	OCR A Extended
Chopped tomatoes	Perpetua
Raspberries	Ransom
Spaghetti bolognaise	Wingdings
Treacle pudding	Gill Sans MT Ext Condensed Bold
Chicken in white wine	Holidays MT
Steak and kidney	Stencil
Runner beans	Impact MT Shadow
Mackerel	Goudy Old Style
Big breakfast	Tahoma
Three bean salad	Eurostile
Mandarin slices	Viner Hand ITC
Mussels	Bell MT
Anchovies	Courier New
Cherries	Flexure
Artichokes	Maiandra GD
Fruit salad	Snap ITC
Salmon	Trebuchet MS
Irish stew	Wide Latin
Gooseberries	Matura MT Script Capitals
Ravioli	Windings2

50 Signs and Symbols

Om
Swastika
%
American bald eagle
No smoking
♫
Skull and crossbones
Highly inflammable
White dove with olive branch
Fire exit
Shrug of the shoulders
Way out
©
'V' for victory
Road works
No cycling
Star of David
♂
No entry
Zebra crossing
St. Christopher
40 mile an hour speed limit
&
A handshake
'P' for parking
Lapel poppy
Barber's pole
?
Rabbit's foot
The holy cross
National flag
A wave
@
Thumb-up
Pawnbroker's balls
Nod of the head
£
Waving a white hankie
Car indicator
Weathercock
⅓
Buoy
Wreath
Coat of arms
=
Hammer and sickle
A wink of the eye
Totem pole
Raise one's eyebrows
!

50 Shapes

Circle
Equilateral triangle
Pyramid
Star
Chevron
Isosceles triangle
Icosahedron
Square
Rectangle
Pentagonal pyramid
Square prism
Quadrangle
Regular pentagon
Cube
Trapezoid
Cuboid
Cylinder
Regular hexagon
Pentagon
Oval
Octagon
Hexagon
Lozenge
Rhomboid
Quadrature
Triangular prism
Semi-circle
Regular heptagon
Heart
Dodecahedron
Pentagonal prism
Tetrahedron
Scalene triangle
Cone
Hexagonal prism
Square-based pyramid
Diamond
Sphere
Regular octagon
Trigon
Spherical triangle
Wedge
Heptagon
Oblong
Parallelogram
Right-angled triangle
Decagon
Trapezium
Rhombus
Kite

50 Haircuts and Hairstyles

Bob
Short back and sides
Crop
Eton crop
Pageboy
Crew-cut
Shingle
Cut en brosse
Curls
Urchin cut
Baby doll cut
Bouffant
Ponytail
Chignon
Suedehead
Skinhead
Bun
Pompadour
Beehive
B52
Afro
Canerow
Ringlets
Dreadlocks
Warlocks
Shampoo and set
Mullet
Beckam haircut
Mohican
Bunches
Plaits
Quiff
Perdy cut
Basin haircut
Coiffure
Corkscrew
Wig
Frizz
Blow wave
Marcel wave
Perm
Toupee
Mop top
Curly locks
Tresses
Spiky
Braids
Pigtail
Topknot
Widow's peak

50 Racing Greyhounds

Mick the Miller
Dusty Trail
Ballylanigan Tanist
Shanes Legacy
Booked Out
Hi Joe
Gulf of Darien
Maryville Hi
Ballyregan Bob
Endless Gossip
Forward Flash
Long Hop
Kilbeg Kuda
Westpark Mustard
Yellow Printer
Newdown Heather
Maryville Hi
Duleek Dandy
Trev's Perfection
The Grand Canal
Low Pressure
Mile Bush Pride
Lauries Panther
Lucky Hi There
Glenroe Hiker
Gentle Touch
Fodda Champion
Wired To Moon
Cranog Bet
Crazy Parachute
Crazy Paving
Magourna Reject
Palms Printer
Westpark Quail
Oregon Prince
Clonalvy Pride
Scurlogue Champ
Ataxy
Faithful Hope
Brave Enough
Pigalle Wonder
Wild Woolley
Ace of Trumps
Pat Seamur
Santolina
Myrtown
Yankee Express
Greenane Flash
Dromin Glory
Tric Trac

50 Supermarkets

Tesco
A&P
Fine Fare
Waitrose
SuperValu
Makro
LiDL
McColl's
Budgens
Liptons
International
Harry Tuffins
Subway
Sainsbury's
Wavy Line
Bejam
Wing Yip Oriental Superstore
Jackson's Europa Foods
Netto
Planet Organic
Asda
Alldays
SPAR
Carrefour
Co-Op
Costcutter
Day & Nite
Iceland
Savacentre
Kwik-Save
Winn-Dixie
David Greig
Gateway
Somerfield
Safeway
Aldi
Booths
Walmart
Marks & Spencer Foodhall
Hillards
Costco
Walmart Supercentre
Morrisons
Londis
One Store Shop
Cullens
Wal-Mart
Centra
Dunnes Stores
Pricerite

50 London Churches in the Middle Ages

All Hallows Honey Lane
St. Alphage
House of Franciscan Grey Friars
St. Dionis Backchurch
St. Augustine Papey
St. Bartholomew the Little
St. Martin in the Vintry
St. Botolph Billingsgate
St. Christopher
All Hallows Bread Street
House of Carmelite White Friars
St. Clement Eastcheap
St. Michael Paternoster in the Riole
St. Faith under St. Paul's
St. Stephen Walbrook
Priory of Holy Trinity Aldgate
St. Helen
St. Thomas the Apostle
St. James Garlickhithe
St. Leonard Eastcheap
St. Margaret Bridge Street
St. Anne Aldersgate
St. Mary at Axe
St. Mary Magdalen Old Fish Street
St. Michael Crooked Lane
Convent of St. Helen
St. Nicholas in the Shambles
House of Friars of the Cross
St. Olave by the Tower
St. Pancreas
St. Peter the Little Paul's Wharf
St. Swithin
St. Benet Woodwharf
All Hallows on the Wall
Priory of St. Bartholomew
St. Vedast
St. Andrew Holborn
St. Botolph without Aldgate
St. Bride
St. Dunstan in the West
St. Giles without Cripplegate
St. Sepulchure
St. Clement Danes
St. Matthew Friday Street
St. Mary Savoy
Chapel of St. James by Cripplegate
House of Dominican Black Friars
All Hallows Grasschurch
St. Katherine Colemanchurch
St. Mildred Poultry

50 London Parks

Hyde Park
Primrose Hill
Regent's Park
Kensington Gardens
Green Park
Kew Gardens
St. James's Park
Hampstead Heath
Holland Park
Parliament Hill
Southwark Park
Hackney Downs
Battersea Park
London Fields
Alexander Park
Wanstead Flats
Finsbury Park
Walthamstow Marshes
Victoria Park
Queen Mary's Gardens
Lambeth Palace Gardens
Huntsmoor Park
Lincoln's Inn Fields
Gunnersbury Park
Wormwood Scrubs
Fryent Country Park
Tabard Gardens
Haggerston Park
Weavers Fields
Mudchute Park
King's Stairs Gardens
Mile End Park
Bethnal Green Gardens
Great Fields Park
Petersham Meadows
Marble Hill Park
Gray's Inn Gardens
Putney Heath
Richmond Park
Hurlingham Club Gardens
Boston Manor Park
Wandsworth Common
Prospect Park
Royal Victoria Gardens
Avenue Park
Meath Gardens
Syon Park
Myatt's Fields
Brockwell Park
Wimbledon Common

50 Ballets

The Age of Gold
Bacchus and Ariadne
Coppélia
Don Quixote
Miracle in the Gorbels
Edward II
Le Festin de l'araignée (Spider's Banquet)
Peer Gynt
Gayane
Nutcracker
Les Deux Pigeons
Swan Lake
La Création du Monde
Ondine (Undine)
Giselle, or the Wilis
Petrushka
Salome
Homage to the Queen
Jeux (Games)
The Wise Virgins
Madame Chrysanthème
Billy the Kid
Nobilissima Visione
The Tales of Hoffmann
Orpheus
Scaramouche
The Rite of Spring
Parade
Josephslegende (Legend of Joseph)
Appalachian Spring
Pulcinella
The Fairy's Kiss
The Haunted Ballroom
The Box of Toys
Romeo and Juliet
The Four Temperaments
The Sleeping Beauty
La Ventana
The Triumph of Neptune
A Wedding Bouquet
The Wooden Prince
Checkmate
Fall River Legend
Horoscope
Les Mariés de la Tour Eiffel
Soleil de Nuit
Le Pas d'Acier
Pineapple Poll
Raymonda
Les Sylphides

50 Golfers	*50 Musicals*
Ernie Els	The Woman in White
Tiger Woods	Oklahoma
Lee Westwood	South Pacific
Thomas Bjorn	The Sound of Music
W. Park	Oliver
Sergio Garcia	Chitty Chitty Bang Bang
Ian Woosnam	Cats
Gary Player	Phantom of the Opera
Jack Nicklaus	Les Miserables
Colin Montgomerie	Tommy
T. Morris (senior)	Carousel
Padraig Harrington	The King and I
Mark O'Meara	Hair
Vijay Singh	Miss Saigon
Corey Pavin	Jesus Christ Superstar
J. Anderson	Joseph and His Technicoloured Dreamcoat
Nick Faldo	The Pyjama Game
Steve Elkington	The Blood Brothers
P. Michelson	Mamma Mia
Jeff Sluman	Lilac Time
Arnold Palmer	Spring in the Park
Lee Trevino	Annie get your Gun
I. Baker-Finch	West Side Story
Bernhard Langer	Grease
Severiano Ballesteros	Fame
Sandy Lyle	Guys and Dolls
Greg Norman	Mary Poppins
D. Duval	Porky and Bess
Nick Price	Mac and Mabel
Mark McNulty	Fiddler on the Roof
J. M. Olazabal	42nd. Street
Ben Crenshaw	Sunset Boulevard
Isao Aoki	The Lion King
Simon Owen	Chicago
D. Love III	The Vagabond King
Ray Floyd	Desert Song
Hale Irwin	Starlight Express
Ted Ray	Gigi
P. Lawrie	Barnum
Al Geiberger	The Wizard of Oz
Graham Marsh	The Rocky Horror Show
M. Calcavecchia	My Fair Lady
Gene Littler	Camelot
Bob Charles	We Will Rock You
J. Barnes	The Producers
Peter Thomson	Half a Sixpence
C. Strange	Rhapsody in Blue
Neil Coles	Salad Days
David Graham	Chess
Tom Weiskopf	The Woman in Black

50 Salvador Dali Paintings	**50 Picasso Paintings**
The Rose	Violin and Guitar
Mercury and Argos	Blue Nude
The Persistence of Memory	Guernica
Madonna of Port Lligat	The Old Guitarist
Apparatus and Hand	Don Quixote
Still Life Fast Moving	Femme
Archeological Reminiscence of Millet's Angelus	Sunflowers
Clothes Automobile	Dove of Peace
Dream Caused by Flight	Aficionado
The Enigma of Desire	Head
Galatea of the Spheres	The Pigeons
Leda Atomica	Weeping Woman
Morning Ossification of the Cypress	Child Holding a Dove
Portrait of Picasso	The Red Armchair
Surrealist Poster	The Studio
Young Virgin	Femme à La Fleur
Soft Construction with Boiled Beans	Woman with a Blue Hat
Hallucinogenic Torreador	Petit Fleurs
Harlequin	Motherhead
St. John on the Cross	The Rest
The Sacrament of the Last Supper	Carnet Toros Y Toreros'
Girl Standing at the Window	Girl Before a Mirror
Les Montres Molles	La Visage De La Paix
The Elephants	La Ronde
Napoleon's Nose	Nude Seen from Behind
Mystery of Sleep	La Colombe
The Burning Giraffe	Three Musicians
The Path of Enigmas (second version)	Dora Maar November 1937
Crucifix or Corpus Hypercubis	Enamel Saucepan
Mae West's Face which may be used as a	Mediterranean Landscape
-Surrealist Appartment	Tete D'une Femme Lisant
The Pharmacist of Ampurdan in Search of	Self Portrait
-Absolutely Nothing	Death of Casagemas
Figure on the Rocks (Penya Segats)	Nu Couche
Landscape with Butterflies	The Absinth Drinker
Moses Saved from the Water	La Vie
Galatea of the Spheres	Girl in Chemise
The Famine	Les Demoiselles d'Avignon
Without Hope	Three Women
Cannibalism in Autumn	Woman with a Fan
Soft Self-Portrait with a Rasher of Grilled Bacon	Harlequin and Woman with a Necklace
The Lugubrious Game	Tête et Bras de Plâtre
The Metamorphosis of Narcissus	The Dance
La Mort	Femme à la Fleur
The First Days of Spring	Woman Sitting in an Armchair
Railway Station at Perpignan	Jacqueline Roque
Tristan and Isolde	Musketter with Pipe and Flowers
The Temptation of St. Anthony	The Tragedy
Transcendent Passage	Le Repas Frugal
Coronation of Gala	Garcon a la Pipe
La Tour	
Sleep	

50 Forms of Lighting

Arc light
Torch
Starlight
Street lighting
Standard lamp
Halogen lighting
Candle
Uplight
Desk lamp
Chandelier
Overhead lighting
Strip lights
Table lamp
Sunlight
Sodium lighting
Tiffany lamp
Headlights
Floor lamp
Lighthouse
Firelight
Acetylene lamp
Moonlight
Lantern
Reading light
Gas lighting
Strobe
Ceiling light
Taper
Lanthorn
Wall light
Gaselier
Neon light
Phosphorescent lighting
Laser light
Flare
Tail light
Mercury vapour lamp
Ultra violet light
Chinese lantern
Reed light
Flashlight
Oil lamp
Electric light
Searchlight
Foglamp
Fairy lights
Candelabra
Fluorescent light
Daylight
Lightship

50 Forms of Heating

Coal fire
Hot water bottle
Radiator
Air-conditioning
Thermal insulation
Central heating
Gas fire
Range
Space heating
Storage heaters
Oil stove
Furnace
Oven
Convector heater
Kiln
Panel heater
Incinerator
Brazier
Stove
Microwave
Cooker
Bunsen burner
Blowlamp
Log fire
Oxyacetylene lamp
Paraffin heater
Solar panel
Hot-air duct
Immersion heater
Boiler
Warming pan
Electric blanket
Primus stove
Foot warmer
Oasthouse
Sunlight
Pellet heater
Hydro-heat
Camp fire
Quartz heater
LPG gas
Fan heater
Wood stove
Underfloor heating
Cavity wall insulation
Halogen heater
Oil-filled radiator
Bar heater
Body warmth
Barbecue

50 Computer Commands

Open
Print
Save
Page set-up
Cut
Copy paste
Undo
Clear
Select all
Send
Go to
Full screen
Zoom
Page break
File
Style
Word count
Auto summarise
Auto correct
Customise
Draw table
New
Print preview
Spell check
Format painter
Tables and borders
Columns
Font
Font size
Bold
Italic
Underline
Centre
Justify
Numbering
Increase Indent
Highlight
Minimise window
Restore window
Close window
Next page
Show hidden icons
Page layout view
Run
Search
Ruler
Header and footer
Auto field
Symbol
Close

50 Science Fiction B-Movies

The Astounding She-Monster
Attack from Space
The Blob
The Crawling Eye
Devil Girl from Mars
Earth Vs the Flying Saucers
I Married a Monster from Outer Space
Invasion of the Body Snatchers
It Came from Outer Space
It Conquered the World
Mars Needs Women
Plan 9 from Outer Space
Robot Monster
Teenagers from Outer Space
It! The Terror from Beyond Space
Rocketship X-M
Voyage to the Planet of Prehistoric Women
The Crawling Hand
The Incredible Melting Man
Night of the Blood Beast
The Day of the Triffids
The Day the Sky Exploded
Panic in Year Zero
X the Unknown
The Abominable Dr. Phibes
The Cabinet of Dr. Caligari
Doctor X
4D Man
How Awful about Allen
The Mad Monster
The Brain from Planet Arous
The Amazing Transparent Man
Attack of the 50ft. Woman
The Incredible Shrinking Man
Attack of the Crab Monster
The Beast from 20,000 Fathoms
Earth Vs the Spider
The Giant Gila Monster
It Came from Beneath the Sea
The Killer Shrews
One Million Years BC
Attack of the Giant Leeches
Empire of the Ants
The Alligator People
Invasion of the Bee Girls
Creature from the Black Lagoon
Track of the Moon Beast
I Saw What You Did
The Wasp Woman
Them

50 Best selling Novels

Watership Down – Richard Adams
Pride and Prejudice – Jane Austen
Jane Eyre – Charlotte Bronte
The Hound of the Baskervilles – Arthur Conan Doyle
The Grapes of Wrath – John Steinbeck
Star of the Sea – Joseph O'Connor
Harry Potter & the Philosopher's Stone – JK Rowling
Oliver Twist – Charles Dickens
Capt. Corelli's Mandolin – Louis De Bernieres
Tom Jones – Henry Fielding
Trainspotting – Irvine Welsh
1984 - George Orwell
Tess of the d'Urbervilles – Thomas Hardy
The Carpetbaggers – Harold Robbins
The Firm – John Grisham
Ulysses – James Joyce
Lolita – Vladmir Nabokov
Frankenstein – Mary Shelly
The Da Vinci Code – Dan Brown
A Clockwork Orange – Anthony Burgess
The Jungle Book – Rudyard Kipling
The Canterbury Tales - Chaucer
Lady Chatterley's Lover – D.H. Lawrence
Roses are Red – James Patterson
Love Story – Erich Segal
Around the World in 80 Days – Jules Verne
Hannibal – Thomas Harris
The Colour Purple – Toni Morrison
Christine – Stephen King
The War of the Worlds – H. G. Wells
Wuthering Heights – Emily Bronte
The Satanic Verses – Salman Rushdie
Robinson Crusoe - Daniel Defoe
Patriot Games – Tom Clancy
Smiley's People – John Le Carré
The Three Musketeers – Alexandre Dumas
Hollywood Wives – Jackie Collins
Dr. Jekyll and Mr. Hyde – Robert Louis Stevenson
The Name of the Rose – Umberto Eco
Gulliver's Travels – Jonathan Swift
The French Lieutenant's Woman – John Fowles
Brighton Rock – Graham Greene
Gone with the Wind – Margaret Mitchell
Hotel – Arthur Hailey
The Thorn Birds – Colleen McCullough
Jaws – Peter Benchley
The Day of the Jackal – Fredrick Forsyth
To Kill a Mockingbird – Harper Lee
On the Beach – Nevil Shute
Dr. Zhivago – Boris Basternak

50 Frank Sinatra Songs

Pennies from Heaven
Some Enchanted Evening
My Way
The Good Life
Hello Dolly
Summer Wind
Strangers in the Night
New York, New York
Chicago
I Get a Kick Out of You
Somthin' Stupid
Moon River
Fly Me to the Moon
What Now My Love
For Once in My Life
Love and Marriage
They Can't Take that Away from Me
My Kind of Town
This Town
I've Got You Under My Skin
All or Nothing at All
The Best is Yet to Come
It Was a Very Good Year
Mack the Knife
Come Fly with Me
That's Life
The Girl from Ipanema
The Lady is a Tramp
Bad, Bad Leroy Brown
Love's Been Good to Me
L. A. is My Lady
Young at Heart
(Love is) The Tender Trap
I Will Drink the Wine
High Hopes
The World We Knew (Over and Over)
Learnin' the Blues
Songs for Swingin' Lovers
All the Way
Witchcraft
Mr. Success
Nice 'N' Easy
It Happened in Monterey
You're Getting to be a Habit with Me
On a Clear Day (You Can See Forever)
The Most Beautiful Girl in the World
Don't Sleep in the Subway
More
Wives and Lovers
Makin' Whoopee

50 Star Wars Characters	*50 Simpson's Characters*
4-LOM	Zutroy
Anakin Skywalker	Barney Gumble
Leia Organa Solo	Dr. Nick
Biggs Darklighter	Apu Nahasapeemapetilon
C-3PO	Homer
Dorsk 81	Yendor
Exar Kun	Frank
Fox (Clone Commander CC-1010)	Milhouse Van Houten
Galak Stari	Marge
Naga Sadow	Itchy – The Psycho Mouse
Darth Vader	Waylon Smithers
King Terak	Patty Bouvier
Wat Tambor	Martin Prince
Yarna D'al Gargan	Duncan (Furious D)
Grakchawwaa	Clancy Wiggum
Han Solo	Willie the Groundskeeper
Tarkin	Jimbo
HK-47	Krusty the Clown
Chewbacca	Snowball II
Mungo Baobab	Lisa
Rute Gunnay	Nelson Muntz
IG-88	Bart
Jabba the Hutt	Ned Flanders
R2-D2	Ling Bouvier
Sharad 'Howlrunner' Hett	Lenny Leonard
Kaan	Selma Bouvier
Luke Skywalker	Moe Szysiak
Boc	Quimby – The Mayor of Springfield
Poggle the Lesser	R. Terwilliger
WA-7	Seymour Skinner
Xizor	Uncle Arthur
Zett Jukassa	Rod Flanders
Magaloof	Santa's Little Helper – Bart's pet
Jar Jar Binks	Troy McClure
Nym	Uter
Fang Zar	C. M. Burns
Iaco Stark	Dr. Julius Hibbert
Tilak Hord	Carl Carson
Obi-Wan Kenobi	Comic Book Guy
Vodo-Siosk Baas	Todd Flanders
OOM-9	Edna Krabappel
Pax Bonkik	Otto Mann
Queen Organa	Abraham Simpson
Sio Bibble	Scratchy the Cat
Ludo Kressh	Ralph Wiggum
TK-421	Radioactive Man
Ulic Qel-Droma	Princess Kashmir
V-Tan	The Three-Eyed Fish
Xaverri	Kent Brockmann
Pic	Maggie

50 Beans and Pulses	*50 London Bus Routes*
Chick peas	73
Butter beans	88
Green lentils	110
Baked beans	X26
Split peas	190
Runner beans	C2
Sugar Snap peas	209
Royal Burgundy Purple Heirloom beans	1
Soya beans	94
Petit Pois	36
Haricot beans	PR2
Early Onward peas	24
Red lentils	E2
Broad beans	29
Mangetout	134
Blue Lake beans	92
Puy lentils	15
Black-eyed beans	N31
Mushy peas	243
Coffee beans	266
Lincoln peas	E6
Black beans	444
Marrowfat peas	N279
French beans	N7
Large brown lentils	945
Red kidney beans	248
Processed peas	E11
Adzuki beans	A10
Rattlesnake Heirloom Pole beans	C3
Garden peas	H17
Carob beans	R62
Southern peas	H50
Mung beans	969
Garbanzo beans	W6
Chinese peas	H1
Jelly beans	699
Fava beans	U10
Yellow lentils	N253
Lady peas	6
Wax beans	33
Haricot verts	4
Yellow beans	302
Dragon Tongue beans	195
Green beans	U3
Bush beans	240
Lima beans	50A/50B
Snow peas	PR1
Pinto beans	52
Dwarf French beans	81
Borlotti beans	148

50 Vegetarian Dishes

Bean burger
Bean casserole
Vegetable stew
Acorn squash filled with savoury spinach
Baked corn timbales
Cavatappi with spinach, garbanzo and feta
Calabacitas
Falafel and salad
Cannellini parmesan casserole
Parsley spaghetti
Cauliflower cheese
Cheesy spinach bake
Broccoli quiche
Veggie burger
Chickpea macaroni salad
Leek and taleggio risotto
Caribbean sweet potato and bean stew
Coconut lentil soup
Macaroni cheese
Nut roast
Garbanzo bean patties
Vegetable stir-fry
Potato, cheeses and beans
Cheddar and leek strata
Couscous, artichoke heart and walnut salad
Lentil loaf
Mexican bean burgers
Navratan korma
Stuffed peppers
Cheese ravioli with mushrooms
Vegetable lasagne
Quorn and chickpea curry
Brownbag burritos
Sweet and sour tofu veggies
Ratatouille
Three bean salad
Courgette and aubergine bake
Chilli bean lasagne
Roasted vegetable risotto
Veggie goulash
Cheddared farmhouse chowder
Chunky garden stew
Crispy orange vegetable and tofu
Fettuccine gorgonzola with sun-dried tomatoes
Garden omelette
Vegetable pizza
Mexican hot pot
Middle eastern grilled vegetable wraps
Stuffed vine leaves
Pasta with pesto and goat cheese

50 Butterflies and Moths

Small Blue
Brown Argus
Ringlet
Painted Lady
Large Skipper
Small Pearl Bordered Fritillary
Green Veined White
Pale Clouded Yellow
Common Blue
Speckled Wood
Small Tortoiseshell
Comma
White-Letter Hairstreak
White Admiral
Meadow Brown
Gatekeeper
Peacock
Dark Green Fritillary
Common Clouded Yellow
Chequered Skipper
Silver-Washed Fritillary
Brimstone
Adonis Blue
Purple Emperor
Scotch Argus
Large White
Black Hairstreak
Grizzled Skipper
Small Copper
Orange-Tip
Queen of Spain Fritillary
Purple Hairstreak
Large Blue
Small White
Greyling
Wall
Marbled White
Dingy Skipper
Red Admiral
Chalk-Hill Blue
Small Heath
Silver-Studded Blue
Green Hairstreak
High Brown Fritillary
Essex Skipper
Large Tortoiseshell
Berger's Clouded Yellow
Mountain Ringlet
Wood White
Holly Blue

50 Molluscs

Common whelk
Grove snail
Sting winkle
Horse mussel
Oyster
White-Lipped banded snail
Oyster Drill
Baltic Tellin
Cockle
Sandhill snail
Common limpet
Heath snail
Cowrie
Plaited Door snail
Lake limpet
Ormer
Saddle oyster
Roman snail
Flat winkle
Common or Garden snail
Queen scallop
Thin Tellin
Keyhole limpet
Prickly cockle
Ear Pond snail
Actaeon
European cowrie
Common or Edible winkle
River snail
Dog whelk
Freshwater Nerite
White Ram's-Horn
River limpet
Curved Razor
Great scallop
Great Ram's-Horn
Blue-Rayed limpet
Netted Dog whelk
Great Pond snail
Sand Gaper
Slipper limpet
Dwarf Pond snail
Rough winkle
Tortoiseshell limpet
Wendletrap
Moss Bladder snail
Slit limpet
Violet Sea snail
Thick-Lipped Dog whelk
Common Piddock

50 Memorable Days and Dates

Farming began – 6500 BC
Friday the 13th.
Christmas Day
'Rock Around the Clock,' first No. 1 rock 'n' roll
-single – Nov. 1955
Easter Sunday
First Woolworth's opened - 1909
1812 Overture
1914 – 1918
21st. January – Martin Luther King Day
Cleopatra became queen of Egypt – 69-30 BC
Shredded Wheat introduced - 1908
Black Friday
Good Friday
The 'Pill' available on prescription - 1963
9/11
2nd. September 1666
Mickey Mouse made his film debut - 1928
1939 – 1945
St. Valentines Day
The Iron Age began – 1200 BC
November 5th.
Boadicea revolts against Romans – AD 62
Boston Tea Party – 1773
The Daleks first appear in Dr. Who; The Dead
-Planet - 1963
February 29th.
Your wedding anniversary
First vacuum cleaners become available – 1911
Father's Day – June 16th.
17th. March – St. Patrick's Day
Mother's Day
The 11th. min. of the 11th. hr. on the 11th. Nov.
-1945
First day of Spring – March 20th.
Your own birthday
Decimalisation in Britain – 15th. February 1971
May Day
New Year's Day
April Fool's Day
Princess Diana killed in car crash – 1st. Sept. 1997
Happy new millennium – 2000 AD!
August Bank Holiday
England won the World Cup – 1966
Victoria, Queen of Great Britain – 1837-1901
Winter Solstice – June 21st.
Mars bars arrived – 1932
'Hello' used as official telephone response – 1905
The Twelve of Never
Boxing Day
4th. July
Halloween! – Oct. 31st.
Your Mother's birthday!

50 Slang words for Money

Bob
Shrapnel
Quid
Pony
Nugget
Dough
Brass
Rich
Loaded
Brasic
Monkey
Flush
Loot
Fiver
Tener
2-bob
Well-off
Dosh
Silver
Cash
Tidy sum
Change
Gold
Bullion
Lush
Buck
Spondulix
Minted
Bread
Nickel
Coppers
Dime
Jingle
Treasure
Greens
Stash
Wedge
Grand
Packet
Half-a-crown
Yen
Nest egg
Sorted
Doubloons
Lucre
Fortune
Affluent
Penniless
Rupees
Tin

50 Words for Woman

Girl
Miss
Lady
Dear
Darling
Filly
Woman
Mrs.
Huney
Mistress
Dame
Ms.
Luv
Tigress
Wife
Matron
She
Sheila
Mademoiselle
Doll
Her
Female
Hen
Maiden
Wench
Ma'am
Lass
Fraulein
Spinster
Sister
Widow
Signora
Cow
Sis.
Marm
Chick
Bird
Signorina
Babe
Sweetheart
Missus
Moll
Bint
Gentlewoman
Baby
Madam
Frau
Memsahib
Mare
Vixen

50 Bridges	50 Words for 'Bottom'
London Bridge	Bum
Pont de Normandie	Behind
Huey P Long	Posterior
Tower Bridge	Bam-bam
Bridge on the River Kwai	Arse
Battersea Bridge	Bottom
Yangtze River Bridge	Binky
Forth Road Bridge	Cheeks
Millennium Foot Bridge	Cupcakes
Hell Gate	Rump
Blackfriars Bridge	Bottle and glass
Bridge of Sighs	Derrière
Ironbridge	Rear
Greenwich Bridge	Cushions
Orvieto Viaduct	Sit-me-downs
Brooklyn Bridge	Backside
Queen Elizabeth II	Fanny
Savannah River Bridge	Arse-end
The Bridges of Madison County	Do-nothing stool
Richmond Bridge	Chuff
Salginatobel Bridge	Jacksie
Sydney Harbour Bridge	Khyber Pass
Lower Zambesi	Duff
Putney Bridge	Dutch dumplings
Venice Viaduct	English muffins
Southwark Bridge	Full moon
Akashi Kaikyo Suspension Bridge	Booty
The Bridge at Remagen	Fife and drum
Hungerford Foot Bridge	Botty
Tay	Butt
Waterloo Bridge	Peach
Tarr Steps Clapper Bridge	Tush
Barnes Rail Bridge	Back-porch
Teddington Lock Foot Bridge	Hind-quarters
Severn Road Bridge	Rear-end
Bradford-on-Avon Medieval bridge	Arsebone
Chelsea Bridge	Hot buns
Storstrom	Sweet cheeks
The Bridge of San Luis Rey	Johnson
Chiswick Road Bridge	Buttocks
Old London Bridge	Parking place
Pulteney Bridge	Back-end
Coalbrookdale Cast Iron Bridge	Seat of honour
Westminster Bridge	Tooshie
Humber Bridge	Hindside
Hanging Bridge	Stern
The Bridges at Toko-Ri	Truck-end
Lambeth Bridge	Bott-bott
Tanfield Arch	Slapper
Kew Bridge	Buns

50 Electrical Goods Shops	50 Office Jobs
50 Electrical Goods Shops	*50 Office Jobs*

50 Electrical Goods Shops

Dixon's
Argos
Bose
BT Shop
Curry's
24electric.com
Co-op Electrical Shop
John Lewis
Empire Direct
Focus Kitchen Appliances
Bennett's Electrical
Homecare
Comet
AudioVision
Grundig
Cannings
KitchenLand
Littlewoods
Maplin Electronics
Sound & Vision
Tesco Electrics
Jessop's
PC World
Powerhouse
Bargain Crazy
Sainsbury's Kitchen
Comet Spares
Allders
Sony
Philips
Toshiba
Panasonic
Trade Appliances
Sony Style
Freeman
Grattan
MISCO
PLAY
Amkells
Viatek
Debenhams
K K Electronics
Kays
Marshall Ward
247 Electrical
Audio Visual WOW
Carphone Warehouse
Focus DIY
Appliance City
AJ Electrics

50 Office Jobs

Interviewing
Filing
Invoicing
Ordering
Recruiting
Paying bills
Telephoning clients
Typing
Making the tea
Shorthand
Sharpening pencils
Changing an ink cartridge
Creating Publisher documents
Opening mail
Writing letters
Addressing envelopes
Updating the databank
Shredding
Photocopying
Making appointments
Faxing
Talking to colleagues
Sorting the post
Meeting clients
Calling in the computer technician
Going to the bank
Tidying shelves
Filling out VAT returns
Running errands
Answering the phone
Washing up
Taking dictation
Going out for lunch
Querying bills
Cooking the books
Returning goods
Dictating
Reading documents
Preparing Power Point lectures
Re-loading the photocopier with paper
Filling out tax returns
Giving out orders
Receiving a dressing-down
Brainstorming
Wearing a tie
Administration
Tidying one's desk
Watering the two plants
Hiding bluetac
Firing

50 Words for 'Big'

Huge
Dumpy
Large
Enormous
Colossal
Gigantic
Vast
Awesome
Abundant
Plentiful
Ample
Full
Chunky
Superabundant
Overweight
Excessive
Immense
Boundless
Extensive
Tubby
Roomy
Mighty
Monstrous
Fat
Buxom
Plump
Homely
Massive
Rotund
Podgy
Great
Gargantuan
Substantial
Considerable
Cuddly
Bulky
Broad
Swollen
Generous
Capacious
Spacious
Meaty
Voluptuous
Monumental
Expansive
Weighty
Obese
Corpulent
Stout
Chubby

50 Racing Car Drivers

Sterling Moss
Graham Hill
Jackie Stewart
Michael Schumacher
Mika Hakkinen
Eddie Irvine
Rubens Barrichello
Kimi Raikkonen
Alberto Ascari
David Coulthard
Jacques Villeneuve
Damon Hill
Alain Prost
Nigel Mansell
Ayrto Senna
Michele Alboreto
J. Watson
D. Pironi
Carlos Reutemann
Nelson Piquet
Gilles Villeneuve
Ronnie Peterson
Jody Scheckter
Niki Lauder
Emerson Fittipaldi
Clay Regazzoni
Keke Rosberg
Alan Jones
Mario Andretti
James Hunt
Jacky Ickx
Jack Brabham
John Surtees
Jim Clark
Wolfgang von Trips
Bruce McLaren
Tony Brooks
Jose Gonzalez
Juan Manuel Fangio
Jochen Rindt
Denny Hulme
Phil Hill
Mike Hawthorn
Guiseppe Farina
Maria Teresa de Filippi
Ray Harroun
Andy Green
Louis Rigolly
Ricardo Patrese
Fernando Alonso

50 Words for 'Small'	50 Barbara Cartland Novels
Tiny	A Dual of Hearts
Little	Fire on the Snow
Diddy	Bewitched
Ickle	Dance on My Heart
Minuscule	Elizabethan Lover
Microscopic	The Captive Heart
Insey	Enchanted
Micro	From Hate to Love
Reduced	Lovers in Paradise
Minute	I Search for Rainbows
Scant	Journey to Paradise
Insignificant	A Call to the Heart
Mini	Lessons in Love
Titchy	The Glittering Lights
Minimal	Only Love
Infinitesimal	Who Can Deny Love
Weeny	Lost Love
Wee	Look, Listen and Love
Miniature	Too Precious to Love
Undersized	The Curse of the Clan
Slim	A Fugitive from Love
Slender	Love, Lords and Ladybirds
Fractional	The Little Pretender
Lean	Book of Love and Lovers
Meagre	Love Climbs In
Thin	The Complacent Wife
Wasted	A Safety Match
Slight	I Seek the Miracles
Frail	The Coin of Love
Dainty	The Heart of the Clan
Fragile	Sweet Enchantress
Minikin	The Reluctant Bride
Squat	Royal Punishment
Compact	The Hell Cat and the King
Shrunken	Punishment of A Vixen
Minor	A Game of Love
Trivial	Seek the Stairs
Unimportant	Hidden by Love
Petty	The Impetuous Duchess
Paltry	Love, Lies and Marriage
Marginal	I Reach for the Stars
Humble	A Sword to the Heart
Seck	We Danced all Night
Granule	Tempted to Love
Crumb	Miracle for a Madonna
Wisp	The Kiss of Life
Fragment	Alone in Paris
Snip	The Marquis Wins
Snippet	The Sign of Love
Dot	Escape

50 Things the Wolf might have said to gain entrance to the Three Little Pigs House

Postman; special delivery
What's all this water running down the wall?
I only want to talk
Truffles, truffles. Free truffles today!
It's only me; Little Red Riding Hood
Gas man, …come to read the meter
This letterbox is a bit dirty
Wolf Patrol! You all OK in there?
They're going to build a road right through here…
I can see you all, …hiding behind the sofa
Hello? I'm looking for my wife; I've a picture of
-her here sunbathing topless…
Right; I'll huff and I'll puff and all that nonsense!
There's a wasp's nest in your guttering you know
We could go out, get to know each other better?
Did you mean to throw this out?
Don't make me do it…
Did you know that my mother was sick?
Police! I hear you got trouble!
I'm climbing on the roof now just like in the story
Is that your car rolling down the hill?
Grandma sends her love
Well, well, would you look at this…
"We wish you a merry xmas, we wish you a…"
-Remember what I did to your house made of straw
Parcel for Mr. Pig
Honestly, I'm a vegetarian
I see there's been a flood here
It's OK, bacon gives me indigestion
Extra, extra; wolf killed by pigs! Read all about it!
Hello! Lottery winnings for Mr. Piggy!
…And I've got so much to tell you all
It's the builder come to open up your chimney mate
…How about a pork pie then?
Locksmith!?
Open up or this little piglet gets it
Pig protection unit here
Little pigs, it's mother…
Free cauldrons, only today!
Ok, I'll count to 10. …6, 7,.. 8,… 9,… 9½,…. 9¾
Hello? Local gunsmith at your service
Nobody loves me (sob!) No one cares!
I love pigs (I could even eat a whole one)
Hello? Milkman
I love your garden, especially these yellow…
I'll get cross…
You must do something about this brickwork
Now who's afraid of the big bad wolfie… arh
You'll be sorry
I'm counting to 20 this time…
I'm going now

50 Things you might say if you met Jesus

Well everyone's got their cross to bear I suppose
How d'you do that trick with the loaves and
-fishes?
God, is it really you!
Still wearing the nappy
Lucky you were born right on Christmas day!
Your book's still selling well
Can you still turn water into wine? We could
-maybe go into partnership together?
There's a guy who can bend spoons now
So, …you've come back
We're all still sinning!
You've kept the beard then
Jesus who?
Hi! You staying at the YMCA
Look we all wear these little crosses now
Remind me who you are again?
Hey miracle man! Can you get this stain out?
How's heaven these days?
Can I take a photo?
What's it like being dead?
Have you forgiven Judas?
How's Mary?
And you say the Pope won't see you?
Well things have changed a bit now around here
Now don't get cross! Ha! –Get it?
How's your dad?
Jesus of… what was it, -Norwich?
Can I have your autograph please?
And what's your surname?
There's a firm called, 'Cheeses of Nazareth' in
-Wales
Let's catch up sometime
Mind if I borrow your mobile
You staying long?
I'm an Atheist myself
Looking for work?
You took your time getting back
Nice stigmata
What's it really like being crucified?
Are you for real!
Give my love to Mary
Holy Moses!
Fancy a beer?
Sorry I can't stop, catch you next time
Let me do a quick sketch
About time you had a haircut
I'm Italian
Hey! The Crown of Thorns was a cool touch man!
You look like Hell!
Give me your mobile number
Was Peter gay by the way?
God still alive?

50 Parts of the Eye

Iris
Lacrimal gland
Lacrimal sac
Lateral rectus muscle
Vitreous humour
Macula
Eyeball
Central retinal nerve
Central retinal artery
Pia mater
Arachnoid mater
Lens
Dura mater
Optic nerve
Eye orbits
Retina
Choroid
Sclera
Retinal blood vessels
Medial rectus muscle
Cornea
Ora serrata
Ciliary body
Iridocorneal angle
Eyelids
Sinus venosus sclerae
Zonular ligament
Dilator muscle
Sphincter muscle
Pupil
Eyebrows
Aqueous humour, anterior chamber
Aqueous humour, posterior chamber
Levator palpebrae superioris
Lacrimal canaliculus
Tear duct
Blind spot
Conjunctiva
Lacrimal punctum
Optic disc
Rods and cones
Eyelashes
Tear film
Nerve impulses
Superior rectus
Trochlea
Inferior oblique
Lateral rectus
Annular tendon
Medial rectus

50 Things taught at School

English
Maths
Textiles
Geography
Biology
Good behaviour
Chemistry
Food Technology
How to tell the time
Physics
Organisation
Tolerance
Swimming
History
How to tie your shoe-laces
PE
Good manners
RE
Latin
Home Economics
Working as a team
Information Systems
Turn-taking
Visual Education
Careers Advice
Metalwork
Care of the Environment
Sex Education
Woodwork
How to revise
Commerce
Resistant Materials
Sharing
Research skills
Drama
French
Listening skills
Music
Personal, Social and Health Education
How to respect others
Spanish
Technology
Note-taking
Art
Information Technology
How to use the Library
Exam skills
Technical Drawing
Punctuality
German

50 Danielle Steele Novels	50 Nautical Terms
Star	All aboard
Vanished	Full steam ahead
Jewels	Port
Changes	There she blows
Sunset in St. Tropez	Scrub the decks
The Promise	Steady as she goes
Leap of Faith	Hard to starboard
The Cottage	Stern
The Kiss	Weigh anchor
Zoya	Lower the gangplank
Bittersweet	Come about
Seasons of Passion	Ship ahoy!
Summer's End	Mayday
Answered Prayers	To the lifeboats
Malveillance	Man the rigging
Wanderlust	Ship shape
Irresistible Forces	Reverse engines
Remembrance	Stowaway
Once in a Lifetime	Captain's orders
Journey	Keelhaul him
Lone Eagle	Trim the sails
Five Days in Paris	Ship aground
Love; Poems	All hands on deck
The House on Hope Street	Lower the foresails
The Long Road Home	Unleash the jib
The Wedding	Westward ho
The Gift	Man overboard
Family Album	Take the helm
No Greater Love	Lower the lifeboats
Crossings	Enemy ships in sight
Thurston House	Give a wide berth
Palomino	Man the cannon
The Ring	Sealegs
Silent Honor	Cast off
Accident	Hoist the sail
Granny Dan	Make way
Daddy	Hold the helm
The Ranch	Put about
To Love Again	Capsize
Message from Nam	Run for port
Mixed Blessings	Heave to
Now and Forever	Bring to rest
Mirror Image	Sea-worthy
Special Delivery	Captain's table
The Klone and I	Walk the plank
Heartbeat	Belay there
Wings	Yo-heave-ho
Lightning	Land ahoy
Malice	Aft
The Ghost	Abandon ship

50 David Bowie Songs	*50 Famous Numbers*
Wild is the Wind	666
Cold Fire	999
Five Years	2.4 children
Young Americans	1 in 10
Hang onto Yourself	1066
Station to Station	1 and 1 is 2
Changes	Key of the door – never been 21 before
Future Legend	2 + 2 = 4
Win	69
Sons of the Silent Age	50/50
The Jean Genie	2001- A Space Odyssey
Space Oddity	100%
Thursday's Child	9 times out of 10
Starman	1666
Golden Years	77 Sunset Strip
Hallo Spaceboy	AD 63
Sweet Thing	5th. Avenue
Moss Garden	99 red balloons
Drive-In Saturday	12 apostles
The Laughing Gnome	Route 66
The Man Who Sold the World	The M1
Scary Monsters and Super Creeps	10 Downing St.
Stay	7/11
Joe the Lion	6 of one, half a dozen of the other
Chant of the Ever Circling Skeletal Family	3rd, time lucky
1984	901
Right	Unlucky 13
Somebody Up there Likes Me	Into The Valley of Death rode the 600
TVC 15	Boeing 747
Fame	10 0' clock news
DJ	14th. February
Always Crashing in the Same Car	When I'm 64
The Secret Life of Arabia	The year 2000
Up the Hill Backwards	99 ice cream
Seven Years in Tibet	Sweet 16
The Heart's Filthy Lesson	Two fat ladies - 88
Knock on Wood	20,000 Leagues Under the Sea
We are the Dead	76 trombones
Black Tie, White Noise	The 39 Steps
Sound and Vision	Half-a-Sixpence
Beauty and the Beast	1 in a million
Across the Universe	A stitch in time saves 9
Breaking Glass	Legs 11
Boys Keep Swinging	1812
V-2 Schneider	20/20 vision
John, I'm Only Dancing	Henry VIII
Jean Genie	12 days of Christmas
Blue Jean	The 19th. hole
China Girl	2 of a kind
Be My Wife	Kelly's eye; No. 1

50 Possible Wives for Henry VIII

Pink
Twiggy
Anna Friel
Kate Moss
Gweneth Paltrow
Nicole Kidman
Scary Spice
Britney Spears
Florence Nightingale
Pamela Stephens
Betty Grable
Elizabeth Fry
Mary Shelly
Anna Pavlova
Jean Shrimpton
Catherine Zeta-Jones
Virginia Woolf
Charlotte Bronte
Mary Quant
Fay Dunaway
Paula Radcliffe
Debbie Harry
Billie Piper
Brigit Polk
Olive Oil
Goldie Hawn
Marge Simpson
Joan of Arc
Jennifer Aniston
Mata Hari
Cilla Black
Sheena Easton
Cathy Kirby
Cindy Crawford
Julie Andrews
Dolly Parton
Julia Roberts
Leslie Ash
Mary Hopkins
Pamela Anderson
Tina Turner
Victoria Wood
Dawn French
Virginia Wade
Bette Davis
Maria Sharapova
Jennifer Lopez
Sandra Bullock
Jordan
Kate Bush

50 Aerial Terms

Arrivals
Chocks away
Ready for take-off
Bandits at 5 o' clock!
Ready to land
Fasten your seatbelts
Flaps up
Wind-speed good
Coming into land
We have lift-off
This is your captain speaking
Air turbulence
Loop-the-loop
Scramble!
Enemy aircraft in sight
Blast off!
We're losing height
On the wing
Bale out!
We'll have to make a crash landing!
Jetlag
Your in-flight movie
Duty free drinks
Going into a roll
Pull out, pull out!
Approaching the target
Going into orbit
Extinguish all cigarettes
Stow all baggage
Return your seats to the upright position
Bombs away!
Airspeed good
She's going down!
She's caught in a spin!
80,000 ft. and climbing
I can see the red tail-lights, heading for Spain
Now we're flying by wire
I gotta full moon in my port sight
I ordered a vegetarian
Maximum velocity
We're losing altitude
They're flying out of the sun Captain!
Please use the 'airsick' bag
I see the landing lights
We're flying into restricted airspace
It's one of ours!
White wine please
Welcome to the 'Mile High Club'
Please remain calm
Departures

50 Mints and Chewing Gums

Trebor extra strong mints
Murray mints
Wrigley's spearmint gum
Trebor mint imperials
After Eight mints
Bazooka Joe
Polo mints
Trebor softmints
Wrigley's juicy fruit
Smint
Dentyne, cinnamon chewing gum
Mintoes
Orbit, sugar-free gum
Air Waves vapour release
Bubblicious, watermelon
Wrigley's Extra, cool mint fresh
Clarnico mint creams
Everton mints
Crystal mints
Bubble Yum gum
Nicotinell mint
Wrigley's double mint gum
Fox's glacier mints
Mint humbugs
Chowards spearmint chewing gum
Freedent spearmint
Magic mints
Chickets fruit chewing gum
Eclipse Winterfresh
Mojo chews
Bubblicious, sour apple
Eclipse polar ice
Wrigley's big red
Freshen Up, peppermint
Hubba Bubba
Wrigley's Extra, cool green apple
Dentyne ice arctic chill
Doubble Bubble bubble gum
Blanx
Eclipse Flash
Wrigley's Extra, mountain frost
Freedent peppermint
Orbit white
Alpine
Wrigley's P. K.
Mastic gum
Chickets tiny bubble gum
Xylitol gum
Icebreaker peppermint
Trident bubble gum

50 Lollies and Ice-Creams

Wall's cream of Cornish
Ben & Jerry's caramel chew
Carte D'or strawberry
Fab
Cornetto choc chip and hazelnut
Snofruit lemon
Zoom
Orbit
Wall's banoffee pie
Ben & Jerry's New York super fudge
Magnum almond
Solero exotic
Viennetta biscuit tirami
Rev
Lyon's Maid sea jet
Carte D'or vanilla
Big Wiz
Funny Faces
Cornetto strawberry
Raspberry split
Cola Rola ice lolly
Twango
Wall's neapolitan
Jumbo
Choc-top woppa
Wall's vanilla
Ben & Jerry's cherry garcia frozen yogurt
Viennetta chocolate
Lyon's Maid king sundae
Kinky
Orange Maid
Magnum intense
Snocream raspberry
Carte D'or spagnola
Sky Ray
Heart
Orange sparkle
Cornetto cappuccino and Irish cream
Magnum seven deadly sins, gluttony
Magnum taste
Solero get fresh
Viennetta vanilla
Cornish mivvi
Wall's choc bar
Choc ice
Woppa
Lyon's Maid Cornish dairy brick
Raspberry ripple
Strawberry fayre
Sundae cup

50 Police-Drama/Detective Programmes

The Bill
Z-Cars
A Touch of Frost
The Sweeney
The Professionals
Dixon of Dock Green
Starsky and Hutch
Prime Suspect
Indelible Evidence
Cagney and Lacey
Softly, Softly
The Rockford Files
Miami Vice
The X Files
Juliet Bravo
Ally McBeal
Police Woman
Magnum PI
The Avengers
The Man from U.N.C.L.E.
Twin Peaks
Minder
Callan
Charlie's Angels
The Chinese Detective
Cracker
Crime Traveller
C.A.T.S. Eyes
Dalziel and Pascoe
Dempsey and Makepeace
Department S
The Detectives
Dial 999
Dragnet
The Dukes of Hazzard
The Equalizer
The FBI
The Gentle Touch
Special Branch
Hart to Hart
Hawaii Five-O
Heartbeat
Hill Street Blues
NYPD Blue
The Thin Blue Line
Knight Rider
The Persuaders
LA Law
A Man Called Ironside
The Streets of San Fransisco

50 Boxers

Joe Louis
Marvin Haggler
Sandy Saddler
Ray Winstone
Sugar Ray Robinson
Lennox Lewis
Jersey Joe Walcott
Alexis Arguello
Henry Cooper
Dave Charnley
Don Cockell
Gene Tunney
Carlos Monzon
Georges Carpenter
Joe Baksi
Gus Lesnevich
Barry McGuigan
Dick McTaggert
Max Baer
Rinty Monaghan
Rocky Marciano
Jake La Motta
Max Schmeling
George Foreman
Terry Spinks
Archie Moore
Randolf Turpin
Benny Leonard
Muhammed Ali
Terry Downes
Floyd Patterson
Bruce Woodcock
Barney Ross
Freedie Mills
Henry Armstrong
Ted 'Kid' Lewis
Ingemar Johannson
Willie Pep
Sonny Liston
Lloyd Honeygan
Joe Bugner
Billy Walker
Jack Dempsey
Emir Khan
Jimmy Wilde
Mike Tyson
Jack Johnson
Ray Leonard
Thomas Hearns
Joe Frazier

50 British Towns and Villages with Silly Names A-G

An T-òb
Angle
Ardtoe
Ashby de la Zouch
Badlipster
Balgown
Battle
Beer
Boat of Garten
Box
Braintree
Bridge of Allan
Cardigan
Catbrain
Cheddar
Chopwell
Collin
Crouch End
Diss
Crossmichael
Devil's Bridge
Dial Post
Digg
Dishes
Dog Village
Doll
Dollar
Donkey Town
Drums
Dull
East-the-Water
Egypt
Eye
Fail
Fence
Field
Fingerpost
Fir Tree
Fishnish
Fishpond Bottom
Five Turnings
Floors
Foulbog
Frisby on the Wreake
Frog Pool
Garden
Gass
Gay Street
Gibraltar
Glasshouses

50 British Towns and Villages with Silly Names G-N

Godmanchester
Grabhair
Great Heck
Great Snoring
Greenheads
Guide Post
Guy's Head
Ham
Hammer
Hatt
Headless Cross
Hill
Hole-in-the-Wall
Hook-a-Gate
Horsehouse
How Man
Indian Queens
Inkpen
Jump
Keith
Kettlesing Bottom
Killiecrankie
Kilmichael of Inverlussa
Knockdown
Leatherhead
Letters
Leysdown-on-Sea
Lickey End
Little Badminton
Little Snoring
Little Town
Littlemore
Lizard
Loans
Loose
Lover
Lower Down
Matching Tye
Mid Yell
Middle Wallop
Mill of Fortune
More
Moscow
Mousehole
New Houses
New Invention
New Orleans
New York
Nidd
Nobottle

50 British Towns and Villages with Silly Names N-Z

Oil Terminal
Old Crombie
Oliver
Over
Pan
Pant-Pastynog
Paul
Peebles
Pity Me
Playing Place
Queen Camel
Red Dial
Redscarhead
Rise
Rosebush
Royal British Legion Village
Saltburn-by-the-Sea
Sand Hole
Seal
Second Coast
Sexhow
Sharpness
Sheepwash
Sheet
Shelf
Shop
Simonsbath
Six Mile Bottom
Sixpenny Handley
Skidby
Slackhead
Snailbeach
Sockburn
Spital in the Street
Sticker
Talybont-on-Usk
The Bog
The Shoe
Thong
Three Leg Cross
Tongue
Trevor
Triangle
Trumpet
Twelveheads
Twenty
Upper End
Water
Waterloo
Windy Yet

50 Oceans and Seas

Arctic
South China
Mediterranean
Aegean
Indian
Bering
Sulu
Tyrrhenian
Gulf of Mexico
Banda
Okhotsk
Sea of Japan
Atlantic
Beaufort
Hudson Bay
Arabian
East China
Sea of Okhotsk
Andaman
Adriatic
Baltic
Pacific
Laccadive
Bismarck
Caribbean
Azov
Celebes (Sulawesi)
East Siberian
Coral
Black
Red
Yellow
White
Flores
Solomon
Ligurian
Ionian
Tasman
Irish
Java
Kara
Laptev
Molucca
North
Chukchi
Norwegian
Phillippine
Savu
Sea of Marmara (Propontis)
Timor

50 Lakes

Superior
Windermere
Van
Lake of the Woods
Edward (Idi Amin Dada)
Michigan
Great Slave
Erie
Winnipeg
Ontario
Chad
Volta
Hövsgöl
Victoria
Tonie Sap
Po-ssu-t'eng (Baghrash)
Torrens
Albert
Kariba
Koko Nor
Great Salt
Tana
Caspian Sea
Peipus
P'o-yang
Uvs
St. Clair
Poopó
T'ai
Frome
Leopold II (Mai-Ndombe)
Lama
Vättern
Huron
Chiquita
Tangra (T'ang-ku-la-yu-mu)
Har Us
Tengis
Sevan
Vyrnwy
Ness
Morar
Geneva (Lac Léman)
Derwent Water
Chapala
Dead Sea
Balaton
Bitter Lakes
San Martin (O'Higgins)
Lesser Slave Red

50 Drawing, Painting and Writing Implements

2B pencil
Fountain pen
Biro
Charcoal stick
Cartridge pen
Ruler
Wax crayon
Paint brush
4H pencil
Highlighter
Easel
Felt tip pen
Permanent marker
Pencil pot
Handwriting pen
3B pencil
Oil crayon
Italic pen
Linseed oil
Still life objects
Rubber
4B pencil
Set square
Correction fluid
Pencil sharpener
Ink cartridge
Water pot
2H pencil
Coloured pencils
Writing paper
Oil paints
Palette
3H pencil
Bottled ink
T-square
Studio
Stretched canvas
HB pencil
Palette knife
Indian ink
Pastels
Chinagraph pencil
Line guide
Drawing paper
Model
Paint pot
Compass
6B pencil
Cartridge paper
Measuring stick

50 Gems and Precious Stones

Diamond
Coronelian
Ruby
Pearl
Sard
Topaz
Moonstone
Chrysoprase
Jet
Amethyst
Sapphire
Tourmaline
Turquoise
Emerald
Hyacinth
Amber
Sugilite
Cultured pearl
Sardonyx
Cat's-eye
Zircon
Opal
Girasol
Seed pearl
Beryl
Aquamarine
Pink pearl
Chrysoberyl
Black opal
Alexandrite
Garnet
Chalcedony
Fire opal
Jasper
Tiger's-eye
Agate
Onyx
Heliotrope
Hematite
Bloodstone
Jacinth
Apatite
Chrysolite
Olivine
Peritot
Chrysocolla
Carbuncle
Mother of Pearl
Jade
Lapis Lazuli

50 Items of Jewellery

Pearl necklace
Silver bracelet
Drop earrings
Pendant
Nose-ring
Necklet
Studs
Ladies wristwatch
Wedding ring
Identity bracelet
Rope chain
Bangle
Medallion
Tie-pin
Diamond earrings
Signet ring
Charm bracelet
Silver chain
Engagement bracelet
Sleepers
Broach
Eternity ring
Silver cross
Solitaire ring
Belcher chain
Christening bracelet
Gent's wristwatch
Clip-on earrings
Hatpin
Engagement ring
Gold curb chain
Gate bracelet
Bridal set
Commitment ring
Hoops
Pearl earrings
Body bar
Pocket watch
Silver chocker
Creoles
Cuff-links
T-bar bracelet
Torgue
Ankle chain
Silver locket
Figaro chain
Cluster ring
Fob watch
Dog tag
Toe ring

50 Disasters

Earthquake
Volcanic eruption
Monsoon
Endemic disease
Landslide
Air crash
Drought
Hurricane
Pestilence
Forest fire
Comet collision
Atomic explosion
Tornado
Exploding star
Whirlwind
War
Plague of insects
Disease
Earth tremor
Crop failure
Tidal wave
Mass bombing
Bubonic plague
Famine
Lava flow
Meteor storm
Tempest
Extinction
Genocide
Epidemic
Alien invasion
Flood
Global warming
Radical climate change
Cyclone
Crop desolation
Forest devastation
Sea-level rise
Pandemic
Avalanche
Climate deterioration
Pollution
Ecosystem collapse
Tsunami
Terrorist mass attack
Storm
Bird flu
Mudflow
Dam burst
Dust storm

50 Cakes and Puddings

Sponge cake
Christmas cake
Rice pudding
Treacle tart
Birthday cake
Jam roly-poly
Layer cake
Fresh cream cake
Wedding cake
Bread and butter pudding
Bakewell tart
Spotted dick
Sherry trifle
Christmas pudding
Fruit cake
Bread pudding
Battenberg cake
Swiss roll
Apple pie and custard
Blackcurrant cheesecake
Black Forest gâteau
Semolina
Apple strudel
Rhubarb and custard
Sticky banana pudding
Rhubarb crumble
Banoffee pie
Apple crumble
Tiramisu
Almond cake
Plum pudding
Ginger cake
Chocolate cake
Pecan pie
Brak cake
Pumpkin pie
Sticky toffee pudding
Jelly and ice-cream
Apple tart
Carrot cake
Syrup sponge pudding
Custard tart
Fruit salad
Chocolate mousse
Angel cake
Banana pudding
Tapioca pudding
Blancmange
Lemon meringue pie
Upside down pudding

50 Meats

Tongue
Pork chop
Mince lamb
Sirloin steak
Shoulder of Lamb
Kidney
Sheep's tongue
Lamb chop
Mutton
Rump steak
Chicken
Veal
Turkey
Neck of beef
Duck
Streaky bacon
Gammon
Shoulder of beef
Spare ribs
Bath chap
Cutlets
Haunch of venison
Heart
Leg of mutton
Liver
Boiled bacon
Brisket of beef
Lamb fillets
Silverside of beef
Rissoles
Braised steak
Leg of pork
Rack of lamb
Venison
Pheasant
Haggis
Black pudding
Meatballs
Sausage
Baron of beef
Tripe
Chump steak
Pork pie
Pig's trotters
Fillet steak
Ham
Knuckle
Sweetbreads
Brawn
Oxtail

50 Thoughts from a Burglars Perspective

At least it's not raining
They never leave a downstairs window open!
I'm getting too old for shinning up drainpipes
Hope they haven't got a dog
One day I'll get a proper job
Did I bring my torch?
Through the window and –hell! Down the toilet!
I could be home and tucked up in bed
Sod this for a game of soldiers
Should I leave my card?
Ow! Cut myself! –I'll sue them for that!
No. 41, boiler repairs? Oh, you don't have a
-boiler?
Not another digital camera
Just leave cash out; it's much simpler for us both!
Hope they haven't got a big dog!
And the misses thinks I'm out with me mates
Ooh, nice wallpaper
Let's see if they've got any beer in the fridge
Just got time to use the loo
Hope they don't wake up
This always reminds me of Oliver Twist
Bloody cat!
Heating's still on!
Should I shut the window behind me?
Good, plenty of cloud cover
Back door open? Excellent!
I'm fed up with wearing black all the time
A friendly dog... that's more like it!
I used to sell home alarm systems years ago
Is that their idea of a living room carpet!
Damn! Students! –Nothing here worth stealing!
Yes; I've come to read the gas meter dear... no,
-I'm not Richard. The gas man...arrh!
Could do with a sandwich; -as I'm in the kitchen
An empty room? Minimalist! Hell!
Er! Your son lent me his key!
Bet David Niven never had these problems in The
-Pink Panther
Looks like rain
God! –Er! Yes, it's only me!
Excellent; iPod, MP3, wallet, mobile... all laid out
Now for the panty draw...
Next month I'm going straight
Fancy leaving that on the stairs; I could have
-broken my neck!
Out the window and –hell! Into the flowerbed!
Wish I hadn't worn this Tony Blair mask
Lord! They've come home!
Nice dog. Please take your teeth out of my leg!
Oh, as I'm here; I might as well wash-up for them
Just time to use the lav... Engaged!?
Glass everywhere –and it wasn't even me
Oh. Evening officer...

211

50 Places to find a Crowd

Football match
Robbie Williams concert
Tesco's, Christmas eve.
Trafalgar Sq. on New Year's eve.
Speakers Corner
Oxford Street
Award ceremony
Rally
Christmas party
Night club
Train station
Rush hour traffic
Cinema
Market
Office party
Purgatory
Piccadilly Circus
Riot
Disco
Airport
Theatre
The Grand National
Mecca
Ice rink
Worker's march
Olympics
A metropolis
Outdoor festival
Slave ship
Night bus
Times Square
January sales
World Cup final
Nobel prize giving
Royal wedding
Tokyo
Wembley Arena
Charles I execution
Refugee camp
Jerusalem 999AD (The Last Judgement)
Roman Gladiator games
Beach, August bank holiday
Rolling Stones concert
Tower of Babal
A King's Coronation
Las Vegas
Viking army
School assembly
McDonalds
Hell

50 Places you'd find Deserted

The desert
Sinking ship
A-Ha concert
South Pole
Mars
Scottish Highlands
Pacific Islands
Central Australia
Pyrennes
Ghost ship
Ruined mansion
British Museum at night
The seabed
Abandoned underground station
Lake District in mid-winter
Greenland
Middle of a forest
Haunted house
Catacombs
Bank on a Bank Holiday
Monastery
Gary Glitter concert
The Moon
Power station with radiation leak
Space
Cemetery at night
Leper colony
8-Track cartridge shop
Swamp
The streets on Cup Final day
Jupiter
Country lane after midnight
North Pole
South American rain forests
Russian Steppes
Centre of the Earth
Wreck at the bottom of the sea
Isolation ward
Solitary confinement cell
Peat bog
City offices at the weekend
Bus in a Bus Depot
Pub after closing time
Millennium Dome
Abandoned space station
Cricket pitch in winter
Inside an Egyptian pyramid
Venus
Turkish baths in a heat wave
Seaside on Christmas Day

50 Accidents and Mishaps

Slip on a banana skin
Gravy down your shirt
Spill a cup of tea
Ink blob on your paper
Bite your tongue
Prick your finger
Bang heads together
Stub your toe
Catch your sleeve on a door handle
Drop an easy catch
Tread on a snail
Stung by a wasp
Flat tire
Split your trousers
Dog doo on your shoe
Cut your finger
Fall out with the mother-in-law
Graze your knee
Break a glass
Get on the wrong train
White clothes come out pink in the wash
Lose a button
Splattered on by a seagull
Spider in the bath
Come out of the toilet with toilet paper on your shoe
Caught by ticket inspector without a ticket
Spill gravy down your shirt
Lipstick on your collar
Get a sunburnt nose
Splinter
Bag stolen
Shut your fingers in the door
Water squirted by kids
Bag splits and contents spill out across the pavement
Burp at the dinner table
Lose your phone
Parking ticket
Tape the wrong programme
Flat battery
Forget Mother's Day
Walk into a plate-glass window
Fart in church
Fall down a manhole
Lose your trunks after diving into the pool
Miss an easy goal
Tuck your skirt into your knickers
Forget your coat
Walk into the Ladies
Burn the dinner
Trip over a dog

50 Well-known Soldiers

Boadicea
Bernard Law Montgomery
Horatio Nelson
Napoleon Bonaparte
Dwight D. Eisenhower
Ghengis Khan
William the Conqueror
King John
Duke of Wellington
General Custer
Sitting Bull
King Darius
Sun Tzu
Attila the Hun
Cesare Borgia
Robert E. Lee
Shahrbaraz of Persia
George Brown
Lawrence of Arabia
Cao Cao
Joachim Murat
Heinz Guderian
Surena
Tojo Hideki
George S. Patton
Joan of Arc
Erwin Rommel
Earl Mountbatten
Ulysses S. Grant
Charles de Gaulle
Reza Shah
Toyotomi Hideyoshi
Lazare Carnot
Gebhard Leberecht von Blücher
Harry Truman
King Cyrus
Arkan
Alexander the Great
Hannibal
Julius Caesar
Charlemagne
Belisarius
Gustavus Adolphus
Henry VIII
Marshal Vauban
Duke of Marlborough
Fredrick the Great
Oliver Cromwell
Francis Drake
Richard the Lionheart

50 Gasses	50 Witchcraft Artefacts
Oxygen	Cauldron
Hydrogen	Broomstick
Sulfur hexafluoride	Black cat
Ozone	Witch's hat
Carbon monoxide	Crystal ball
Xenon	Eye of newt
Hydroflourcarbons	Pagan symbols
Dichlorodifluoromethane	Snake's head
Ethylene	Pentagon
Chlorotrifluoromethane	Book of Spells
Desflurane	Spirits
Carbon dioxide	Toad
Propane	Black cloak
Perflourcarbons	Tarot cards
Chloropentafluoroethane	Magic stone
Carbon tetrachloride	Deer horn
Nitrous oxide	Animal bones
Ammonia gas	Sticking pins
Argon	Witch's mirror
Chlorofluorocarbons	Poppet dolls
Halothane	Book of Curses
Tetrafluoromethane	Poppet coffin
Ethane	Human hair
Bromotrifluoromethane	Candles
Butane	Magic lamp
Dichlorotetrafluoroethane	Antler
Isoflurane	Sun symbols
Helium	Charms
Fluoroethane	Mandrake root
Neon	Divination pan
Hexafluoroethane	Corn dollies
Methane	Terracotta witching jars
Trifluoromrthane	Sickle
Sevoflurane	Pitchfork
Cyanide	Herbs
Nitrogen	Zodiac symbols
Difluoroethane	Book of Black Magic
Hydroxyl radical	Pet rook
Trichlorofluoromrthane	Teacup for fortune-telling
Methyl chloroform	Nail clippings
Bromochlorodifluoromethane	Witch's Bellarmine bottle
Halon	Book of Hexes
Fluorine	Lucky heather
Methanol Chloromrthane	Crooked walking staff
Fluorotrichloromrthane	Necklace of snake vertebrae
Hydrogen sulfide	Wind/bull roarers
Toluene	Chalice
Xylene	Book of the Dead
Ethylbenzene	Athame dagger
Naphthalene	Human skull

50 Proverbs

First come, first served
A stitch in time saves nine
Too many cooks spoil the broth
If you can't stand the heat get out of the kitchen
Never look a gift horse in the mouth
You can lead a horse to water but you can't make him
-drink
A chain is no stronger than its weakest link
A bird in the hand is worth two in the bush
Never judge a book by its cover
Don't jump the gun
Don't run before you can walk
Don't rock the boat
Don't count your chickens before they're hatched
A watched pot never boils
Birds of a feather flock together
Give a dog a bad name and he'll always keep it
A fool and his money are soon parted
Don't burn your bridges before you cross them
An apple a day keeps the doctor away
The higher the climb, the harder the fall
It takes one to know one
If the cap fits, wear it
Familiarity breeds contempt
Don't bolt the stable door after the horse has bolted
A rolling stone gathers no moss
Fight fire with fire
All that glitters is not gold
Beggars can't be choosers
Finders keepers, losers weepers
Better the devil you know than the devil you don't
Make hay while the sun shines
Blood is thicker than water
Curiosity killed the cat
Dead men tell no tales
Don't cut off your nose to spite your face
Don't put all your eggs in one basket
Nothing ventured, nothing gained
Every picture tells a story
Faith can move mountains
Give him an inch and he'll take a mile
Don't wash your dirty linen in public
In for a penny, in for a pound
It's no use crying over spilt milk
It never rains, but pours
Jack of all trades, master of none
Let sleeping dogs lie
Lightening never strikes twice in the same place
Look before you leap
Many hands make light work
No news is good news

50 Little-known Animals

Abalone
Babirusa
Cacomistle
Dik-dik
Eyra
Gemsbok
Hellbender
Alewife
Kalong
Wapiti
Zebu
Hamadryas
Kolinsky
Baluga
Thylacine
Manatee
Numbat
Oribi
Katipo
Paddymelon
Capybara
Yapok
Quokka
Ratel
Sea squirt
Gavial
Markhop
Sugar glider
Tayra
Unau
Kiang
Dhole
Wobbegong
Solenodon
Pangolin
Brandling
Cribo
Viscacha
Talpan
Wisent
Potto
Zorilla
Axoloto
Drosophila
Grunion
Muskellunge
Peccary
Suricate
Vicuña
Tokay

50 HMS Ships	50 'Anger' Words
HMS Victory	Mad
HMS Warrior	Rant
HMS Revenge	Seethe
HMS Mayflower	Vex
HMS Leopard	Ire
HMS Verdun	Rage
HMS Dreadnought	Enrage
HMS Agincourt	Huff
HMS Tiger	Umbage
HMS Ludlow	Rancour
HMS Marlborough	Hate
HMS Ulysses	Animosity
HMS Vengeance	Revengeful
HMS Ark Royal	Spite
HMS Belfast	Malice
HMS Peregrine	Grudge
HMS Salisbury	Aggravation
HMS Rooke	Wrath
HMS Vigilant	Irate
HMS Constance	Vehemence
HMS Defiance	Exasperate
HMS Emerald	Choler
HMS Fearless	Fury
HMS Gambia	Cross
HMS Brecon	Temper
HMS Consort	Tantrum
HMS Peterel	Tizzy
HMS Jupiter	Paddy
HMS Hydra	Fume
HMS Implacable	Fit
HMS King George V	Storm
HMS Intrepid	Stew
HMS Keppel	Rampage
HMS Lowestoft	Glare
HMS Mohawk	Scowl
HMS Nottingham	Growl
HMS Neptune	Snarl
HMS Oberon	Gall
HMS Falcon	Miffed
HMS Glenearn	Virulence
HMS Defender	Spleenful
HMS Exeter	Frenzy
HMS Hornbill	Revenge
HMS Juno	Jealousy
HMS Otus	Angst
HMS Repulse	Envy
HMS Sheraton	Ratty
HMS Triumph	Wild
HMS York	Livid
HMS Whippet	Foam

50 'Love' Words

Amour
Affection
Woo
Desire
Fancy
Adore
Caress
Sensual
Endear
Darling
Kiss
Cuddle
Court
Flirt
Valentine
Girlfriend
Beau
Lover
Passion
Fondle
Buff
Hug
Soulmate
Snuggle
Nuzzle
Romp
Canoodle
Fawn
Smooch
Coquette
Lust
Beloved
Truelove
Sweetheart
Sweetie
Sugar
Honey
Precious
Dear
Chéri
Angel
Poppet
Pet
Snog
Embrace
Spoon
Fondest
Cherish
Coo
Enfold

50 Theatrical Terms

Beginners
Curtain call
Lighting angles
Make-up
Costumes
Props
Rigging
Scenic
Sound
Scene shifters
Stage Production
Stage Manager
Wardrobe
Applause
Five minute call
Clearance
Seating
Balcony
Backdrop
Actor
Playwright
Designers
Choreography
Backstage
Front of House
Dry ice
Strobe
Mirror ball
Mime
Follow spot
Radio microphone
Foot lights
Autocue
Prompt
Script
Effects
Gaffer
Grip
Pyrotechnics
Behind the scenes
In the wings
Cue
Show
Audience
Safety curtain
Ticket sales
Loading
Stage hands
Crew
Rider

50 Heavens and Hells

Nirvana
Lower world
Paradise
Nether world
Kingdom of God
Underworld
Abode of the Blest
Sheol
Land of the Leal
Hades
Olympus
Purgatory
Abraham's bosom
Perdition
Valhalla
Place of the Damned
Eternal home
Inferno
Asgard
Satan's Palace
Celestial bliss
Pandemonium
Elysium
Abyss
Eternal rest
Bottomless pit
Blessed state
Place of the Dead
Elysian Fields
Abaddon
Zion
Tophet
Land of Beulah
Place of torment
New Jerusalem
Gehenna
Holy City
Niflheim
Happy hunting grounds
Tartarus
Eden
Avernus
Garden of the Hesperides
Erebus
Islands of the Blest
Acheron
Isle of Avalon
Cocytus
Celestial city
Phlegethon

50 Angels and Fairies

Archangel
Fairie
Heavenly host
Good fairy
Angelic host
Little people
Choir invisible
Fay
Heavenly hierarchy
Peri
Throne
Mab
Principality
Titania
Seraph
Oberon
Seraphim
Puck
Cherub
Spirit of air
Cherubim
Robin Goodfellow
Ministering spirit
Ariel
Michael
Sylph
Gabriel
Sylphid
Raphael
Pixie
Uriel
Elf
Zadkiel
Piskie
Israfel
Brownie
Azreal
Kobold
Guardian angel
Fairy godmother
Tutelary spirit
Sprite
Changling
Lemure
Jinn
Houri
Satyr
Faun
Kelpie
Nixie

50 Devils, Demons and Monsters

Grendel
Satan
Centaur
Ogre
Diabolus
Fiend
Cerberus
Vampire
Lycanthrope
Ghoul
Moloch
Lucifer
Prince of Darkness
Charybdis
Apollyon
Goblin
Abaddon
Chimera
Werewolf
Sprite
Angra
Cyclops
Gorgon
Harpie
Incubus
Mephistopheles
Old Nick
Banshee
Hydra
Leviathan
Imp
Ogress
Beelzebub
Mammon
Gremlin
Kelpie
Zombie
Manasa
Succubus
Lord of the Flies
Saddam Hussein
Minotaur
Baba Yaga
Wyvern
Hobgoblin
Rakshasa
She-demon
Troll
Siren
Sphinx

50 Forms of Torture

The rack
Scourge
Thumb-screw
Cat-o'-nine-tails
Birch-rod
Bride's tongue
Hang in irons
Weights
Iron boot
Flaying
Chinese water torture
Whipping
Put in the stocks
Iron maiden
Strap
Break on the wheel
Lay on the lash
Keelhauling
Knee screw
Talons
Heretic fork
Iron lock jaw
Iron collar of thorns
Chastity belt
Head press
Barrel pillory
Hanging cage
Stocks
Cat's paw
Breast ripper
Scold's bride
Judas cradle
The pear
Red hot poker
Three-beamed harrow
Tongs
Garottes
St. Elmo's belt
Turcas
Bootikens
Eye gougers
Branding
Burning
Boiling
Flogging
The Strappado
Branks
The spider
Impalement
Ducking stool

50 Words and Phrases to express Drunkenness

Brahms and Liszt
3 sheets to the wind
Pie-eyed
Pissed
Tipsy
Tiddly
Inebriated
Rat-arsed
In his cups
Mashed
Out of his skull
Had a skinfull
One too many
Lashed
Under the influence
Intoxicated
Sozzled
Befuddled
One over the eight
Had a drop too much
Soaked
Boozed up
Blind drunk
The worse for wear
Half-seas over
In liquor
Merry
Well-primed
Tanked up
Bevvied up
Roaring drunk
Flushed
Pot-valiant
Tight
Libation to Bacchus
Cut
Well-oiled
Pickled
Canned
Sloshed
Plastered
Legless
Paralytic
In a drunken stupor
Under the table
Dead to the world
Pissed as a newt
Drunk as a lord
Glassy-eyed
Gone

50 Words and Phrases to express Craziness

A complete and utter loony
Mad
Daft as a brush
Insane
Two books short of a library
Loopy
Cuckoo
Of unsound mind
Round the twist
Gone off his crumpet
Two sausages short of a barbecue
Mad as a March hare
Bonkers
Potty
He's got bats in the belfry
Nutcase
Crackpot
Half-baked
Off his head
Two shillings short of a ten bob note
They call him 'Upton Park' coz he's two stops -short of 'Barking'
Do-lally
Not all there
Got a screw loose
She's not the full ticket
Two cakes short of a bakery
Candidate for Bedlam
Off one's rocker
Scatty
Nutty as a fruit cake
Moon-struck
Two words short of a dictionary
Up the pole
Non compos mentis
Out of his mind
Certifiable
Stark staring mad
Mad as a hatter
Dotty
Off his nut
Round the bend
Bananas
Two slices short of a full loaf
Batty
Lost his marbles
A bit touched
Slightly unhinged
Gaga
Crackers
Barmy

50 Relations	50 Receptacles
Son	Dish
Father-in-law	Bowl
Uncle	Box
Cousin	Desk drawer
Grandmother	Plate
Mother	Egg-cup
Grandson	Trunk
Sister	Frying pan
Great-grandmother	Vase
Father	Briefcase
Girlfriend	Filing cabinet
Mum	Larder
Step-mother	Pot
Godchild	Roasting tray
Niece	Saucepan
Nephew	Billie can
Auntie	Basket
Grandfather	Cup
Step-daughter	Purse
Sibling	Sheath
Sister-in-law	Treasure chest
Godson	Pocket
Cousin once removed	Chest of drawers
Daughter	Woc
Godmother	Handbag
Great-grandfather	Rucksack
Dad	Wardrobe
Grand-nephew	Shopping trolley
Wife	Saddle bag
Brother	Mug
Godfather	Quiver
Mother-in-law	Holdall
Distant cousin	Carpet bag
Granddaughter	Envelope
Great-grandson	Kitchen drawer
Step-father	Pantry
Goddaughter	Paper bag
Ancestor	Urn
Next-of-kin	Casket
Great-granddaughter	Carrier bag
Husband	Tankard
Boyfriend	Safe
Brother-in-law	Box file
Betrothed	Suitcase
Lover	Glass
Kissing cousin	Car boot
Grand-niece	Saucer
Step-son	Cupboard
First cousin	Jug
Second cousin	Bin

50 Scottish Clans

Agnew
MacArthur
Hamilton
MacBain
Armstrong
MacCallum
Mitchell
MacDonald
Baxter
MacDougall
Henderson
Macduff
Hunter
MacFarlane
Montgomery
MacGowan
Boyd
MacGregor
Boyle
MacIntyre
Irvine
McAndrew
Johnston
Mackay
Brown
Mackenzie
Burns
Mackinnon
Campbell
Mackintosh
Douglas
Maclachlan
Duncan
McMillan
Stewart
MacLean
Morrison
Murray
MacNab
Buchanan
MacNeil
Lindsay
Macpherson
Malcolm
MacRae
Robertson
Cameron
Scott
MacNicol
Wallace

50 Things to do in a 1950's Sitting-Room

Sit in a relaxing, red, Draylon armchair
Read the newspaper
Listen to the Goons on the wireless
Smoke a pipe
Marvel at your orange G-Plan furniture
Poke the fire
Run fingers through your Brylcreemed hair
Look at your collection of 'I Spy' books
Polish the Dansette stereophonic record player
Watch the Queen's 1953 Coronation on your
-brand new b/w Bush television set
Play a card game
Sip at a bottle of Babycham
Polish the sideboard
Leaf through a John Bull magazine
Wear your slippers
Chuckle at The Eagle comic
Repeat Macmillan's; 'we've never had it so good.'
Eat a bar of Fry's Punch chocolate
Discuss the Monarchy
Admire your new, red striped Polyester shirt
Darn some socks
Watch Tommy play with his 'Muffin the Mule'
Tie your tie in the mirror
Look out at your shiny, new Vauxhall Victor
Wind up the mantelpiece clock
Enjoy a mug of Bourn-vita
Tut over the disgraceful antics of Elvis Presley
Look at a copy of the Radio Times
Watch the children playing cowboys and Indians
Eat Spam sandwiches
Bath baby in front of the fire
Smoke a Capstan, navy cut cigarette
Bring some coal in from the outside coal bunker
Hum a popular jingle, 'Murray mints, Murray
-mints, to good to hurry mints.'
Arrange the b/w photographs on the mantelpiece
Take the best china out of the sideboard
Cheer on Stanley Matthews getting his cup
-winners medal
Stroke the dog
Open your Week-End assortment chocolates
Have a go at a Rag, Tag and Bobtail jigsaw
Curtain twitch
Chide Janet for getting plastercine on the carpet
Count up your spare shillings
Leaf through your copy of Practical Householder
Turn on the tan, Formica shaded, standard-lamp
Listen to Pat Boone on the radio
Wonder if two TV channels might be a little
-excessive
Look at the orange, swirly wall-to-wall carpet
Tread on a Dinky car toy
Call out to the new wife cleaning in the kitchen

50 Sounds we can make with our Voices

Sob
Shout
Gargle
Cry
Mutter
Tut
Scream
Talk
Call
Cluck
Grunt
Roar
Chatter
Rant
Howl
Screech
Whisper
Whine
Gasp
Cough
Choke
Hack
Growl
Groan
Burp
Bawl
Breathe
Weep
Slurp
Guzzle
Hiccup
Scoff
Rasp
Wheeze
Coo
Kiss
Snort
Click
Sigh
Moan
Whinny
Woof
Laugh
Giggle
Pop
Pah
Moo
Mumble
Snuzzle
Snigger

50 World Leaders

Alexander the Great
Julius Caesar
Fidel Castro
Winston Churchill
Emperor Hirohito
Boadicea
Adolf Hitler
Saddam Hussein
Helmut Kohl
Nikita Khrushchev
Lenin
Nelson Mandela
Karl Marx
Bernito Mussolini
Napoleon Boneparte
Benazir Bhutto
Joseph Stalin
Margaret Thatcher
Leon Trotsky
Jesus Christ
Boris Yeltsin
George Bush
Pope Benedict
George Washington
Martin Luther King
Tariq Aziz
Constantine
Mahatma Ghandi
President Chirac
Charlemagne
William the Conqueror
Charles de Gaulle
Moses
Golda Meir
Benjamin Disraeli
Buddha
Hammurabi
Queen Hatshepsut
Augustus Caesar
Lech Walesa
Mikhail Gorbachev
Mao Zedong
David Levy
Confucius
John Wesley
Pope John Paul II
Dalai Lama
Empress Theodora
Chairman Mao
Flavius Tiberius

50 Political Parties

Liberal
Conservative
Whig
Labour
Liberal-Democrat
Green Party
British Nationalist Party
Republican
National Front
Tory
Nazi Party
Democrat
Communist
Humanist
Socialist
European People's Party
Social-Democrat
Confederate
National Party
Socialist Workers
Irish Republican Socialist
Popular Front
Christian Democrats
People's Party
Democratic Unionist Party
Plaid Cymru
Respect
Scottish National Party
Sinn Féin
Ulster Unionist
Britannia Party
British National
Chapter 88
Christian People's Alliance
England First Party
Freedom Party
Greenpeace UK
Imperial Party
Monster Raving Loony Party
Rainbow Dream Ticket Party
Red Action
Black Panther
Centrist Reform Party
Freedom Alliance
Solidarity
Friends of the Earth
New Alliance
General People's Congress
Workers International Vanguard League
Win Party

50 Places to have Fun

Cinema
Pub
Greyhound stadium
Restaurant
Beach
Night club
Swimming pool
Gym
Living room
Park
School playground
Canoe club
Ice-ring
Brothel
Café
Holiday camp
Horse racing track
Crazy golf
Bingo
Theatre
Bedroom
Football field
Boating lake
Disco
Adventure playground
Pot-holing expedition
Zoo
Cruise ship
Bowling alley
Skating rink
Comedy club
Golf course
Garden
Speedway
Ski slopes
Yacht club
Cliff-face
Rugby ground
Olympic stadium
Sand-pit
Amusement arcade
Theme park
Absailing centre
Tennis court
Running track
Pitch and putt
Wine bar
City farm
Caving expedition
Museum

50 Houses of Detention

Devil's Island
Alcatraz
Hull
Château d'If
Angola
Tower of London
Atlanta Fedral Penitentiary
Nottingham
The Clink
Attica
Eastern State Penitentiary
Ashfield
Dartmoor
Folsom State Prison
Wormwood Scrubs
Leavenworth
Bedford
Dover
McNeil Island
Holloway
San Quentin
Chelmsford
Sing Sing
Pentonville
Full Sutton
The King's Bench
Exeter
Robben Island
Lubyanka
The Bastille
Grendon
Spandau
Fleet
Newgate
Camp Crame
Kingston
Kingston Penitentiary
Wandsworth
Isla Isabela
Vacaville
The Mount
Butyrka
Lancaster Castle
Whitemoor
Manchester
Parkhurst
Colditz
Stock Heath
The Verne
Warren Hill

50 Traditional Cocktails

The Apple Jack Rabbit
Blue Devil
Cecil Pick-Me-Up
Depth Charge
Earthquake
Fallen Angel
Grand Slam
H. and H.
Ichbién
Jabberwocky
Kicker
Charlie Lindbergh
The Magnolia Blossom
New York
Sex on the Beach
Oh Henry!
Pall Mall
Prohibition
Rattlesnake
Temptation
Union Jack
Vermouth and Curaco
White Way
Xanthia
Yellow Rattler
Absinthe Drip
Brainstorm
Corpse Reviver No. 1
Dolly O' Dare
Eye Opener
Fifty-Fifty
Gasper
Hanky Panky
The 100%
The Judge
Knickerbocker Special
Little Devil
Martini Dry
The Nose-Dive
Oriental
Pink Lady
Quarter Deck
Rock and Rye
Satan's Whiskers
White Zombie
T. N. T.
Velocity
Whizz Doodle
X. Y. Z.
Zaza

50 Gods and Goddesses	50 Holy Days
Mayan	St. Patrick's Day
Anubis	Good Friday
Luna	Easter Sunday
Allah	Shavot
Ceres	Day of Pentecost
Thoth	Christmas Day
Pan	Diwali
Poseidon	Trinity Sunday
Shiva	Corpus Christi
Vishnu	Tisha B'Av
Amun-Ra	Assumption Day
Jehovah	Eid-ul-Fitr
Odin	Rosh Hashanah
Silvanus	Ramadân
Flora	Yom Kippur
Apollo	Succot
Hephaistos	Thanksgiving Day
Ahura Mazda	Solemnity of Mary, Mother of God
Attis	Days of Repentance
Artemis	Shemini Atzeret
Cupid	Simchat Torah
Gaia	Makar Sankrant
Priapus	All Saints Day
Ormuzd	Pentecost Monday
Proserpina	St. Andrew's Day
Cybele	Rei-sai
Isis	Advent Sunday
Ishtar	Hanukkah
Cerberus	Ascension Day
Hades	Eid-ul-Adha
Athena	Lent
Venus	Maundy Thursday
Aphrodite	Rogation Sunday
Krishna	Yom Hashoah
Juno	St. George's Day
Ares	Holi
Serapis	Easter Monday
Osiris	Palm Sunday
Antlered	Purim
Persephone	Shrove Tuesday
Durga	Tu B'Shevat
Loki	Ash Wednesday
Thor	Islamic New Year
Mars	Guru Nanek
Demeter	Epiphany
Tezcatlipoca	All Soul's Day
Ra	Shichigosan
Astarte	Annunciation
Pluto	Candlemas
Ge	Passion Sunday

50 Vitamins, Minerals and Nutrients

Calcium	E101
Cholecalciferol (Vitamin D)	E515
Pyridoxine (Vitamin B6)	E529
Phosphorus	E553(b)
Cobalamine (Vitamin B12)	E104
Pentothenic acid (Vitamin B5)	E621
Creatine	E626
Magnesium	E640
Ascorbic acid (Vitamin C)	E107
Choline	E120
Folic acid (Vitamin B8)	E905
Tocopherol (Vitamin E)	E913
Selenium	E122
Chromium	E100
5 HTP	E585
Retinol (Vitamin A)	E303
L-Methionine	E110
Fluorine	E319
Menadione (Vitamin K)	E440(b)
Iron	E4120
Zinc	E469
Omega-6 Primrose oil	E123
L-Phenylalanine	E200
Potassium	E292
Thiamin (Vitamin B1)	E102
Riboflavin (Vitamin B2)	E262
Sodium	E150(a)
Amino acids	E228
Biotin (Vitamin B7)	E124
Cyanocobalamin	E637
L-Lysine	E127
Copper	E140
Manganese	E133
Cod Liver oil	E142
Niacin (Vitamin B3)	E161(g)
Adenine (Vitamin B4)	E162
P-aminobenzoic acid (Vitamin B10)	E171
L-carnitine (Vitamin B11)	E174
Orotic acid	E199
Pangamic acid (Vitamin B15)	E181
Amygdalin (Vitamin B17)	E9120
Essential fatty acids (Vitamin F)	E967
Bioflavonoids (Vitamin P)	E931
Allantoine	E1444
Folate (Vitamin B9)	E1518
Linoletic acid	E341
Iodine	E3120
Molybdenum	E357
Omega-3 fish oil	E579
Inositol	E553(a)

The right column falls under the heading:

50 Food Colours and Additives

50 Herbs and Spices

Basil
Zedoary
Caraway
Wintergreen
Balsam
Cinnamon
Vervain
Chilli pepper
Sage
Pennyroyal
Marjoram
Coriander
Dill
Fennel
Cayenne
Ginger
Horseradish
Lemon grass
Cumin
Mint
Saffron
Asafoetida
Thyme
Mustard
Angelica
Nutmeg
Caper
Paprika
Elecampane
Parsley
Bay leaf
Wasabi
Tansy
Fenugreek
Pepper
Rosemary
Khus Khus
Sandlewood
Daun Salam
Sarsaparilla
Tarragon
Bergamot
Turmeric
Vanilla
Garlic
Ylang-Ylang
Spearmint
Cloves
Nasturtium
Water Dropwort

50 Theatre Styles

Musical Theatre
Rock Opera
Theatre for Social Change
Comedy
Postmodern Theatre
Post Style Theatre
Mummer's Plays
Farce
Regional Theatre
Pantomime
Romantic Comedy
Comedy of Situation
Broadway Theatre
Comedy of Manners
Political Theatre
Proletcult Theatre
Commedia Dell'arte
Musical Comedy
Natya
Repertory Theatre
Mime
Who-Done-Its
Opera
Black Comedy
Physical Theatre
Melodrama
Tragedy
Tragicomedy
Summer Stock Theatre
Community Theatre
Reader's Theatre
Temple Dance
Domestic Drama
Passion Plays
Fantasy
Morality Play
Dinner Theatre
Off-Broadway
Theatre of the Absurd
Existentialist Theatre
Meta-Theatre
Grand Guignol
Street Theatre
West End Theatre
Mystery Plays
Improvisational Theatre
Fringe Festival
Vanguard
Art Deco Style Theatre
In-Yer-Face Theatre

50 Things you might find at the Bus Stop

Litter
Pram
Bus shelter
Bus timetable
Girl
Girl's satchel
Chewing gum on the floor
Old newspaper
Baby
Dropped dummy
Pavement
Advertisements
Woman
Woman's handbag
Old woman
Shopping basket
Ticket machine
Tree
Leaves
Graffiti
Manhole cover
Railings
Bush
Man
Man's briefcase
Old man
Roadside
Parked car
Bus lane markings
Boy
Boy's bike
Night bus timetable
View
Litter bin
Ticket inspector
Bench
Lamppost
Forgotten carrier bag
Left umbrella
Chip wrappers
Curb
Curb markings
Dropped hat
Man with sandwich board
Red route
Road works
Passers by
Hovering traffic warden
Small talk
Bus

50 Sweeteners

Jam
Saccharin
Honey
Syrup
Sucrose
Lemon juice
Lactose
Galactose
Cane sugar
Sugar beet
Malt sugar
Glucose
Icing sugar
Candied peel
Dextrose
Xylitol
Milk sugar
Fructose
Invert sugar
Demerara
Molasses
Treacle
Marmalade
Granulated sugar
Julep
Nectar
Mead
Metheglin
Lemon peel
Marzipan
Castor sugar
Jelly
Sucralose
Fruit juices
Maple syrup
Barley malt
Apartame
Stevia
Condensed milk
Neotame
Evaporated cane juice
Acesulflame-K
Rice syrup
Cyclamates
Licorice root
Refined sugar
Fructooligosaccharides
Amasake
Vegetable glycerin
Sorbitol

50 Packets of Crisps

Tayto
Walker's crisps
Smith's crisps
Pringles
Lay's Stax
Fritos
CCs
Doritos
Wotsits
Quavers
Monster Munch
Sensations
Potato Heads
Frazzles
Frisps
Smith's bacon fries
Brannigans
Phileas Fogg
Seabrook
Hola Hoops
McCoy's
Mini Cheddars
Skips
Go Ahead! crisps
Pipers crisps
Golden Wonder crisps
Jacob's crisps
Smith's scampi fries
Kettle crisps
Marks & Spencer crisps
Nik Naks
Tyrells
Roysters
Tesco crisps
Golden Lights
Golden Skins
Ringos
Wheat Crunchies
Chicksticks
Square crisps
Smith's cheese Moments
Pringles Mini crisps
Golden Wonder light crisps
Cheese Puffs
Discos
Nobby's crisps
Reh Hill crisps
Jacob's twiglets
Humdinger apple crisps
Mr. Porky Crackles

50 Types of Fuel

Wood
Colour gas
Pink paraffin
North Sea gas
Electricity
Petroleum
Oil
Diesel
Phosphoric acid
Fat
Methane gas
Kerosene
4 star petrol
Bituminous (soft coal)
Kindling
Liquified natural gas (LNG)
Coke
Gasoline
Alkaline
2 stroke
Marine diesel
Homefire ovals
Molton carbonate
Petrol
Esso blue
Anthracite (hard coal)
Gas oil
Red diesel
Solid oxide
3 star petrol
Bituminous sands
Briquettes
ARCO gas
Biodiesel
Peat
Aviation gasoline
Hydrogen
Liquefied petroleum gas (LPG)
Charcoal
Crude oil
Hydro
Jet kerosene
Oil shale
LPG
Natural gas
Firelogs
Coalite
Tar sands
LBL nuts
White gas

50 People that come to our Door

Postman
Water meter reader
Delivery boy
Christian worshippers
Carol singer
Burglar
'Penny for the guy' kids
Friends
Friendly neighbours
Door-to-door salesman
Maths tutor
Avon lady
Pizza delivery boy
Plumber
Coalman
'Rag and bone' man
Landscape garden salesman
Boyfriend
Builder
Electrical appliance delivery men
Bailiffs
Dustman
Jehovah's witness
Double-glazing salesman
Gas man
English tutor
Social worker
Someone playing 'knock-down-ginger'
Delivery man
Paper boy
Electrician
Parent
Football coupon man
Hari Krishna worshipper
Catalogue lady
Boy for his ball, kicked into your garden
Milkman
Electric meter reader
Complaining neighbours
Girlfriend
Indian curry delivery man
Painter and decorator
Leaflet distributor
Motorcycle messenger
Confidence trickster
Police officer
Re-cycling collectors
Landlord
Piano tutor
Midwife

50 Farm Crops

Oats
Runner beans
Beans
Cocksfoot
Barley
Sugar beet
Radishes
Turnip
Peaches
Meadow fescue
Sainfoin
Fodder cabbage
Maize
Wheat
Celery
Carrots
Brown mustard
Mangold
Potatoes
Rye
Cherries
Corn
Common wild oat
Fodder rape
Red Dutch clover
Tomatoes
Broccoli
Swede
Beetroot
Pears
Common reed
Fodder beet
Field beans
Plums
False-brome
Wood millet
Peas
White mustard
Lettuce
Marram
Cabbage
Oilseed rape
Sand couch
Kale
Brussels sprouts
Apples
Parsnip
Common vetch
Buckwheat
Lupin

50 Clergy Terms	**50 Clocks and Timepieces**
Bishop	Big Ben
Clergyman	Rolex
Christian ministry	Alarm clock
Dean	Wrist-watch
Holy orders	Wall clock
Lay minster	Mileometer
Liturgy	Fob-watch
Deacon	Astronomical clock (Prague)
Holy bible	Half-hunter
Absolution	Mantelpiece clock
Friar	Speedometer
Christian teachings	Stop-watch
Vicar	Grandfather clock
The church	Eastgate clock (Chester)
Parish	Taxi meter
Parson	Nurses fob watch
Rectory	Cuckoo clock
Priest	Salomon Coster clock
Prayer	Sundial
Baptism	Carriage clock
The Gospel	St. Mark's clock (Venice)
Pope	Bracelet watch
Cardinal	Clock/radio/clock
Doctrine	Pocket watch
Monk	Termo calendar clock
Canon law	Ahasuerus Fromanteel clock
Chaplain	CD/radio/alarm clock
Pastor	Digital clock
Diocese	Water clock
Abbot	The Four Liars (Cork)
Confirmation	Shelton clock
Congregation	Pendulum clock
Archbishop	Omega
Cloister	Accutron
Archdeacon	Jessop's clock (San Diego)
Parsonage	NBS-1 atomic clock
Curate	Cesium clock
Biblical teachings	Quartz clock
Parishioners	Projection clock
Pastoral	Swatch
House of Laity	Wells Cathedral clock (Wells)
Teaching of scripture	Antique clock
Penance	Huygens' clock
Doctrinal discipline	Longcase clocks
Church of England	Chronometer
Reverend	Table clock
Cathedral	Atomic clock
Genuflection	Moondial
Verger	Synchronome clock
Amen	The speaking clock

50 Nursery Rhymes

Baa baa black sheep
Dr. Foster
Goosey goosey gander
Hark, hark, the dogs do bark
I had a little nut tree
Hickory, dickory dock
Jack be nimble, Jack be quick
Little Bo-Peep
Georgie Porgie
Little Boy Blue
Humpty Dumpty
Little Polly Flinders
Bobby Shafto
Wee Willie Winkie
Mary had a little lamb
Ring-a-ring o' roses
Little Jack Horner
Mary, Mary, quite contrary
Lucy Locket lost her pocket
This little piggy went to market
Old King Cole
Hey diddle diddle
There was an old woman who lived in a shoe
Old Mother Hubbard
Jack Sprat
See-saw Margery Daw
Oranges and Lemons
Pat-a-cake, pat-a-cake, baker's man
Little Miss Muffet
Dance to your daddy
Twinkle, twinkle, little star
Polly put the kettle on
Ride a cockhorse to Banbury Cross
Yankie Doodle came to town
Little Tommy Tucker
Rub-a-dub dub
The Queen of Hearts
One, two, three, four, five
Simple Simon
Sing a song of sixpence
Pease pudding hot
Solomon Grundy
On the twelfth day of Christmas
The Grande Old Duke of York
The man in the moon
As I was going to St. Ives
There was a crooked man
Walky round the garden like a teddy bear
Tom, Tom, the piper's son
Pussy cat, pussy cat, where have you been?

50 Snakes

Grass snake
Boa Constrictor
Speckled Racer
Python
Red Diamond Rattlesnake
Wagler's Temple Pitviper
Sea snake
Ringed Snail-Eating snake
Tree Boa
Smooth snake
Texas Blind snake
European Asp
Water snake
Red-Tailed Racer
Common Milk snake
Cottonmouth
Sidewinder Viper
Puff Adder
Green Tree Python
Deadly Coral snake
King Cobra
Tree snake
Hamadryad
Slow worm
Mamba
Horned Viper
Ground snake
Anaconda
Spitting Cobra
Desert Viper
Burrowing Blindsnake
Sea Krait
Ornate Flying snake
Timber Rattlesnake
Black-Banded snake
Green snake
Africian Egg-Eating snake
Gaboon Viper
Monocled Cobra
Copperhead
Giant Madagascan Hognose
Grey-Banded King snake
Cornsnake
Western Long-nose
Green Anaconda
Californian King
Burmese Rock Python
Boomslang
Common EusasianViper
Whip snake

50 Things to put on a Shelf

Book
Ornament
CD
DVD
Video
Magazine
Cassette
Bottle
Jar
Doily
Clock
Ashtray
Fruit bowl
Radio
Pot
Hi-fi
Photoframe
Tin
Vase
Sculpture
Egg timer
Plant
Bowl
Condiments
Pens
Teapot
Papers
Lamp
Best crockery
Photo album
Book ends
Telephone
Pot pourie
Scanner
Jewellery box
Keys
Air freshener
Biscuit barrel
Toys
Camera
Saucepans
Tray
Printer
Games
Candle
Phone book
Sewing basket
Sunglasses
Sugar bowl
Spare change

50 Tacky Christmas Presents

Socks
Pants
Soap-on-a-rope
Brut aftershave
Simpson's socks
Comb for a bald man
Red polka-dot bow-tie
Cub scout diary
I love the '80's CD
Oven glove
Photo album
70's comedy compilation video
Shampoo for 'Him'
Family box of Quality Street chocolates
100 sports games on DVD
Glass crystal animal ornament
Tea towel set
Stapler and refill pack
Set of six £1 shop paint brushes
Scented candles from Barclays Bank
Magazine rack
Wicker bin
Set of brown flannels
Plaid pyjamas
Decorative plate from Cornwall
Oxfam Christmas card
Travel 'Scrabble'
Back scrubbing brush in the shape of a fish
Teapot table lighter
Willie warmer
Bath cubes
'I Love You Mummy' teddy
Paisley wash-kit bag
Marzipan
Marilyn Monroe wall clock
Set of 4 Harry Potter mugs
Spacehopper
Set of Ian Fleming's 'James Bond' novels
Plastic garlic crusher
China 'deer in the forest' ornament
Mantelpiece clock
Pouffe
3-piece bathroom set
Dog and cat shaped salt & pepper set
Plastic fruitbowl
3-slot wine rack
Doily
Mobile phone belt pouch
NYC cap
Talcum powder

50 Weird and wonderful Band Names

The Orange Cardigan
Death From Beyond 1979
God Speed You Black Emperor
Flock of Seagulls
The Presidents of the United States of America
A
The Yeah, Yeah, Yeahs
The The
Matching Moles
Albertos Y Los Trios Paranois
Scrapping Foetus Off the Wheel
JJ 42
Again Again
X-Ray Spex
Z Z Top
At the Drive In
UB40
And You Will Know Us by the Trail of Dead
L7
Orchestral Manoeuvres in the Dark
Curiosity Killed the Cat
3T
Half Man, Half Biscuit
Zig and Zag
BBM
A-HA
Yes
Trashcan Sinatras
80's Matchbox B-Line Disaster
Gaye Bikers on Acid
Me Me Me
Gay Dad
Younger Younger 28's
Pavement
Shut Up and Dance
The Band
Cud
!!!
Mr. Blobby
10,000 Maniacs
Wubble-U
Herman's Hermits
The Dead Kennedy's
Dave Dee, Dozy, Beaky, Mick and Tich
4-Skins
Test Icicles
S-J
Crispy Ambulance
Y & T
A Homeboy, A Hippie and A Funki Dredd

50 Bands, Groups and Musicians beginning with 'U'

Ultravox
U2
The Undertones
Ugly Kid Joe
UB40
UFO
UK Decay
Urban Cookie Crew
Usher
Utah Saints
Uk Subs
Tracy Ullman
Ultrasonic
Ultra Vivid Scene
Umboza
Underworld
UHF
Midge Ure
Up Yer Ronson
Upsetters
Utopia
UK Players
Uriah Heap
US3
Urban Soul
U.T.F.O.
UBM
UK Apachi
Ultimate Chaos
Ultra High
Piero Umiliani
Unation
Ultra
Unbelievable Truth
Uncanny Alliance
Ultramarine
Ultrasound
Undertakers
Undisputed Truth
U96
Unit Four Plus Two
Upside Down
Urban All Stars
Urge Overkill
Usura
Urban Shakedown
Unitone Rockers
Unique 3
Uncle Sam
UK Mixmasters

50 Sayings

The early bird catches the worm
Look before you leap
Never judge a book by its cover
You can't get blood out of a stone
A stitch in time saves nine
Fools rush in where angels fear to tread
You can't make an omelette without breaking eggs
Beauty is only skin deep
An apple a day keeps the doctor away
Never a borrower nor a lender be
Absence makes the heart grow fonder
As plain as the nose on your face
He who laughs last laughs longest
Here today, gone tomorrow
Act your age and not your shoe size
Strike while the iron is hot
Out of sight, out of mind
Money can't buy you love
You can't run with the hare and hunt with the hounds
Failure teaches success
If you can't do the time, don't do the crime
I'm a poet and I didn't know it
If you want a job done well do it yourself
He who hesitates is lost
April showers bring forth May flowers
Bad news travels fast
The tailor maketh the man
The pen is mightier than the sword
You can't teach an old dog new tricks
All's well that ends well
Good things come to those that wait
Faith can move mountains
A man's home is his castle
Patience is a virtue
One swallow does not a summer make
You can't make a silk purse out of a sow's ear
Barking dogs seldom bite
Cleanliness is next to godliness
Do as I say and not as I do
A nod's as good as a wink to a blind horse
The farther they climb, the harder they fall
Ignorance is bliss
Good fences make good neighbours
You can't have your cake and eat it
The best things in life are free
Two heads are better than one
Great minds think alike
Too slow to catch a cold
It's not over till it's over
Easier said than done

50 Things to be found in a Victorian Kitchen

Potato peeler
Cerebos table salt
Wringer
Larder
Sausage mincing machine
Dolly peg
Washboard
Bryant & May's flaming fuses
Fry's cocoa
Carpet sweeper
Brasso
Bovril fluid beef
Treadle sewing machine
Alfred Bird's custard powder
Coal
Jacob & Co. cream crackers
Tub
Edwards' desiccated soup
Copper pans
Crosse & Blackwell anchovy paste
Chamber pot
Lipton loose tea
Bucket
Lifebuoy soap
Water filter
McCall & Co. ox tongues
Range
Colman's mustard
Lark spit
Rose's lime cordial
Sugar nippers
Cadbury's cocoa essence
Marmalade cutter
Sinclair's baking powder
Spice tin
Coomb's eureka self-raising flour
Mangle
Mrs. Beeton's cookery book
Water pump
Rinso
Pantry
Cherry blossom boot polish
Bed warming pan
Water-filled iron
Oil lamp
Scullery
Cast iron pots
White glazed pottery
Tin mugs
Sunlight soap

50 Primary Schools in London	50 Paris Street Names
Jubilee	Avenue de L'Opera
Sir Thomas Abbney	Rue de Rivoli
William Patten	Avenue des Champs Elysees
Avondale Park	Rue de Caire
London Fields	Boulevard de Sebastopol
St. Cuthbert with St. Matthias C of E	Rue Saint Paul
Walnut Tree Walk	Parc du Champ de Mars
Newington Green	Q. D'orsay
Our Lady of Victories RC	Rue Charlemagne
Highbury Quadrant	Boulevard Saint Germain
Canonbury	Place Daphine
Ambler	Boulevard des Invalides
English Martyrs Junior	Rue de Clignancourt
Fox	Place de L'Opera
Fleet	Boulevard Montmartre
Victory	Rue Lepic
Osmani	Rue de Petit Musc
Paddington Green	Boulevard Diderot
Kobi Nazrul	Pont Sully
Queensbridge Infants	Place Pigalle
St. Francis of Assisi	Boulevard des Batignolles
Smithy Street	Avenue Friedland
Vauxhall	Boulevard Houssmann
St. Joan of Arc	Rue de Berri
Michael Faraday	Boulevard Raspail
Oratory RC	Place Blanche
Hague	Rue de Lyon
St. John the Divine JMI	Avenue de République
St. Mary's the Angel RC	Place d'est D'orves
Ivydale	Avenue de Wagram
Johanna	Place Charles de Gaulle
St. Vincent de Paul RC	Parvis Notre Dame
Ashmole	Pont Alexandre III
Bigland Green	Place de la Concorde
Charles Dickens	Rue des Jeuneure
Hill House International	Quai de la Mégisserie
Rhyl	Rue Saint Dominique
St Paul's with St Michael's C of E JMI	Boulevard Poissonniére
Wilberforce	Avenue Jean Jaures
Christchurch Benedick C of E	Rue La Fayette
Harry Gosling	Rue Puperre
Copenhagen	Avenue Trudaine
De Beauvoir	Rue de Bellefond
Dulwich Hamlet	Boulevard des Capucines
Hermitage	Place des Victoires
Snowfields	Rue Coquilliére
Tufnell Park	Rue Soufflot
St Aloysius RC	Rue Piat
Barrow Hill Junior	Boulevard Saint Martin
Crampton	Rue Notre Dame de Nazareth

50 Biggest things on Earth	**50 Dead Pop Stars**
Elephant	Freddie Mercury
Russia	John Lennon
Microsoft	Les Grey
Empire State Building	Brian Conolly
Pacific Ocean	'Mama' Cass
Blue whale	Frank Sinatra
Michael Jackson	Jerry Garcia
A0 paper size	Nat King Cole
JK Rowling book sales	Lee Brilleaux
Pyramid	Johnny Cash
Sahara Desert	Gene Vincent
Bird flu	Marc Bolan
Red double-decker bus	John Bonham
Madonna	Joe Strummer
Big Mac	Janis Joplin
Yotta	Micky Finn
Greenland	Sonny Bono
HSBC	Roy Orbison
Melchior bottle of champagne	Nico
Marilyn Monroe	Sammy Davis Junior
Boeing 747	Joey Ramone
Asia	Jeff Buckley
Royal octavo book size	Tim Buckley
Mount Everest	Paul Kossoff
Elton John	Karen Carpenter
World War Two	Kurt Cobain
Lake Superior	Sam Cooke
Great Dane	Sid Vicious
Dodecagon	King Curtis
17½" men's shirt collar size	Marvin Gaye
£50 note	Kirsty MacColl
Statue of Liberty	Lowell George
Double bass	Jimi Hendrix
Marks & Spencer	Buddy Holly
Christmas	Michael Hutchence
The Loch Ness monster	Brian Jones
Tom Cruise	Louis Armstrong
The Harrods sale	Joe Meek
Stretch limo	Dennis Wilson
Hollywood	Keith Moon
Christianity	Jim Morrison
Tarantula	'The Notorious' B.I.G
Poverty	Elvis Presley
London	Otis Redding
The Titanic	J. P. Richardson
The Olympic Games	Tupac Shakur
Cancer	Vivian Stanshall
Red-wood tree	Richie Valens
Dessert spoon	Dean Martin
Soldier ant	Stevie Ray Vaughan

50 Smallest things on Earth

Ant
Atom
Grain of sand
Farthing
Full stop
Raindrop
Mini skirt
Blackcurrant
Finger nail
Bacteria
Baked bean
Tick
Teabag
Door knob
Grape pip
Mite
Mini disc
Font size point 4
Tiddlywink
Dust
Nail
Daisy
Polly Pocket
Pea
Peppercorn
Bullet
Sweetcorn
Keyhole
Peanut
Eyelash
Earring
Drawing pin
Toenail clipping
Egg cup
Crumb
Paper clip
Needle
Orange pip
Student bank account
Acorn
Maggot
Crisp
Washer
Wasp
Screw
Belly button
Plectrum
Button badge
Dice
Spoonful of sugar

50 Forms of Greeting

Hi
Watcha
Mingala ba
Good day
Bonjour
Bula
Alright?
Konnichiwa
Here's looking at ya
Halito
Geezer
Sawubona
Man
Hola
Dobar dan
Morning
Hejsan
Welcome
Salaam alikam
Talofa
Jambo
Privet
Bawoni
Greetings
Prijatno
How are ya?
Wimafa shoo
Ni hao
Ciao
Guten tag
What ho
Hei
Wassuup!
Poolah
Gamarjobat
Yo
Shalom
Luv
Keeping well?
Namaste
How's life treating you then?
Look what the cat dragged in
Dzien dobry
Talk of the devil
How you going
'ello
Zdravo
Giv me five
Annyong
Nunga

50 Roman Numerals

XX
II
M
IV
V
CC
CD
I
LI
DCCC
MM
III
VI
X
X̲
IX
LX
LXXX
CVI
CIV
D
DIX
VIII
CM
V̲
D̲
VII
XXX
C
XL
L
DC
LXX
XC
DCC
M̲
DIV
DXX
CV
MLI
V̲IX
LXXVII
CDXXIX
DCCCLXXX
M̲DXC
XIX
DCXLIII
X̲XXX
XCIX
XXIX

50 Things to think about when playing Centre Forward

'Heads,' we kick-off
Here they come
That blonde defender looks nice
Hope my bum looks good in these shorts
God! I'm knackered already
Good crowd this week
I count three ambulances
That stand needs repainting
Not another advert for haemorrhoid cream
Did I leave the immersion on?
What if I miss an easy goal?
It's getting chilly; glad I'm wearing my thermals
Did I pay my gas bill?
Good tackle Cheasley
I'm sure that defender just smiled at me
Haven't these people got anything better to chant?
Should I buy that new iPod?
Wonder what me partner Simon's up to
I count four sparrows
Am I going to be playing here every Sunday?
Those clouds look ominous
That defender's following me
Must concentrate
Interesting hot-dog stand
Simon said he'd be back at five
Good, close tackle from that blond defender
Hope I don't get blocked-in
I'll be the last one inside if it suddenly rains
Getting thirsty now
That defender definitely smiled at me
Two ice-cream vans…is that unlucky
Is that Timothy in the red top?
Simon was out very late last night
Oh, gosh! That defender's ran right into me
He's put his hand up my shorts!
Must start going to the gym more often
How come the referee knows where Simon was
-last night
What's he staring at
That defender's just slipped me his phone number
There goes ol' bandy legs
Those peppers are repeating on me
Did I close down the internet?
Uh-oh, ere comes a 'winger!'
Shit…-well you try better!
Now it is raining
Hope I've not pulled a tendon
Come to think of it wasn't the referee's whistle in
-the back of Simon's car last week!
I don't feel like playing centre forward next week
Can't wait to get in those communal showers with
-that defender

240

50 'In' and 'On' Phrases	50 Liqueurs
In the pink	Advocaat
On the ball	Bailey's Irish Cream
In two minds	Benedictine D. O. M.
On a roll	Raki
In at nine	Pernod
On the game	Sambuca Luxardo
In a tiz	Bols Blue Curacao
On my life	Cachaca Yipioca
In the red	Stones Ginger wine
On the make	Green Chartreuse
In good time	Malibu
On good form	Cointreau
In one room	Drambuie
On the stage	Freezomint
In the oven	Galliano
On at last	Amaretto
In and out	Grand Marnier Reserve Flacon
On the spot	Irish Mist
In for it	Marie Bizzard Crème de Cacau dark
On the rocks	Ouzo
In the doghouse	Ricard
On-going	Saki
In his cups	Southern Comfort
On the job	Tia Maria
In-between	Van der Hum
On and off	Xanath
In a jam	Aquavit Linie
On and on	Bramwell
In the throes	Crème de Menthe white I. Legout
On my own	De Kuyper cherry brandy
In the running	Eau de Vie Fraise Kirsch
On the town	Frangelico
In at night	Grappa Julia
On the side	Jägermeister
In mutual favour	Kahlua
On something	King's Ginger
In the market	Limoncello Luxardo
On the way	Mandarin Napoleon
In itself	Nocello
On top form	Pisco
In excelsis	Royal Mint chocolate
On the tracks	Somerset Royal
In front of	Tia Luso
On the bench	Wallace
In need of	Watermelon Monin
On for tonight	Midori
In loco parentis	Calvados
On every corner	Cherry Herring
In situ	Arak
On your side	Lochanora

50 Women Wimbledon Players	50 Bicycles
Martina Hingis	Penny-farthing
Virginia Wade	Boneshaker
Venus Williams	Mountain bike
Maria Sharapova	Unicycle
Serena Williams	Tandem
Steffi Graf	Raleigh bike
Lindsay Davenport	BMX bike
Jana Novotna	Pedal cycle
Conchita Martinez	Push bike
Martina Navratilova	Velocipede
Amelie Mauresmo	Ordinary
Chris Evert	Chopper
Evonne Goolagong	Safety
Billie Jean King	Racer
Margaret Smith	Tourist
Ann Haydon Jones	Roadster
Maria Bueno	Randem
Karen Susman	Monocycle
Angela Mortimer	Tricycle
Jennifer Capriati	Trike
Althea Gibson	Quadricycle
Gabriela Sabatini	Motorized bicycle
Shirley Fry	Cycle rickshaw
Louise Brough	Trishaw
Maureen Connolly	Sociable
Doris Hart	White's improved bicycle
Margaret Osbourne	Cooly tricycle
Justine Henin Hardenne	5-speed Peugeot
Pauline Betz	Draisine
Alice Marble	Hobbyhorse
Helen Wills Moody	Pedespeed
Dorothy Round	Two-wheeler
Helen Hull Jacobs	Duplex Excelsior tricycle
Cilly Aussem	Cycledrome
Kitty Godfree	Exercise bike
Suzanne Lenglen	Vélo-douche
Dorothy Douglass Lambert-Chambers	Eiffel Tower bicycle
Ethel Larcombe	Samuel's patent hand crank velocipede
Dora Boothby	American velocipede
Charlotte Cooper Sterry	Motor bicycle
Kerry Reid	Steam tricycle
Petr Korda	Criterium racer
May Sutton	Triple tandem
Muriel Robb	Pedicab
Blanche Bingley Hillyard	Kingcycle bean
Lottie Dod	French velocar
Helen Rice	Time-trial bike
Hana Mandlikova	Cannondale SH600, hybrid
Maud Watson	Ladies bike
Kim Clisters	Kiddie bike

50 Female Characters from History

Jane Austen
Nancy Astor
Margaret Thatcher
Edith Cavell
Cleopatra
Lady Jane Grey
Diana, Princess of Wales
Elizabeth I
Florence Nightingale
Margot Fonteyn
Elizabeth Fry
Emily Brontë
Lady Godiva
Mrs. Beeton
Nell Gwyn
Emma Hamilton
Queen Victoria
Virginia Woolf
Joan of Arc
Amy Johnson
Laura Ashley
Lilian Baylis
Vera Lynn
Flora Macdonald
Marie Curie
Madame Tussaud
Mary, Queen of Scots
Anne Boleyn
Salome
Mary I
Emily Pankhurst
Boudicca
Marie Stopes
Elizabeth II
Elizabeth Garrett Anderson
Queen Anne
Annie Besant
Maria Theresa
Enid Blyton
Barbara Castle
Gertrude Jekyll
Elizabeth David
George Eliot
Mary Quant
Margot Fonteyn
Barbara Hepworth
Iris Murdoch
Marie Antoinette
Dorothy L. Sayers
Isabella of Castile

50 Facial Expressions

Smile
Pull a long face
Poker face
Jeer
Grin
Look shocked
Frown
Suck in one's cheeks
Look surprised
Leer
Wrinkle your nose
Pout
Shake your head
Laugh
Go all shy
Cry
Mope
Look tired
Groan
Raise an eyebrow
Rage
Look startled
Suck one's teeth
Wink
Stick out your tongue
Blow a kiss
Look forlorn
Whince
Bat your eyelids
Scowl
Look down your nose
Sneer
Cock an ear
Smack your lips
Scoff
Look frightened
Nod your head
Go all silly
Snap
Look disgusted
Screw up your face
Growl
Smirk
Turn up one's nose
Look hurt
Weep
Huff
Jut your chin out
Turn one's face away
Look cross

50 Tropical Marine Fish

Banded Glowfish
Yellow-tailed Damselfish
Catalina Goby
Long-nosed Butterflyfish
Coral Beauty
Foxface
Clown Triggerfish
Koran Angelfish
Marine Betta
Common Clownfish
Blue-tailed Damselfish
Domino
Powder Blue Surgeon
Regal Tang
Threadfin Butterflyfish
Maroon Clownfish
Black-backed Butterflyfish
Blue Devil
Humbug
Copper-band Butterflyfish
Bicolor Cherub
Firefish
Clown Wrasse
Wreckfish
Birdmouth Wrasse
Cowfish
Royal Chromis
Pakistani Butterflyfish
Cherub Angelfish
Rock Beauty
Lionfish
Blue-ringed Angelfish
Cloudy Damselfish
Picasso Triggerfish
Pearlscale Butterflyfish
Black Neon Damselfish
Yellow-headed Jawfish
Wimplefish
Black Triggerfish
Cleaner Wrasse
Spotted Cardinalfish
Mandarinfish
Long-nosed Hawkfish
Midas Blenny
Pantherfish
Eibl's Angelfish
Yellow Tang
Yellow Seahorse
Tompot Blenny
Blue Chromis

50 Collective Nouns and Group Names

Flock of sheep
Stud of mares
Bevy of quails
Covey of grouse
Clamour of rooks
Cast of hawks
Herd of cattle
Litter of cubs
Muster of peacocks
Parliament of owls
Pack of hounds
Rout of wolves
Pod of whiting
Pride of lions
Rag of colts
Run of poultry
School of whales
Shoal of herring
Skein of geese
Skulk of foxes
Sleuth of bears
Flight of swallows
Down of hares
Clowder of cats
Paddling of ducks
Barren of mules
Brace of bucks
Cete of badgers
Charm of goldfinches
Chattering of choughs
Colony of gulls
Desert of lapwings
Exaltation of larks
Fall of woodcocks
String of racehorses
Covert of coots
Dule of doves
Gang of elks
Host of sparrows
Kindle of kittens
Labour of moles
Leap of leopards
Nest of rabbits
Plump of wildfowl
Murder of crows
Catch of fish
Sounder of boars
Swarm of insects
Troop of kangaroos
Drove of oxen

50 Greyhound Racing Trainers	50 Some Historical Events
Bobby Burls	World War I – 1914-1918
Wilf France	September 11th attack, New York – 2001
Barbara Tomkins	Neil Armstrong lands on the moon – 1969
John Coleman	Edmund Hilary conquers Mount Everest – 1953
Barney O'Connor	Vikings raid Britain – 700+
Denis Hannafin	Black Death kills over 30% of Europeans - 1345+
John Honeysett	First writen evidence, Mesopotamia – 2500 BC+
Tom Johnston	Printing introduced in Europe – 1456
Jack Hedley	Vietnam War – 1945-1975
George Curtis	Magellan sails around the world – 1517-22
Joe Pickering	Hiroshima bombing – 1945
Jack Harvey	Homo Sapiens first appeared – 50,000 BC
Norman Chambers	Newton discovers gravity – 1665
Ray Wilkes	Charles I executed – 1649
Jim Singleton	London's population in 1600 equals 200,000
Pam Heasman	Hebrews settle in Canaan – 2000 BC+
Norman Oliver	World economic depression – 1929-33
Gunner Smith	140,000 slaves a year shipped to America – 18[th]C.
Brian Clemenson	Pilgrim fathers sail to New England, – 1620
Leslie Reynolds	American Civil War – 1861-1865
John McGee	Life emerges from the sea – 400,000,000 BC
Jim Syder	Romans invade Briton – 63+
Ernie Wiley	Angles and Saxons settle in England – 407
Noreen Collin	Muhammad founds Islam – 590+
Frank Melville	1st. King of England, Egbert (Saxon) – 829-839
Norman Merchant	First real man emerges – 5,000,000 BC
Tom Reily	The Incas emerge in Peru – 1400+
Nora McEllistrim	World War II – 1939-1945
Adam Jackson	Napoleonic Empire falls – 1815
Paddy Keane	Adam and Eve expelled from the Garden of Eden
John Basset	-4003 BC
George Waterman	Berlin Wall torn down – 1989-1990
Paddy Gordon	Salem witchcraft trials – 1692
Clare Orton	Sinking of the Titanic – 1912
Syd Mann	1st. war recorded, between Egyptians – 3100 BC
Arthur Hitch	Chernobyl nuclear disaster – 1986
Dal Hawkesley	Spanish Civil War – 1936-1939
Nick Savva	Greeks hold 1st Olympic Games, Olympia – 776
Terry O'Sullivan	-BC
Brian Jay	Gunpowder invented in China – 1044
Ray Peacock	Doomsday book published – 1086
Linda Jones	Pharaoh's buried in Valley of the Kings – 1600
Charles Lister	-BC+
Terry Duggan	Great fire of London – 1666
Les Parry	American Goldrush – 1848
Jimmy Jowett	Man learns to farm – 12,000 BC
Bob Thomson	English Civil War – 1625-49
Molly Redpath	Darwin's 'Origin of the Species' published – 1859
Nora Gleeson	Martin Luther King delivers 'I Have A Dream
Colin West	-Speech' – 1967
	Collapse of the Soviet Union – 1991
	Nelson Mandela elected 1st. Black President of
	-South Africa – 1994
	War of the Roses – 1461
	Falklands War – 1982

50 Aesop Fables

The Wolf and the Lamb
The Dog and the Shadow
The Lion's Share
The Man and the Serpent
The Town Mouse and the Country Mouse
The Fox and the Crow
The Ass and the Lapdog
The Lion and the Mouse
The Frogs Desiring a King
The Swallow and the Other Birds
The Hares and the Frogs
The Wolf and the Kid
The Woodman and the Serpent
The Fox and the Stork
The Jay and the Peacock
The Frog and the Ox
The Bat, the Bird and the Beasts
The Hart and the Hunter
The Man and the Wood
The Dog and the Wolf
The Fox and the Grapes
The Horse, Hunter and Stag
The Peacock and Juno
The Fox and the Lion
The Lion and the Statue
The Ant and the Grasshopper
The Tree and the Reed
The Fox and the Cat
The Wolf in Sheep's Clothing
The Man and the Wooden God
The Fisher
The Shepherd's Boy
The Young Thief and his Mother
The Nurse and the Wolf
The Tortoise and the Birds
The Two Crabs
The Ass in the Lion's Skin
The Two Fellows and the Bear
The Two Pots
The Four Oxen and the Lion
The Fisher and the Little Fish
Avaricious and Envious
The Crow and the Pitcher
The Goose with the Golden Eggs
The Labourer and the Nightingale
The Wind and the Sun
The Fox without a Tail
The Hare and the Tortoise
The Bundle of Sticks
The Eagle and the Arrow

50 Animal Homes

Bird nest
Fox earth
Badger sett
Rabbit warren
Beaver lodge
Bat roost
Sheep fold
Dog kennel
Horse stable
Lion den
Gopher burrow
Otter holt
Grey squirrel drey
Bear cave
Owl hole
Ant hill
Bee hive
Mole burrow
Spider web
Wasp byke
Snake nest
Chicken coop
Dove cote
Eagle erie
Tiger lair
Hare form
Woodpecker tree hole
Pigsty
Termite mound
Cattle barn
Prairie dog burrow
Wolf den
Cat lair
Worm hole
Gorilla nest
Kangaroo pouch
Duck pond
Game bird covert
Morey eel cave
Rat nest
Skunk burrow
Red squirrel hole
Mouse hole
Goat pen
Cow shed
Jackal den
Skunk nest
Pigeon loft
Rabbit hutch
Hen coop

50 Rooms

Attic
Kitchen
Living room
Study
Bedroom
Drawing room
Lean-to
Stockroom
Dining room
Utility room
Hall
Smoking room
Pantry
Billiard room
Sitting room
Vestibule
Bathroom
Store room
Loft
Music room
Ballroom
Library
Computer room
Staff room
Conservatory
Basement
Galley
Guest room
Orangery
Front room
Sun lounge
Lounge
Classroom
Parlour
Washhouse
Boudoir
Tea room
Nursery
Office
Back room
Games room
Changing room
Chat room
Hotel room
Scullery
War room
Box room
Cloakroom
Larder
Cellar

50 Things in a Forest

Deer
Trees
Badger
Owl
Worms
Poacher
Fox
Stoat
Litter
Rabbit
Streaker
Beetles
Trails
Bushes
Hiker
Campers
Leaves
Game keeper
Insects
Mouse
Horse rider
Bird watcher
Tracker
Wild flowers
Mole
Shrew
Wanted criminal
Weasel
Sunshine
Moss
Rat
Woodpecker
Rain
Stream
Bluebells
Earth
Escaped convict
Lichen
Squirrel
Old hunting lodge
Picnickers
Fruit
Acorns
Elk
Blackbird
Abandoned Norman church
Rocks
Bees
Finches
Wolf

50 Things to Drop

Anchor
A clanger
An easy catch
In on the neighbours
Something into the conversation
In for tea
A line
Mother-in-law-s best china
A bomb
Someone in it
On someone from a great height
Kick
Off
And do 50 press-ups
One's trousers
A glove
A penny
A player from the team
An artist from the record company
A glass
A vase
Your keys down a drain
Your wallet
Your gaze
One's guard
Your head in shame
Your concentration
The ball
Your gun
Someone off
A plumb-line
Anything you're doing
It in the post
Everything
2, pearl 1
Shields
Shot
The Dead Donkey
In nursery
Them over enemy lines
The weakest one
A hint
Goal
By
Round for a natter
Supplies
Off a parcel
The baby
Open
Back

50 Things Charles I might have thought on the morning of his Beheading

Hope that blade's sharp enough
Looks a bit chilly; better wear two shirts
Hope there's a big crowd
Don't I know that henchman?
Should I have a hearty breakfast?
This scaffolding seems a bit richerty
Charles Stuart, prepare to meet thy maker… gulp!
Better give my neck a good wash
Hope someone's recording this
Did I leave the fire burning?
Wonder if these cuff links will glint in the light?
Hope it doesn't rain
Am I afraid of heights?
Hope my head rolls handsomely
Please don't let my tongue hang out of my severed
-head like a simpleton's
If only I'd been a better king
Will I shiver even in two shirts?
Damn that Cromwell
Will my body look silly without a head?
24 years as king… at least it's an even number!
Mum!
Now I must keep calm; mustn't lose my head, lol!
Still time for a shave?
There's more people here than at my coronation!
Mustn't trip
There's still time for a last minute reprieve
At least I'll get into the history books
Mustn't whimper
Will I babble after I've lost my head?
Should I wink at the crowd?
Will I dribble?
Should I tip the henchman?
Will my eyes pop out?
Oliver I'm really sorry, it'll never happen again
Please, no complications; one clean cut
Should I wash my hair?
What do I do with this loose change in my pocket?
Should I text my lawyer?
Did I cancel the tailor?
Did I leave my prison cell neat and tidy?
Perhaps three shirts?
Help!
Hope my body doesn't twitch after I'm dead
If I get reincarnated, please, no responsibilities; let
-me be a housemaid
I feel sick
Should I go to the toilet first?
What an ugly looking crowd
Do I get a cushion for my knees?
Hope my head lands in a nice, clean basket
Remember…

50 Guitar Manufacturers

Fender
Modulus
Gibson
Carvin
Wolff Erickson
Hofner
BC Rich
Applause
Breedlove
Mike Lull
Burns
Daisy Rock
Tacoma
Lakland
Dean
Epiphone
Roberts
Ibanez
Sadowsky
Jackson
Martin
Olympia
Vox
Peavey
Guild
PRS
Richenbacker
Schecter
Rodriguez
Seagull
Takamine
Black Dog
Aria
Traveler
Danelectro
Treker
Gecko
Washburn
Gretsch
Hohner
Warwick
Vintique
Musicvox
MXG
Yamaha
Norton
Parker
Status Graphite
Blade
Alvarez

50 Things to sit On

Ottoman
Regency chair
Settee
Couch
Stool
Windsor chair
Throne
Sofa
Chaise longue
Bench
Hepplewhite
Settle
Rocking chair
Hassock
Bucket seat
Divan
Swivel seat
Tabouret
Love seat
Office chair
Sheraton
Fence
Dentists chair
Box seat
Pew
Easy chair
Saddle
Prie-dieu
Car seat
Basket chair
Form
Ladder-back chair
Pouffe
Toilet seat
Bar stool
Armchair
Studio couch
Sociable
High-chair
Lounger
Foot stool
Deckchair
Bean bag
Dining chair
Campstool
Chippendale
Balloon-backed chair
Pillion
Choirstall
Country style chair

50 Metals and Metal Compounds	**50 Things in a Ladies Handbag**
Lithium	Tissues
Beryllium	Lipstick
Sodium	Oyster card
Iron	Mints
Magnesium	Eyeliner
Aluminium	Condoms
Potassium	Perfume
Bronze	Tampons
Tantalum	Magazine
Calcium	Sunglasses
Titanium	P45
Arsenite	Filofax
Vanadium	Pen
Chromium	Chewing gum
Phenyltins	Bottle of water
Technetium	Mobile
Methylmercuric chloride	Spare tights
Manganese	Money
Brass	Keys
Selenium	Umbrella
Cobalt	Camera
Phenylmercuric acetate	MP3 player
Nickel	Letter from the boss
Copper	Hairspray
Zinc	Hairband
Arsenic	Deodorant
Zirconium	Shopping list
Molybdenium	Diary
Silver	Mace spray
Cadmium	Purse
Antimony	Chocolate bar
Barium	Soiled panties
Steel	Credit cards
Osmium	Nail varnish
Nickel silver	Compact mirror
Rhenium	Scarf
Arsenate	Payslip
Platinum	Blood donor card
Nitrilotriacetate	Paracetamol
Alkyltins	Rennies
Mercury	Blusher brush
Thallium	Mascara
Lead	Tweezers
Uranium	Hairbrush
Gold	Contact lens case
Silicon	Suncream
Tungsten	List of boyfriends
Niobium	Nail clippers
Iridium	Toilet roll
Tin	A – Z

50 Things in a Man's Pocket	50 Made-up Words
50 Things in a Man's Pocket	*50 Made-up Words*

Wallet	Bok
Keys	Qexopple
Fluff	Swoodinp
Marble	Tefcuig
Money	Oot
Credit cards	Blitshangwun
Handkerchief	Wurterterker
Cash cards	Cleep
Elastic band	Fujiino
Football programme	Jiwg
Condoms	Pyppun
Mobile	Gliphertave
Tie	Duddle
List of ex-girlfriends	Ugfikllwerd
Conker	Foob
Gig flyer	Rangleshangle
Comb	Ezzongthunf
Glasses	Hiffduvblinsheeg
Organ donor card	Igox
iPod	Lanblaminflam
Chewed nail clippings	Vrachillwaddquem
Badge	Kiidoon
Shirt button	Maztechraphej
Compass	Yaanglajeekot
Tube map	Nufdugex
Gum	Pojite
Cricket scores	Bezelweff
Betting slip	Aabalartam
Phone number of a local plumber	Zaxoon
Reminder to buy Mother's Day flowers	Xasweet
Picture of his dog	Kaaytach
Beer stains	Rolibolibertol
One cuff-link	Shashasash
Half eaten falafel	Twib
Pencil stub	Lillittell
Dog-eared novel	Miminsulartum
IOU	Bakatakolateenox
Newspaper	Carchatazbiloot
Dry cleaning ticket	Pokjalolatran
Scratch card	Rarrdinam
Cigarettes	Gug
Lighter	Vivestac
Mini-camera	Ballywangdassal
Half a mint	Nonononon
Unfulfilled dreams	Glung-glung
His hands	Yayatamaran
Argos pen	Agtavash
Foreign coins	Counert
Cheque book	Dododopillion
Broken watch	Guskinapollonid

50 Bushes	50 Floor Coverings
Bluebeard - blue mist	Carpet
Spiraea - snowmound	Lino
Burning bush – compacta	Cobbles
Rose of Sharon - paeonyflorus	Ceramic tiles
English oak bush	Crazy paving
Buttonbush	Tarmac
Garden rose	Floorboards
Chokeberry – black	Stone
Dogwood – isanti	Decking
Coral berry – amethyst	Earth
Euonymus – blondy	Straw
Forsythia – lynwood gold	Sawdust
Hancock coralberry	Cork tiles
Hydrangea –nikko blue	Gravel
Indigo bush – false indigo	Concrete
Ninebark – darts gold	Vinyl
Pink flowering almond	Flagstones
Lavender	Grass
Pussy willow – French	Astroturf
Quince – Texas scarlet flowering	Wood chippings
Rhododendron - yakushimanum	Metal plate
Russian sage	Rubber
Blackcurrant	Plastic
Sumac – flameleaf	Groundsheet
Viburnum – cardinal candy	Bamboo
Weigela – midnight wine	Marble
Lilac – Persian	Carpet tiles
Barberry – red leaf Japanese	Sand
Wild dewberry	Matting
Burning bush – emerald gaiety	Rugs
Butterfly bush – purple emperor	Newspaper
Chokeberry – red	Pavement
Dogwood – ivory halo	Rushes
Hydrangea –lime light	Brick
Magnolia – winter sun	Wood
Crab-apple	Tarpaulin
Rose of Sharon – chiffon white	Parquet
Rhododendron - maddenia	Oak
Sumac – smooth	Topsoil
Viburnum – mohican	Quarry tiles
Weigela ruby queen	Duckboards
Bluebeard – sunshine blue	Asphalt
Gooseberry	Persian carpet
Butterfly bush – white bouquet	Coconut mats
Dogwood – silky	Doormat
Hydrangea – grandiflora	Red carpet
Potentilla – Katherine Dykes	Loose chippings
Rose of Sharon – Lucy	Prayer mat
Spiraea – pink parasols	Hearth rug
Dog rose	Tigerskin rug

50 Council Departments

Advice
Benefit
Emergency Services
Business and Regeneration
Community, People and Living
Education
Environment
Health
Housing
Jobs and Careers
Arts and Leisure
Street Cleaning
Libraries
Museums and Heritage
Entertainment
Grants
Community Services
Social Care
Refuse Collecting
Transport
Under 5's Services
Animal Welfare
Elderly Services
Birth, Deaths and Marriages
Fire and Rescue Services
Pest Control
Drainage
Building Control
Waste Disposal
Parking Control
Care in the Community
Harassment
Child Care
Health and Safety
Social Services
Children and Families
Community Inspection and Advisory Service
Complaints
Police Service
Parks and Wardens
Council Tax
Council Tenants
Crime Prevention and Neighbour Watch
Developments and Demolitions
Disabled People
Dog Control
Educational Psychology Department
Electoral Registrar
Events
Finance

50 Areas in the Houses of Parliament

Victoria Tower
Queen's Robing Room
Lord Chancellor's Department
Royal Court
Royal Gallery
Peer's Library
Prince's Chamber
Commons' Corridor
Peer's Court
House of Lords
State Officer's Court
Restaurant
Chancellors Court
Serjeant at Arms Offices
St. Stephen's Hall
Moses Room
Peer's Lobby
Peer's Inner Court
Government Front Bench
Member's Dining Hall
Sovereign's entrance
Bar
Stranger's Dining Hall
Hairdressers
Peer's Dining Hall
Central Lobby
Whips
Westminster Hall
Members' Lobby
Star Chamber Court
Peer's Guest Room
House of Commons
Chess Room
Aye
Big Ben
Back benches
Clerk of the House
Speaker's Court
Speaker's State Rooms
Gymnasium
Common's Court
Member's Tea Room
Common's Library
Common's Inner Court
Member's Smoking Room
Shooting Range
Opposition Front Bench
Bar of the House
Victoria Tower Garden
Peer's Corridor

50 Times of the Day	**50 Sharks**
2.30pm	Basking shark
Noon	Cookie-cutter shark
Five past twelve	Grey Nurse shark
1.15am	Dusky shark
Midnight	Blue shark
Half past five in the afternoon	Porbeagle shark
A quarter to seven	Mandarin shark
Midday	Tiger shark
Tea time	Crested Horn shark
Evening	Frilled shark
9.30pm	Blindshark
Bed time	Draughtboard shark
8 o' clock at night	Epaulette shark
Just coming up to 6 o' clock	Scalloped Hammerhead
16.43	Leopard shark
10 o' clock in the morning	Goblin shark
19 hundred hours	Bull shark
4.15pm	False shark
Breakfast time	Blacktip Reef shark
20.20	Grey Whaler shark
Twenty to six	Australian Angekshark
3am	White shark
Dinner time	Gummy shark
A quarter past nine in the morning	Pacific Sleeper shark
Afternoon	Herbst's Nurse shark
4.45pm	Sandtiger shark
2.30am	Japanese Bullhead shark
The early hours	Sharpnose Sevengill shark
5.30pm	Large-toothed Cookie-cutter shark
Mid-morning	Megamouth shark
6.26pm	Carpet shark
Mid-afternoon	Ornate Wobbegong
5.05am	Great White shark
Early evening	Port Jackson shark
8pm	Whale shark
Ten past the hour	Grey Reef shark
10.15pm	Prickly shark
Ten and twenty past five	Shortfin Mako
13.00	Brier shark
Night time	Catshark
14.30	Silky shark
Half past the hour	Spotted Wobbegong
16.06	Thresher shark
17 hundred hours	Greenland shark
4.20am	Broadnosed Sevengill shark
Morning	Varied Carpetshark
6.30am	Whitetip Reef shark
7.45am	Ganges shark
8.30 in the morning	Zebra shark
10 to three	Lemon shark

50 Card Games	**50 Things to look Through**
Uno	Glasses
Snap	Monacle
Cheat	Sunglasses
Old maid	Contact lenses
Happy Families	Goggles
Solitaire	Binoculars
Rummy	Telescope
Whist	Microscope
Hearts	A book
Patience	A glass darkly
Beggar-My-Neighbour	A spy-hole
Pontoon	The window
Black Jack	Glass
Brag	A visor
Poker	Someone without seeing them
Seven Card Stud Poker	Photochromic glasses
Pairs	A camera
Tarot	The keyhole
Bridge	Zoom lens
Canasta	A catalogue
Skat	A viewfinder
Euchre	A porthole
Nap	A magazine
Spades	Field glasses
Gin Rummy	Kaleidoscope
Free Cell	Pin-hole camera
Crazy Eights	A two-way mirror
Top Trumps	Skiascope
Napoleon	Some old letters
Harry Potter Trading card game	Eyeglass
Pokémon	Bifocal lenses
Numero	Telephoto lens
Pit	Ophthalmoscope
Bezique	Wide-angle lens
Pinocle	Retinoscope
Casino	Ocular
Speculation	Eyepiece
Spite and Malice	Optometer
Chase the Ace	Helioscope
Racing Demon	Fisheye lens
Pelmanism	Prism
Housey-Housey	Spectroscope
Faro	Magnifying glass
Concentration	Diffraction grating
Conquain	Polariscope
Baccarat	Slide viewer
Egyptian Ratscrew	Periscope
Pasur	Spectacles
Scopone	Pince-nez
52 Card Pickup	Opera glasses

50 Sums	50 Well-known Plays
2 + 2 = 4	Waiting for Godot
Red + yellow =	Romeo and Juliet
10/- + 10/- =	A Streetcar Named Desire
3 score years + 10 =	The Cherry Orchard
800 m + 200 m =	Boys from the Blackstuff
Copper + tin =	The Threepenny Opera
9 – 18 =	The Three Sisters
Advocaat + lemonade =	Orpheus
270° + 90° =	Electra
Sand, cement + water =	No Sex Please, We're British
2x + 4x =	The Accidental Death of an Anarchist
Long hair + scissors =	Noises Off
9 lbs + 5 lbs =	Le Misanthrope
A quaver + a quaver =	A Flea in Her Ear
-1 + 1 =	The Crucible
2 baker's dozen =	Faust
£1 + 1/- =	An Inspector Calls
Champagne + orange =	She Stoops to Conquer
¾ + ½ =	Les Liaisons Dangereuses
Flour, yeast + salt =	A Doll's House
Yellow + blue =	Peer Gynt
7 x 8 =	Bartholomew Fair
Knitting needles and wool =	Arsenic and Old Lace
Red + white =	Abigail's Party
16% + 34% =	Cat on a Hot Tin Roof
Zinc + copper =	Doctor Faustus
8 + 18 =	Death of a Salesman
A crotchet + a crotchet =	Tartuffe
⅝ + ⅞ =	A Voyage Round My Father
3 farthings + 1 farthing =	When the Wind Blows
9 x 9 =	Madame Bovary
57p + 89p =	Entertaining Mr. Sloane
Beads + string =	What the Butler Saw
4x + 4y =	Look Back in Anger
Petrol + flame =	Hamlet
44 – 44 =	Phèdre
Black + white =	Blood Brothers
Semi-breve + a minim =	Educating Rita
7" + 5" =	Shirley Valentine
Flour, butter, eggs, sugar + baking powder =	Sleuth
11am + 90 mins =	Arms and the Man
3 quarts + 1 quart =	Man and Superman
Bread and flame =	Pygmalion
11 oz + 5 oz =	Sweet Charity
Half a century =	Oedipus Rex
737 + 876 =	Rosencrantz and Guildenstern are Dead
900 yds + 860 yds =	Under Milk Wood
Blue + yellow =	Chips with Everything
6 fl oz + 14 fl oz =	Salome
88 + 88 =	Lady Windermere's Fan

50 Countries in Africa	50 Bizarre Beliefs

50 Countries in Africa

Chad
Tunisia
Egypt
Sudan
Morocco
Algeria
Libya
Mauritania
Western Sahara
Mali
Niger
Eritrea
Ethiopia
Somalia
Djibouti
Senegal
Gambia
Guinea Bissau
Guinea
Sierra Leone
Liberia
Ivory Coast
Burkina
Ghana
Togo
Benin
Nigeria
Cameroon
Central African Republic
Equatorial Guinea
Gabon
Congo
Zaire
Uganda
Rwanda
Kenya
Tanzania
Carbinda
Burundi
Angola
Zambia
Malawi
Mozambique
Zimbabwe
Botswana
Namibia
South Africa
Swaziland
Lesotho
Comoros

50 Bizarre Beliefs

That the earth was flat
That you can get a sun tan through glass
That the end of the world is nigh
That Hitler would bring Germany to prosperity
That if you spared the rod you'd spoil the child
That Kings and Queens ruled by divine right
That a sweet 'posy' would ward off the plague
That Elvis still lives
That torture would bring forth a true confession
That Nostradamus could predict the future
That crop circles are created by aliens
That there really is a Loch Ness monster
That an apple a day will keep the doctor away
That time travel will one day be possible
That UFO's really exist
That the Bermuda triangle is a real phenomenon
That base metals could be turned into gold
That lucky charms could ward off infections
That bloodletting could drive out evil spirits
That werewolves exist
That a comet was a sign of a coming catastrophe
That coloured light had miraculous healing
-powers
That the sun orbited the Earth
That Ouija boards really work
That the Turin Shroud really exists
That the position of planets affects your character
That butter spread on a 'bump' reduces swelling
That the UN has a secret fleet of black helicopters
That Father Christmas exists
That Iraq held 'weapons of mass destruction.'
That the USA covers-up all UFO sightings
That the Inca's worshipped the Sun as a God
That monsters really existed
That the world should be converted to Christianity
That hell resided at the centre of the Earth
That man could fly
Reincarnation
That the US are bombarding Jupiter with anti-
-matter weapons
That there is a 10th. planet in orbit around the sun
That 'portals' exist, leading us into other worlds
That suicide bombers will go to heaven
That humans descended from apes and space men
That most women in medieval times were witches
That in 1602 a judge declared 'an apple'
-possessed by demons
That animals could be guilty of murder and
-consequently a pig was hanged in France, 1438
That Dean Martin could sing
That the dead can walk
That the first printing presses were seen as
-instruments of the devil
That Fairy Rings were caused by alien landings
That plants have emotions

50 Fast-Food Outlets

Wimpy Bar
McDonalds
Burger King
Pizza Hut
Kentucky Fried Chicken
Wendy's
Subway
Benjy's
Domino's Pizza
Tacco Bell
Pizza Express
Aberdeen Steak House
Southern Fried Chicken
Little Chef
Perfect Pizza
Prêt-à-Manger
Starbucks
Harry Ramsden's
Jack in the Box
Premier Pizza Co.
Bella Pasta
Starburger
Spud U Like
Deep Pan Pizza Company
Garfunkel's
Baker's Oven
Eat
Chicken Licken
Easy Pizza
Favorite Chicken
Great British Burger
Gregg's
Mr. D's
Nando's
Happy Eater
7-Eleven
T G I Friday's
A & W
Whataburger
Dunkin' Donuts
Hard Rock Café
Planet Hollywood
Beefeater
Caffé Uno
Frankie and Benny's
Presto
Tootsies
Est Est Est
La Tasca
Red Planet Pizza

50 Useless Lists

50 Useless Lists
50 Arterial Roads
50 Motorways
50 Things to do on a Dark Night
50 Things we Use in the Bathroom
50 Things to 'Hold'
50 Kitchen Items
50 Racing Greyhounds
50 Things to Put on a Shelf
50 Words Beginning with 'X'
50 Greyhound Racing Trainers
50 Roman Numerals
50 Wedding Gifts
50 Star Trek Characters
50 Gooseberry Varieties
50 Things we Use in the Bathroom
50 London Postal Areas
50 Things You'd find on the Dinner Table
50 Easy DIY Jobs
50 Things to do on a Boring Sunday Afternoon
50 Items of Jewellery
50 Receptacles
50 People that Come to Our Door
50 Bands, Groups and Musicians Beginning
-with 'U'
50 Primary Schools in London
50 Computer Commands
50 Forms of Lighting
50 Drawing, Painting and Writing Implements
50 Things You Might find at the Bus Stop
50 Food Colourings and Additives
50 Bottled Waters
50 Things to Put on Your Face
50 Tinned Items
50 Times of the Day
50 Things to Drop
50 Floor Coverings
50 Pets
50 Pets Names
50 Prime Numbers
50 Sails
50 Banks and Building Societies
50 Boys Names
50 Girls Names
50 Well-Known Surnames
50 Obscure Words Beginning with 'Q'
50 Estate Agents
50 Things to 'Catch'
50 Things to 'Throw'
50 Chores
50 Possible Wives for Henry VIII

Index:

50 Accidents and Mishaps..........page 213
50 Aerial Terms..........203
50 Aesop Fables..........246
50 Airlines..........61
50 Alcoholic Drinks..........73
50 Alternative ways to Earn a Living..........38
50 American Baseball Teams..........21
50 Angels and Fairies..........218
50 'Anger' Words..........216
50 Anglers..........150
50 Animal Homes..........246
50 Archers..........155
50 Areas in the Houses of Parliament..........253
50 Armed Forces..........90
50 Arterial Roads........16
50 Baby Items..........151
50 Bacteria and Viruses..........119
50 Ballets..........184
50 Bands and Groups from the 1970's..........175
50 Bands and Groups from the 1990's..........176
50 Bands and Singers from the 1950's..........174
50 Bands, Groups and Musicians beginning with
   -'S'..........10
50 Bands, Groups and Musicians beginning with
   -'U'..........235
50 Banks and Building Society Names..........117
50 Barbara Cartland Novels..........198
50 Battles..........75
50 Beans and Pulses..........191
50 Beatles Songs..........98
50 Beers and Lagers..........138
50 Best selling Novels..........189
50 Bicycles..........242
50 Biggest things on Earth..........238
50 Bizarre Beliefs..........257
50 Board and Table Games........12
50 Bones in the Human Body..........10
50 Book Publishers..........130
50 Books of the Bible..........124
50 Boring things to do at Home on a Dark Night
   -..........68
50 Bottled Waters..........110
50 Boxers..........205
50 Boys Names..........136
50 Breakfasts..........27
50 Breeds of Cats..........33
50 Breeds of Cattle..........121
50 Breeds of Dog........9
50 Breeds of Horses and Ponies..........35
50 Breeds of Pig..........121
50 Bridges..........195
50 British Fish..........41
50 British Prime Ministers..........34
50 British Seaside Towns..........67
50 British Towns and Villages with Silly Names
   -A-G..........206
50 British Towns and Villages with Silly Names
   -G-N..........206
50 British Towns and Villages with Silly Names
   -N-Z..........207
50 Bushes..........252
50 Butterflies and Moths..........192
50 Cakes and Puddings..........210
50 Capital Cities of the World..........28
50 Car Manufacturers..........46
50 Card Games..........255
50 Cartoon Characters..........92
50 Castles..........114
50 Central London Street Names..........34
50 Chain-Stores..........122
50 Characters from Classical Mythology..........79
50 Characters from the Bible..........104
50 Cheeses..........119
50 Chemical Elements..........53
50 Chocolate Bars..........72
50 Chores..........156
50 Church Features..........17
50 Circus Acts..........100
50 Cities and large Towns in the UK..........66
50 Classical Composers..........69
50 Cleaning Implements..........152
50 Clergy Terms..........232
50 Clock and Timepieces..........232
50 Cockney Rhyming Slang Phrases..........86
50 Collective Nouns and Group Names..........244
50 Colours..........20
50 Comedians..........101
50 Comedy Films..........148
50 Comic Characters..........93
50 Common Ailments..........57
50 Common Medicines..........127
50 Computer Commands..........188
50 Contemporary Film Stars..........178
50 Contemporary Illnesses and Diseases..........37
50 Coronation Street Characters..........50
50 Council Departments..........253
50 Counties in Britain and Ireland..........113
50 Countries in Africa..........257
50 Countries..........39
50 Cowboy Films..........126
50 Cricketers who have played for England..........111
50 Criminal Offences..........20
50 Cubs and Scouts Badges..........161
50 Dances..........83
50 Danielle Steele Novels..........201
50 Darts Players..........166
50 David Bowie Songs..........202
50 Days out with the Kids..........158
50 Dead Pop Stars..........238
50 Designer Labels..........131
50 Devils, Demons and Monsters..........219
50 Dicken's Characters..........106
50 Different 'Balls'..........169

50 Different Ages..........140
50 Different Meals..........11
50 Dinosaurs..........49
50 Disaster Movies..........149
50 Disasters..........210
50 Discoveries and Inventions..........46
50 DIY Tools..........15
50 Double-Acts..........103
50 Dr. Who Monsters..........125
50 Drawing, Painting and Writing
    -Implements..........208
50 Easy DIY Jobs..........118
50 Electrical Appliances..........95
50 Electrical Brand Names..........132
50 Electrical Goods Shops..........196
50 Embarrassing things to Buy..........40
50 English Authors..........37
50 Estate Agents..........142
50 Explorers..........104
50 Facial Expressions..........243
50 Famous Deaths..........117
50 Famous Numbers..........202
50 Farm Crops..........231
50 Fashion Accessories..........168
50 Fashion Designers..........53
50 Fast-Food Outlets..........258
50 Feelings..........51
50 Female Characters from History..........243
50 Fictional Detectives..........106
50 Film Actors..........36
50 Film Actresses..........45
50 Film Directors..........77
50 Film Genres..........58
50 Film Monsters..........23
50 Film Stars from the 1960's..........178
50 Films starring Bette Davies..........149
50 Films starring Jack Nicholson..........150
50 Films starring John Wayne..........128
50 Films starring Katherine Hepburn..........151
50 Floor Coverings..........252
50 Flowers..........41
50 Fonts..........180
50 Food Colourings and Additives..........227
50 Football Grounds..........130
50 Football League Managers..........78
50 Football Teams..........59
50 Footballers who have played for England
    -..........110
50 Foreign Footballers..........81
50 Forms of Evening Entertainment..........64
50 Forms of Greeting..........239
50 Forms of Heating..........187
50 Forms of Lighting..........187
50 Forms of Small-Talk..........111
50 Forms of Therapy..........87
50 Forms of Torture..........219
50 Frank Sinatra Songs..........189
50 Freshwater Aquarium Fish..........77

50 Fruits..........16
50 Funeral Items..........154
50 Gangster Movies from the 1930's and
    -'40's..........26
50 Gangster Movies from the 1960's and
    -'70's..........25
50 Gasses..........214
50 Gems and Precious Stones..........209
50 Geographical Features..........65
50 Geographical Terms..........170
50 Girls Names..........136
50 Gods and Goddesses..........226
50 Golfers..........185
50 Good People..........143
50 Gooseberry Varieties..........54
50 Grand National Winners..........26
50 Green things to Eat..........139
50 Greyhound Racing Trainers..........245
50 Guitar Manufacturers..........249
50 Haircuts and Hairstyles..........182
50 Heavens and Hells..........218
50 Herbs and Spices..........228
50 Historical Terms..........171
50 HMS Ships..........216
50 Hobbies..........162
50 Holy Days..........226
50 Houses of Detention..........225
50 Illnesses and Diseases in the Middle Ages..........18
50 'In' and 'On' Phrases..........241
50 Indoor Games..........58
50 Infamous People..........147
50 Insects..........49
50 Items of Clothing..........28
50 Items of Furniture..........93
50 Items of Jewellery..........209
50 Items of Street Furniture..........65
50 Jobs, Trades and Professions A-L..........173
50 Jobs, Trades and Professions M-Z..........174
50 Kid's Programmes..........162
50 Kinds of Coats and Jackets..........95
50 Kings and Queens of England..........13
50 Kitchen Items..........17
50 Knots..........118
50 Lakes..........208
50 Languages..........74
50 Liqueurs..........241
50 Little-known Animals..........215
50 Lollies and Ice-Creams..........204
50 London Bus Routes..........191
50 London Churches in the Middle Ages..........183
50 London Parks..........184
50 London Postal Areas..........100
50 London Theatres..........84
50 London Underground Stations..........171
50 'Love' Words..........217
50 Made-up Words..........251
50 Madonna Songs..........99
50 Magazines..........89

50 Mammals..........40
50 Materials and Fabrics..........39
50 Mathematical Terms..........169
50 Meats..........211
50 Medals and Awards..........161
50 Memorable Dates and Days..........193
50 Metals and Metal Compounds..........250
50 Michael Jackson Songs..........97
50 Mildly Blasphemous Expressions..........61
50 Mints and Chewing Gums..........204
50 Miss World Winners..........54
50 Modes of Land Transport..........14
50 Molluscs..........193
50 Moon Crater Names..........173
50 Moons..........45
50 More Discoveries and Inventions..........76
50 Most useless Items..........55
50 Motorways..........64
50 Mountains and Volcanoes..........44
50 Mr. Men..........60
50 Muscles of the Body..........52
50 Mushrooms and Fungi..........68
50 Musical Instruments.......... 9
50 Musical Terms..........115
50 Musicals..........185
50 Names not to call your Funeral Service..........153
50 Names of Stars..........124
50 Nautical Terms..........201
50 Newspapers..........88
50 Novel Characters..........105
50 Number One Song Titles..........19
50 Nursery Rhymes..........233
50 Nuts..........85
50 Obscure words beginning with 'Q'..........141
50 Oceans and Seas..........207
50 'Off' and 'Out' Phrases..........32
50 Office Jobs..........196
50 Old London Street Cries..........33
50 'Ologies..........107
50 Olympic Events..........108
50 Olympic Gold Medallists..........55
50 Operas..........86
50 Outdoor Leisure Pursuits..........112
50 Outdoor Sports and Games..........57
50 Packets of Crisps..........230
50 Painters and Artists..........32
50 Painting Movements..........59
50 Paintings by Botticelli..........42
50 Paris Street Names..........237
50 Parts of a Bicycle..........89
50 Parts of the Body..........156
50 Parts of the Ear..........116
50 Parts of the Eye..........200
50 Parts of the outside of a House..........157
50 Patterns..........85
50 People that come to our Door..........231
50 Perfumes..........131
50 Pet Names..........137

50 Pets..........109
50 Philosophers/Political Thinkers..........71
50 Phobias..........127
50 Picasso Paintings..........186
50 Pieces of Armour..........122
50 Places to find a Crowd..........212
50 Places to have Fun..........224
50 Places worth a Visit..........102
50 Places you'd find Deserted..........212
50 Playstation Games..........172
50 Playwrights..........99
50 Poets..........107
50 Police-Drama/Detective Programmes..........205
50 Political Parties..........224
50 Popes..........82
50 Popular Sayings and Phrases..........158
50 Popular Zoo Animals..........101
50 Possible Wives for Henry VIII..........203
50 Primary Schools in London..........237
50 Prime Numbers..........115
50 Proverbs..........215
50 Pubs with Silly Names..........83
50 Races..........74
50 Racing Car Drivers..........197
50 Racing Greyhounds..........182
50 Radio Shows from the 1930's – 1960's..........103
50 Ranks within the Armed Forces..........22
50 Reality TV Shows..........153
50 Receptacles..........221
50 Record Labels..........129
50 Relations..........221
50 Religious Festivals around the World..........168
50 Rivers..........44
50 Rocks and Minerals..........56
50 Rolling Stones Songs..........98
50 Roman Emperors..........62
50 Roman Numerals..........240
50 Roman Towns..........96
50 Rooms..........247
50 Rugby Teams..........62
50 Sails..........116
50 Salvador Dali Paintings..........186
50 Satellite TV Channels..........172
50 Savoury Meat Dishes..........42
50 Sayings..........236
50 Science Fiction B-Movies..........188
50 Scientific Terms..........170
50 Scottish Clans..........222
50 Scottish Football Teams..........175
50 Serial Killers..........43
50 2nd. World War Films..........134
50 Shakespeare Characters..........51
50 Shakespeare Insults..........112
50 Shapes..........181
50 Sharks..........254
50 Signs and Symbols..........181
50 Silent Movie Stars..........177
50 Simpson's Characters..........190

50 Sins..........75
50 Skip Hire Firms..........159
50 Slang words for Money..........194
50 Smallest things on Earth..........239
50 Smells..........145
50 Snakes..........233
50 Soft Drinks..........72
50 Some Historical Events..........245
50 Songs with the word 'Boy' or 'Girl' in the Title
-..........135
50 Songs with the word 'Love' in the Title..........135
50 Sounds we can make with our Voices..........223
50 Sounds..........145
50 'Space' Films..........134
50 Species of Birds..........31
50 Sports Items..........91
50 Sports Personalities..........177
50 Star Trek Characters..........18
50 Star Wars Characters..........190
50 States of America..........14
50 Styles of Music..........73
50 Sums..........256
50 Supermarkets..........183
50 Supermodels..........90
50 Sweeteners..........229
50 Sweets..........70
50 Swords..........144
50 T. Rex Songs..........12
50 Tacky Christmas Presents..........234
50 Tastes..........144
50 Theatre Styles..........228
50 Theatrical Terms..........217
50 Things 'not to say' when entering a Church
-..........67
50 Things a man shouldn't say when present at
-the Birth of his Child..........165
50 Things Charles I might have thought on the
-morning of his Beheading..........248
50 Things Cinderella might have done if the
-Glass Slipper hadn't Fit..........148
50 Things Guy Fawkes might have done while
-waiting to blow up Parliament..........11
50 Things in a Forest..........247
50 Things in a Ladies Handbag..........250
50 Things in a Man's Pocket..........251
50 Things not to do on a 'First Date'..........160
50 Things not to say in an Interview..........143
50 Things not to say on your Wedding
-Night..........165
50 Things not to say when stopped by the
-Police..........179
50 Things not to say when you first meet your
-Girlfriend's Parents..........166
50 Things Red Riding Hood might have taken to
-Grandma's..........29
50 Things Sleeping Beauty might have said
-when woken by the Prince..........35
50 Things taught at School..........200

50 Things that make our lives just that little bit
-Easier..........79
50 Things the Queen might say when
-Waking..........167
50 Things the Seven Dwarfs might have done if
-Snow White hadn't woken Up..........147
50 Things the Wolf might have said to gain
-entrance to the Three Little Pigs House..........199
50 Things the World could do Without..........22
50 Things the World couldn't do Without..........78
50 Things to 'Catch'..........154
50 Things to 'Hold'..........30
50 Things to 'Throw'..........155
50 Things to be found in a Victorian
-Kitchen..........236
50 Things to Collect..........109
50 Things to do as an Eskimo..........82
50 Things to do at 'Camp'..........126
50 Things to do at the Seaside..........114
50 Things to do in a 1950's Sitting-Room..........222
50 Things to do in the Town..........141
50 Things to do on a boring Sunday Afternoon
-..........108
50 Things to do on a hot Summer's Day..........70
50 Things to do on Summer Holiday..........140
50 Things to Drop..........248
50 Things to look Through..........255
50 Things to put on a Shelf..........234
50 Things to put on your Face..........47
50 Things to put on your Head..........48
50 Things to say if you ever met the Queen..........43
50 Things to sit On..........249
50 Things to think about when fielding 'Deep
-Fine Leg'..........23
50 Things to think about when playing Centre
-Forward..........240
50 Things to use in the Gym..........113
50 Things we do with our Bodies..........157
50 Things we use in the Bathroom..........91
50 Things you can buy at the Bakers..........87
50 Things you could buy from a Victorian Chemist
-..........84
50 Things you might find at the Bus Stop..........229
50 Things you might find in a Castle..........163
50 Things you might say if you met Jesus..........199
50 Things you might say when arriving at the
-Gates of Hell..........164
50 Things you should never, ever, ever Do..........52
50 Things you'd find on a Farm..........21
50 Things you'd find on the Dinner Table..........146
50 Thoughts from a Burglars Perspective..........211
50 Times of the Day..........254
50 Tinned Items..........180
50 Tiny Islands around the World..........47
50 Touchy/Feely Words..........146
50 Traditional Children's Story Characters..........105
50 Traditional Children's Toys..........92
50 Traditional Cocktails..........225

50 Traditional Trades and Professions..........63
50 Triple-Barrel Words and Phrases..........29
50 Tropical Marine Fish..........244
50 TV Catchphrases..........129
50 TV Comedy Programmes..........66
50 TV Presenters and Personalities..........176
50 TV Programmes from the 1960's..........19
50 TV Programmes from the 1980's..........102
50 Types of Aircraft..........88
50 Types of Bags and Cases..........139
50 Types of Biscuit..........179
50 Types of Dwelling..........69
50 Types of Footwear..........94
50 Types of Fuel..........230
50 Types of Hats..........94
50 Types of Seacraft..........15
50 Types of Skirts and Dresses..........97
50 Types of Tea..........163
50 Types of Weather..........120
50 Types of Weights and Measures..........48
50 Useless Lists..........258
50 Vampire Films..........125
50 Varieties of Trees..........13
50 Vegetables..........30
50 Vegetarian Dishes..........192
50 Virtues..........76
50 Vitamins, Minerals and Nutrients..........227
50 Waters around the UK..........60
50 Ways to avoid People..........81
50 Ways to Communicate..........80
50 Ways to Die 31
50 Ways to get Arrested..........80
50 Ways to Murder Someone..........38
50 Ways to say 'I Love You'..........27
50 Ways to shout 'Run'..........159
50 Weapons..........50
50 Wedding Gifts..........152
50 Weird and wonderful Band Names..........235
50 Well-known 'Sayings' from the Cinema..........120
50 Well-known Buildings..........36
50 Well-known Cricketers from 1938..........24
50 Well-known Films..........96
50 Well-known Novels..........63
50 Well-known Plays..........256
50 Well-known Ships and Boats..........56
50 Well-known Soldiers..........213
50 Well-known Surnames..........137
50 Whiskeys..........138
50 White Wines..........25
50 Witchcraft Artefacts..........214
50 Women Wimbledon Players..........242
50 Words and Phrases to express
   -Drunkenness..........220
50 Words and Phrases to express Craziness..........220
50 Words beginning with 'Sun...'..........167
50 Words beginning with 'X'..........128
50 Words beginning with 'Zoo...'..........142
50 Words for 'Big'..........197

50 Words for 'Bottom'..........195
50 Words for 'Dark'..........133
50 Words for 'Dirt'..........132
50 Words for 'Small'..........198
50 Words for 'White'..........133
50 Words for Man..........71
50 Words for Woman..........194
50 Words to describe 'Cold'..........24
50 Words to describe 'Hot'..........123
50 Words to use instead of 'Nice'..........123
50 World Leaders..........223
50 World Record Holders..........160
50 Yellow Things to Eat..........164

…And that's about it for now! Of course these lists are inexhaustible and I'm sure you've come up with dozens yourself!

Feel free to send them in if you fancy; and watch this space for,… who knows,… maybe another 500 lists of 50 words!

LaVergne, TN USA
10 August 2010
192767LV00004B/75/A